Marlborough's Campaigns & Battles

JOHANNES baro de CHURCHILL, dux et comes de MARLBOROUGH,

Marlborough's Campaigns & Battles

In the Netherlands, Germany & France during the
War of Spanish Succession, 1702-11

ILLUSTRATED WITH MAPS

An Outline of Marlborough's Campaigns
F. W. O. Maycock

The Battle of Blenheim
Hilaire Belloc

LEONAUR

Marlborough's Campaigns & Battles
In the Netherlands, Germany & France during the War of Spanish Succession, 1702-11
An Outline of Marlborough's Campaigns
by F. W. O. Maycock
The Battle of Blenheim
by Hilaire Belloc

ILLUSTRATED WITH MAPS

FIRST EDITION

First published under the titles
An Outline of Marlborough's Campaigns
and
The Battle of Blenheim

Leonaur is an imprint of Oakpast Ltd

Copyright in this form © 2025 Oakpast Ltd

ISBN: 978-1-917666-54-1 (hardcover)
ISBN: 978-1-917666-55-8 (softcover)

http://www.leonaur.com

Contents

An Outline of Marlborough's Campaigns

Contents

Notes on the Topography of the Theatre of Operations 1702—1711

Even before the commencement of the eighteenth century, the low-lying tract of country enclosed between the French frontier, the Meuse and the North Sea had fully established its unenviable reputation as 'The Cockpit of Europe.' Great Britain, France, Spain and Holland fought their differences on its fertile well-watered plains, without the slightest regard to the misery they inflicted on the unfortunate inhabitants. The Spanish Netherlands were drained by two great river systems. On the west, the Scheldt, joined by the Lys at Ghent and the Dender at Dendermonde, eventually emptied itself into the North Sea. Farther to the eastward, the Demer, rising near Maestricht, and picking up the Geete on its way, flowed into the Dyle, near Louvain, and the latter river, joined by the Senne near Mechlin, eventually united itself with the Scheldt some distance south of Antwerp.

On the eastern boundary of the theatre of operations, the Meuse, which was joined by the Sambre at the strongly fortified city of Namur, flowed eastward past the fortresses of Huy and Liege, then turning northward passed Maestricht, Maeseyck, Stevenswaert, Roermond and Venlo, then, again changing its course, flowed westward past Grave into the estuary of the Rhine.

An important canal connected Ghent and Bruges, from which city one branch ran northward into the estuary of the Scheldt and the other continued its course to Ostend. The latter town was also connected with Dunkirk by a canal, which ran through Nieuport, roughly parallel to the coast.

These rivers were thickly studded with fortified cities, situated either at the junction of the streams or where they were crossed by the main roads connecting the more important towns; these fortresses, repeatedly changing hands during the progress of the previous campaigns, had been continually strengthened by either Vauban or Cohorn, the two foremost engineers of their time. Hence sieges and operations for the relief of the various important cities became more and more a predominant feature of the campaigns and exercised a paramount influence on the strategy of the opposing commanders.

Decisive battles seldom took place, and, though the rival leaders manoeuvred for position with considerable skill, the idea of seeking out the enemy's field army, and crushing it, was entirely foreign to their method of waging war. Even when the hostile forces met, the usual procedure was for one commander to entrench himself as strongly as possible, while his adversary either furiously assaulted the position, much as he would have endeavoured to storm a fortress, or sat himself down in a fortified camp to wait until starvation forced his opponent to evacuate his lines.

As a result of the long-continued struggle, the frontier between France and the Spanish Netherlands was thickly studded with fortresses; on the French side were the fortified cities of Dunkirk, Lille, Conde, Valenciennes and Mauberge, supported by Aire, St. Venant, Bethune, Douai, Bouchain and Quesnoi, with Arras, Cambrai and Landrecies still farther in rear. On the Spanish side were situated Nieuport, Ypres, Menin, Tournai, Mons, Charleroi and Namur, with Ostend, Courtrai and Ath in the second line. The frontier between the Sambre and the sea was divided into three zones by the Lys and the Scheldt, the more important, through which the direct road to Paris and the heart of France ran, being situated between the two latter rivers, here some fifty miles apart.

The whole theatre of operations was extremely cramped, the distance from Dunkirk to Maestricht being only about a hundred and fifty, and from Arras to Antwerp about a hundred, miles. For more than a century the 'Low Countries' had been the training-ground of the British Army and the school in which its officers had learned the art of war. First making her appearance, more or less unofficially, in support of the Dutch in their heroic efforts to free themselves from the Spanish yoke, Great Britain had then aided France in her conflict with Spain and had been finally drawn into the long and deadly struggle waged by William III. to protect the United Provinces from the aggression of Louis XIV.

The British soldier had already fully established his reputation for bull-dog courage and capability for enduring an enormous amount of punishment without flinching, while Morgan and Francis Vere had proved themselves singularly able commanders. (*Vide Sir Francis Vere: Elizabeth I's Greatest Soldier and the Eighty Years War.* Leonaur 2016.) In fact, the fertile fields of the 'Low Countries' had been well watered by good British blood, before the great Duke of Marlborough led his army from victory to victory during ten hard-fought campaigns. The theatre in which operations were about to commence was equally familiar to the leaders of both the rival armies; in fact, most of the senior officers, and a large proportion of the rank and file, in both the French and Allied forces must have known intimately almost every yard of the ground over which they were about to fight.

Preface

This little work makes no pretence of throwing any fresh light on the stirring events of the war of the Spanish Succession or on the life of the great Duke of Marlborough; its sole object is to give a brief and concise outline of the campaigns in which he and the British Army played such a glorious part. Though the campaigns of Wellington are to a great extent familiar to the soldier and the civilian alike, those of Marlborough seem, for some unaccountable reason, to have been almost entirely neglected.

The latter's method of waging war was entirely free from the formality and pedantic adherence to rules which so often make the military operations of the eighteenth century, at any rate prior to the revolutionary era, somewhat dry and uninteresting. Marlborough's grasp of the great principles of strategy, his power of manoeuvre, and the certainty with which he handled his troops on the field of battle, closely resemble the methods of the great Napoleon, and it is no disparagement to his brilliant successors, who have so often led the British Army to victory in every quarter of the globe, to rank him as the greatest general that England has ever produced. He owed much to the training he received in the art of war from Turenne, but when he was entrusted with supreme command, at the age of fifty-two, his exploits far outshone those of his famous master.

The details of the great duke's political career do not come within the scope of this little work, but in justice to his memory it must be pointed out that the charge of needlessly prolonging the war for his own ends is flatly contradicted by the whole tone of both his official and private correspondence. It is interesting to note that Napoleon thought so highly of his military abilities that in 1808 he ordered his staff to prepare a history of Marlborough's campaigns. The principal authorities referred to have been: Alison's *Life of the Duke of Marlborough*, the Hon. J. Fortescue's splendid *History of the British Army*, (see

Sir John Fortescue's 'The Sun Surmounted': Leonaur 2014), and Lord Wolseley's *Life of Churchill*, while numerous other works have been consulted for the detail of the battles, etc. It is hoped that the rough sketch maps and plans compiled by the author may serve their purpose, that of rendering the text more easy to follow.

F. W. O. M.

Bury St. Edmunds
July 1912

CHAPTER 1

Introduction

At the close of the seventeenth century the one subject of absorbing interest to the rulers and statesmen of the principal European Powers was the question of who should succeed the childless Charles II. as the ruler of the vast Spanish possessions on the Continent.

The rival claimants were France and Austria, and the success of either would completely upset the Balance of Power, but the union of France and Spain would be peculiarly distasteful to Great Britain, as it would give the French almost entire control of the Mediterranean.

At the beginning of 1700 a treaty, in the framing of which the Emperor of Austria had not been consulted, was signed by England, France and Holland. It was arranged that the Archduke Charles, the second son of the emperor, was to receive the crown of Spain and her possessions in the Netherlands and the New World. France was to obtain the Spanish territories in northern Italy, while Great Britain and Holland were to be compensated with valuable commercial privileges in America and the West Indies.

The cold-blooded partition of his dominions was bitterly resented by the Spanish monarch and his people, while the emperor was furious at the idea of Louis XIV. obtaining the Italian territories; in fact, it seemed probable that the Empire and Spain would find themselves in alliance against England, France and Holland. However, shortly before his death, Charles II., with the full consent of his Council, made a will leaving the throne to Philip of Anjou, the grandson of Louis XIV., in the hope that the latter monarch would be strong enough to save the Spanish dominions from disintegration.

Charles II. died towards the end of the year 1700, and under the terms of his will Louis XIV. accepted the Spanish throne for his grandson, and promptly disavowed the partition treaty. William III. and the Grand Pensionary Heinsius, who practically ruled Holland, were furious at being over-reached by the French king, more especially as their own greed for colonial expansion had, to a certain extent, contributed to their downfall.

At first England cared little for the destruction of the Balance of Power caused by the union of France and Spain, but when she realised that her commerce was seriously menaced, by the granting of several valuable monopolies in the New World to French companies, public opinion veered round and set steadily in favour of a war with France.

The Emperor of Austria was most eager to revive the former alliance against France, and in 1701 a treaty was signed at The Hague, between England, Holland and the Empire, by which his second son, Charles, was to receive the crown and the Spanish territories in Italy, the fate of the Netherlands was allowed to remain in abeyance, and England and Holland were to retain any conquests made in America or the West Indies.

The King of Prussia was bound by the terms under which he had been raised to the throne to support the emperor, and the bulk of the rulers of the smaller German states, including Hanover, Baden and Hesse-Cassel, joined the Alliance, though the electors of Bavaria and Cologne decided to throw in their lot with France. Louis XIV. struck the first blow by seizing the barrier fortresses of Namur, Luxemburg, Mons, Charleroi, Ath, Oudenarde, Nieuport and Ostend without any declaration of war, and retained the Dutch troops forming the garrisons, amounting to some 15,000 men, as prisoners.

The quarrel was thus forced on Holland whether she wished it or not, and she promptly applied to Great Britain for the 10,000 men which the latter was bound by treaty to supply for the defence of the Low Countries.

William III.'s task was made easier by the fact that on the death of the exiled James II. his son had been recognised by Louis XIV. as King of Great Britain, and this move caused the greatest indignation in England, as both the Whigs and the moderate Tories were enraged by having a ruler foisted on them by the King of France. Parliament promptly voted a force of 40,000 men, of whom 18,000 were to be British and the remainder mercenaries, for carrying on the war on land, while a similar number were to take part in the naval operations.

But unfortunately, the fact that such a force was sanctioned by Parliament did not make the men easy to obtain, for after the Peace of Ryswick the army had been tremendously reduced, and the officers and men so shamefully treated that they showed not the slightest eagerness to come forward again, and it was only by sweeping vagrants, debtors and minor criminals wholesale into the ranks that the regiments could be brought up to anything like their proper strength. For the first time in his long and deadly struggle with Louis XIV., William found himself in a position to use the full power of England, and in spite of his failing health he set himself energetically to organise the forces of the Grand Alliance for the coming campaign.

In June 1701, twelve battalions, consisting of the 1st Guards, both battalions of the 1st Royals (Royal Scots), the 8th, 10th, 13th, 16th, 17th, 18th, 23rd and 24th Regiments (Fortescue's *History of the British Army*), were ordered to Holland under the command of the Earl of Marlborough, and shortly afterwards six more battalions of infantry and eight regiments of cavalry were sent to join him.

For the ensuing campaign the Allies could count the forces of England, Holland, the Empire, Hanover, Baden, Hesse-Cassel and some of the minor German states, the Prussian contingent, and the auxiliaries hired from Denmark and Holstein. The British and Dutch armies, though numerically weak, were composed of excellent troops, the majority of whom were veterans who had served under William in his previous campaigns in the Low Countries and had proved their worth on many a hard-fought field. The armies of the Empire were formidable in point of numbers, and, as far as the personnel was concerned, of excellent quality, but owing to the chronic bankruptcy of the Imperial treasury, they were wretchedly equipped.

The contingents of the other nations were made up of thoroughly trained professional soldiers, who had learned their trade in the numerous campaigns which marked the close of the seventeenth century. The efficiency of the Allied Army was, however, seriously impaired by the fact that it was composed of such a number of small contingents of different nationalities, and it was obvious that, at all events at the commencement of the campaign, little cohesion could be expected in a force drawn from such a variety of sources.

On the other hand, France, during the long reign of Louis XIV., had become by far the most powerful nation in Europe, and with such ministers as Colbert and Louvois, her resources had increased enormously in spite of the incessant wars brought about by Louis' boundless ambition.

Led by Turenne, Conde and Luxemburg her armies had for years proved almost invincible, while the fortresses they had captured had been strengthened by Vauban, the greatest engineer of his time.

Though France had undoubtedly felt the severe drain of men and money caused by the continual wars in which she had been engaged, and her famous ministers and generals had passed away, it appeared that her powerful armies, composed of veteran troops, whose morale had been heightened by a long series of victories, would be more than a match for the heterogeneous forces of the Allies.

In spite of Madame de Maintenon's sneer that 'Louis had many courtiers but no generals,' it seemed that with such able commanders as Villars, Vendôme, Boufflers and the young Duke of Berwick, the French Armies would gather fresh laurels in the forthcoming campaign. Moreover, by her union with Spain, France obtained the command of the Spanish troops and fortresses in the Netherlands, while the dominions of the Duke of Savoy furnished her armies with a secure base in northern Italy and her alliance with Bavaria secured a powerful ally and a strong advanced post in the heart of Germany. Her frontiers were also amply protected by the Rhine, the fortress-studded line of the Maas and the barrier cities of the Spanish Netherlands, while the powerful and homogeneous French Army, occupying a central position, could act on interior lines against the forces of the Allies, assembled in three main groups: in the Netherlands, the valley of the Rhine and northern Italy.

Moreover, the inherent weakness of all coalitions made itself felt even before the commencement of hostilities: England was sincerely anxious to prevent the union of France and Spain; the emperor bent on obtaining the Spanish territories in northern Italy for the House of Hapsburg; Holland desired a strong barrier against French aggression in the Netherlands, and Prussia and Denmark had little interest in the quarrel.

It needed all William III.'s great diplomatic abilities to reconcile the conflicting interests of the Allies and to bring them to co-operate in furthering the common object, but in spite of his shattered health his labours were successful, and he was about to sail to take command of the army assembling in the Low Countries when a fall from his horse caused his death. Fortunately, he had already practically completed all the necessary preparations, and the accession of Queen Anne caused no alteration in the British policy, while through her husband, Prince George, it tended to bind Denmark more firmly to the Alliance.

The Earl of Marlborough, whose abilities William had always thoroughly appreciated, but whose loyalty he had, not without reason, distrusted, had been engaged in negotiations with the Allies in the

Netherlands, and he was now, at William's express wish, appointed Captain-General of the British Forces in Holland, and later to the supreme command of the Allied Army in the Low Countries. He was not, however, allowed a free hand, as he was fettered by the instructions of the governments who had supplied the various contingents and hampered by the presence at his headquarters of the Dutch deputies, who had the right of vetoing his suggestions.

John Churchill was, however, singularly fitted for the difficult role which he was to be called upon to play, for not only was he to command the Allied forces in the field, but he was also destined to become the guiding spirit of the coalition. Born in 1650, he had at the age of twelve been appointed as page to the Duke of York, afterwards James II. His handsome appearance and charming manners had soon made him extremely popular at the Court, and four years later he was given an ensign's commission in the Guards. He at once volunteered for service at Tangiers, which was besieged by the Moors, and even at that early age gave promise of remarkable ability; while five years later, serving with the British contingent under Turenne in the Low Countries, he gained his company by his conspicuous gallantry at the siege of Grave.

Next year he still further distinguished himself at the siege of Maestricht by leading the storming party and planting the British standard on the summit of the breach, where he held his position in spite of desperate odds until he was supported. He was publicly thanked for his gallantry, promoted Lieutenant-Colonel, and given command of a regiment, and though no doubt he owed something to the fact that his sister Arabella had become the mistress of the Duke of York, his advancement on the whole had been thoroughly well earned, and he had moreover gained the good opinion of Turenne, the foremost general of his time. On the accession of James II., Marlborough was promoted to the rank of Brigadier-General and became a Baronet. He speedily justified his promotion by the able handling of a small force, which did much to stamp out Monmouth's rebellion; while at Sedgemoor it was only his ability and the discipline of his brigade which saved the Royal troops under the incompetent Faversham from disaster.

Though he thoroughly disapproved of James' determination to restore the Catholic religion, he still retained command, but took an active part in the intrigues with William of Orange, and on the latter landing in England he used his influence entirely in his favour, and eventually joined him with the bulk of the army. He was created Earl of Marlborough and selected to command the British contingent sent to aid the Allies in the Low Countries; but the latter were too weak to engage in any important operations, and he had little chance of distinguishing himself.

However, the brilliant way in which he handled his men at Walcourt made a most favourable impression on Waldeck, who commanded the Allies, and by curious coincidence Villars, whom he was so often to encounter later, also greatly distinguished himself on the same occasion. Marlborough refused to take the field against his former benefactor in Ireland, but after James, hopelessly defeated at the Battle of the Boyne, had returned to France, he commanded an expedition which reduced Cork and Kinsale in a remarkably short space of time and finally crushed the Jacobite cause in Ireland.

He was afterwards appointed to command a large camp formed near Brussels, but falling into disfavour on account of his suspected intrigues with the Jacobites and his openly expressed disgust at William's galling but not unnatural partiality for his Dutch generals and troops, he was deprived of his command and banished from the Court. However, after the death of Queen Mary, he again returned to favour, no doubt owing to the influence his wife had obtained over the Princess Anne, who, as her sister had died childless, had become heir to the throne. On the 1st of June 1701, William appointed him Ambassador Extraordinary and Commander-in-Chief of the British Forces in the Netherlands, and it was almost entirely owing to his great diplomatic ability that preliminary negotiations for the formation of the Grand Alliance met with success.

One of his most difficult tasks was the arrangement of the numbers to be supplied by the different states, but eventually the strength of the various contingents was fixed. The emperor was to furnish 90,000 men; England, 40,000, of whom 18,000 were to be British and the remainder mercenaries; Holland was to provide 10,000 Dutch troops and to pay for 12,000 Danish auxiliaries, and Prussia to send a contingent 15,000 strong. At William's earnest recommendation Marlborough was appointed to succeed him in command of the Allied forces in the Netherlands, and after attending the late king's funeral he set sail to take up his command in the spring of 1702.

Such, briefly, was the record of the great Earl of Marlborough, who was destined to lead the Allies from victory to victory, humble the proud spirit of Louis XIV., and make the scarlet coat of the British Army dreaded on many a hard-fought field throughout Europe.

CHAPTER 2

The Campaign of 1702-1703

The theatre of operations extended from the North Sea to the Mediterranean, embracing the Netherlands, the valley of the Rhine and northern Italy. The opposing forces were distributed in three main groups. The right wing of the Allies, consisting of the contingents of Great Britain, Holland, Prussia and Denmark, held the Low Countries; in the centre, Lewis of Baden, a brave but by no means brilliant general, whose successes against the Turks had given him an exaggerated idea of his own military abilities, commanded the main body of the Imperial Army which was destined for the invasion of Alsace. In northern Italy, Eugene of Savoy, with a detachment of the Imperial forces, was endeavouring to make good the emperor's claim to the Milanese territories belonging to the Spanish monarchy.

In the Netherlands, Cohorn, the famous engineer, with some 10,000 men, was watching the mouth of the Scheldt and threatening Bruges, while a considerable distance farther west the main body of the Allies, roughly 35,000 strong, lay round Cleves to protect the Dutch frontier and cover the siege of Kaiserworth. As Marlborough was still engaged in his diplomatic labours at The Hague, and unable to take the field, the main force of the Allies was commanded by Ginkel, Earl of Athlone, a gallant veteran who had received his title from William III. as a well-merited reward for his valuable services in Ireland some ten years previously.

On the French side a detachment under the Marquis de Bedmar, Governor of the Spanish Netherlands, was observing Cohorn, while the main body, some 60,000 strong, nominally under the Duke of Burgundy but really commanded by the veteran Marshal Boufflers, was quartered in the northern portion of the bishopric of Liege. Marlborough decided to open the campaign by reduction of the small but strong fortress of Kaiserworth, situated on the right bank of the

Rhine, which had been handed over to the French by the Elector of Cologne.

The place was of considerable importance as it commanded the communications between Holland and Westphalia, consequently its reduction was entrusted to the Prince of Nassau with 25,000 Dutch and Prussian troops. The Allies had been compelled to assemble their forces in northern Brabant, as Louis XIV. had seized all the barrier fortresses prior to the declaration of hostilities, and had also occupied the strongholds on the Maas, with the exception of Maestricht.

Boufflers determined to make an unexpected attack on Nimeguen, an important fortress on the Waal commanding the waterways of Holland, but which, owing to the supineness of the Dutch government, had been left without a garrison, and in pursuance of his plan the French commander left his camp on the evening of the 9th of June. Though Ginkel only heard of the hostile advance twenty-four hours later, he managed to overtake his opponent after a rapid forced march, and under cover of a running cavalry fight, of which the Allies had rather the worse, to throw his infantry into the town. The *burghers* aided the troops by dragging the guns up to the ramparts, and as the fortress was now strongly held, Boufflers decided not to risk an assault, but to avenge himself for his disappointment he overran the fertile bishopric of Cleves, extracting a ransom of 500,000 crowns from the unfortunate inhabitants, and carrying off 20,000 head of cattle.

Meanwhile the siege of Kaiserworth had been vigorously pressed, and had made excellent progress in spite of the continual sorties of the garrison and a half-hearted effort of a French force under Tallard to relieve the town. After a desperate struggle, in which they lost heavily, the Allies managed to capture the covered way, and, bringing up their heavy guns to close range, they pounded the ramparts with such effect that the garrison was forced to surrender, after a gallant resistance which had lasted for two months and had cost the besiegers nearly 5,000 men.

Marlborough, having at last completed his difficult negotiations at The Hague, was able to take the field in person at the beginning of July, but immediately found himself confronted by fresh difficulties. Ginkel considered that his services entitled him at least to the joint command of the Allied Army, and made no effort to hide his rage and disappointment, while the Dutch deputies, always timorous in the carrying on of warlike operations, had been badly scared by the French advance. On his arrival at the camp near Nimeguen, Marlborough managed to concentrate a force of some 70,000 men and 70 guns, but though his opponents were barely 40,000 strong, the deputies would not hear of an advance, and neither the Prussian nor Hanoverian commanders would move without first consulting their governments.

It was not until the end of July that these difficulties were overcome, and then Marlborough, determined to force his opponent to abandon the line of the Maas by threatening southern Brabant, crossed the river and camped within a few miles of the French position. His manoeuvre was most successful, for Boufflers hurriedly crossed the Maas at Roermond and Venlo, and moved towards Brabant. The British general wished to attack him during the march, but the scheme was vetoed by the deputies, though, according to the Duke of Berwick, who was with the French Army, the attack would undoubtedly have been successful. Disgusted by the continual opposition of his allies, which rendered success in the field impossible, Marlborough now decided to reduce Venlo, the most northerly of the French strongholds on the Maas, and took up a position with his main body to cover the siege.

Hearing that a convoy containing his opponent's heavy artillery was on its way from Bois-le-Duc, Boufflers advanced to intercept it, but as the Allies were too strongly posted to attack, he ordered an immediate retreat in order to extricate himself from the dangerous position into which he had blundered. This sudden change of plan caused considerable confusion in the French Army, and Marlborough, seeing his opportunity, ordered a general advance, but Opdam, commanding the Dutch troops on the right of the Allies' line, refused to move, and another excellent chance of defeating the hostile field army was lost.

The strong fort of St. Michael, which was situated on the left bank of the Maas and commanded the town of Venlo, was selected as the first point of attack, and within a fortnight a practicable breach had been made in the walls. Lord Cutts, known throughout the army as the 'Salamander,' owing to his reckless gallantry at the capture of Namur, directed the assault, and issued orders to the storming party to rush the fortress as soon as they had captured the covered way. His rash order was carried out to the letter by the 'forlorn hope,' composed of volunteers drawn from the various battalions of the Guards, who dashed at the breach, drove their opponents from the glacis in confusion, and, unchecked by the explosion of a mine, which did considerable damage, scrambled up the counterscarp by means of the long grass, and carried the fort at the cost of less than thirty men.

Heavy batteries were at once opened against the town and the surrender hastened by a curious coincidence: the Prince of Nassau, learning that the Imperialists had captured Landau, ordered the batteries to fire a *feu de joie*, which so terrified the inhabitants that, imagining the bombardment had commenced, they forced the governor to surrender.

Roermond, some fifteen miles lower down the Maas, was captured after a brief resistance, and the two small but strongly fortified towns of Stevenswaert and Maeseyck taken; but Cohorn's slow and methodical siege operations were little to Marlborough's taste, and he determined to possess himself of the important and strongly fortified town of Liege, one of the bulwarks of southern Brabant. His successes on the Maas had already alarmed the French government, who feared that he might march to the Rhine to join the Imperialists, and they consequently despatched Tallard with a large force to protect the important fortified towns of Cologne and Bonn, thus seriously weakening Boufflers, who remained at Tongres, some dozen miles south-west of Maestricht, whence he could watch Liege and the fortified lines covering the frontier of southern Brabant. Convinced that the Allies meditated an attack on the latter city, Boufflers advanced, but found that he had been forestalled by his opponents, who were drawn up in superior force across his route. His position was most critical; in fact, he was only saved from disaster by the intervention of the deputies, who forbade an attack, and once again allowed the French Army to retreat unmolested.

As soon as the Allies appeared before Liege the garrison, amounting to some 5,000 men, abandoned the city, and retreated into the citadel and to the strong fortress of Chartreuse, on the opposite bank of the Maas. The siege of the citadel was pressed with the utmost vigour, and after a severe bombardment it was most gallantly carried by assault, whereupon the commandment of the fortress of Chartreuse, seeing no hope of relief, surrendered without waiting to be attacked. The capture of Liege, which had been accomplished in under a fortnight, brought the campaign to a conclusion, and though he had gained possession of the fortress-studded line of the Maas and freed Holland from the fear of invasion, Marlborough was profoundly dissatisfied.

He had several times been within an ace of crushing the hostile army, but on every occasion the advantage gained by his skilful manoeuvres had been neutralised by the timidity of the deputies, who invariably refused to risk a battle. The absurd system of dual control was obviously impossible, more especially as the deputies, concerned entirely with the defence of the Dutch frontiers and the reduction of a few relatively unimportant fortresses, consistently ignored the broader interests of the campaign. They looked at the situation entirely from their own point of view, and wished to use the forces of the coalition to defend Holland without the least regard to the strategical needs of the situation or the interests of their allies.

In spite of their initial success in the capture of Landau, which de Catinat, commanding the French troops in Alsace, had been too weak to prevent, the Allies had been most unsuccessful on the Rhine. The Elector of Bavaria had thrown in his lot with France and, joined by Villars with a strong force from the Rhine, had seized the important fortress of Ulm, threatened Lewis of Baden's communications with Vienna, and created a formidable diversion in the heart of Germany.

Towards the end of October, the latter fell back to Friedlingen, where he was heavily defeated by Villars, who received his well-earned marshal's baton as a reward for his victory, which, though obtained too late in the year to have any immediate result, went far to neutralise the successes achieved by the Allies in the Netherlands.

In northern Italy, Eugene with a small and wretchedly equipped army had with difficulty held his own against a far superior force under Vendôme, and the campaign in this portion of the theatre of operations dragged on to an indefinite conclusion.

During the winter of 1702, Louis XIV. formed the most comprehensive plans for the ensuing campaign, and made prodigious effort to enable his armies to take the field in overwhelming strength from the North Sea to the Mediterranean. Boufflers and Villeroi with 120,000 men were to assume the offensive in the Netherlands, Villars with 35,000 was to join the Elector of Bavaria in carrying the war into the heart of Germany, Tallard with a large force was to operate on the Rhine, while Vendôme was to drive the Imperial Army out of northern Italy. In February 1703, Villars opened the campaign by investing the strong fortress of Kehl, situated on the right bank of the Rhine opposite Strasburg, and though the place had been considered impregnable, the siege was pressed with such vigour that the garrison were forced to surrender in less than a fortnight.

On his return to The Hague in March, Marlborough, who had been created a Duke in recognition of his services during the previous campaign, wished to invade southern Brabant, capture Antwerp and

Ostend, and eventually carry the war into France; but this scheme was much too daring to appeal to the States General, who were seriously alarmed by the presence of the hostile force at Cologne, and refused to allow their troops to undertake any operations outside their own frontiers. During the winter the veteran Ginkel, Earl of Athlone, died and was succeeded by Overkirk, who had endeared himself to the British troops by his splendid gallantry at Steinkirk, and who was undoubtedly by far the ablest general in the Dutch service.

Eventually, though not without the greatest difficulty, Marlborough induced the States General to agree to a modification of his original plan, but only on condition that he first captured Cologne and Bonn. Leaving Overkirk to protect the line of the Maas and some detachments to watch the hostile force round Antwerp, he marched the main body, some 30,000 strong, to besiege Bonn, but the small garrison under the Marquis d'Allegre made such a gallant resistance that the town did not fall until the beginning of May. Meanwhile Villeroi attempted to make a diversion by an attack on Maestricht and advanced to Tongres, but the garrison, though only consisting of a couple of battalions, held out for two days, and Overkirk, making a rapid forced march, was enabled to take up a position covering Maestricht.

When the French arrived in front of the city in the morning of the 12th of May after a fatiguing night march, Villeroi found the Allies so strongly posted that though he had a considerable numerical superiority, he decided not to risk an attack, and fell back towards Louvain. Hurrying back from the Rhine, Marlborough collected a force of over 50,000 men and prepared to carry out his designs against Antwerp and Ostend, but his scheme was frustrated by Cohorn, who, instead of besieging the latter city, made an incursion into Spanish Flanders. Undismayed by his failure, the duke evolved a brilliant scheme for the capture of Antwerp—leaving detachments under Cohorn, Spaar and Opdam to observe the city, he marched eastward and manoeuvred to keep the main force of the enemy engaged between Liege and Namur.

His intention was to make a rapid forced march to Antwerp and, picking up his detachments on the way, to capture the city by a *coup de main* before Villeroi could arrive to relieve it. Cohorn, however, again upset his carefully laid plans by making a second raid into Flanders and leaving Opdam's detachment at Eckeren entirely unsupported. At once realising the danger of the isolated Dutch corps, Marlborough ordered it to retire and marched with the main body of the Allies to its support; but the incapable Opdam refused to move, and though the duke pressed forward by forced marches, he was too late to avert the disaster. Villeroi had already despatched Boufflers to crush the exposed force, and, joined by the garrison of Antwerp, the French general, with some 30,000 men, suddenly fell on his opponents, whose leader fled in wild panic to Breda, announcing that his corps had been annihilated. Fortunately, Slangenberg, the second in command, was made of sterner stuff; skilfully posting his men behind the hedges and ditches, he managed to hold his own against the French, though the latter pressed home their attack with the greatest gallantry.

The Dutch infantry, fighting with their habitual stolid bravery, maintained their position until long after nightfall, and then, forcing their way through their opponents, who had seized the dykes in their rear, managed to make good their retreat, though at a cost of 4,500 men killed, wounded and missing. The affair had a most disastrous sequel, as Slangenberg, though a brave and capable soldier, possessed a most ungovernable temper, and declaring that Marlborough had intentionally exposed the Dutch force to disaster, he deliberately set himself to thwart his leader's plans.

After considerable difficulty, the States General were induced to agree to an attack on the lines of the Scheldt and to provide 100 heavy guns for the enterprise, but when Marlborough had collected some 64,000 men, and was preparing to carry the entrenchments, the deputies at the last moment vetoed the attack. Reluctantly forced to abandon his schemes by the continual opposition of his allies, Marlborough marched back to the Meuse, and during August and September captured the fortresses of Huy and Limburg; but the season for campaigning was almost over, and as the autumnal rains had set in with unusual severity, he placed the army in winter quarters.

Owing to the constant interference of the deputies, and the incompetence of the Dutch commanders, the only result of the operations in the Netherlands during the summer of 1703 had been the capture of a few fortresses of minor importance, and it was obvious that there was not the least chance of bringing the campaign to a successful conclusion until the vicious system of dual control had been abolished.

On the Rhine the armies of Louis had been most successful; Villars had joined the Elector of Bavaria and, giving up all hope of enticing Lewis of Baden from his entrenched position at Stolhofen, had formed the masterly scheme of marching down the valley of the Danube to Vienna, and forcing the emperor to sue for peace. Fortunately for the Allies, the Elector of Bavaria, led away by the prospect of extending his dominions, made an unsuccessful incursion into the Tyrol, and the brilliant strategic counterstroke devised by the French marshal was not carried out.

Villars meanwhile had heavily defeated a strong force of Imperialists under General Stirum at Hochstädt, on the Danube, but disgusted by his colleague's incompetence, he handed over his command to Marsin. His bold strategy, however, was to a certain extent successful, for Lewis of Baden, alarmed for his line of communications, fell back to Kempten, on the borders of the Tyrol, and the Franco-Bavarian Army captured the important town of Augsburg. Tallard had also been successful; leaving Vauban to besiege New Breisach, he defeated the Prince of Hesse-Cassell at Spires, and recaptured Landau. Vendôme also had gained considerable ground in northern Italy, in spite of the fact that the Duke of Savoy had joined the Allies, who had been reinforced by a strong contingent under the capable Staremberg.

The bold and vigorous strategy of Louis XIV. had been attended with a considerable measure of success: in the Netherlands he had held his most dangerous opponent in check, on the Rhine his armies had been uniformly successful, and had Villars' daring scheme been carried out in its entirety, the emperor, harassed by the rebellion in Hungary, would have been forced to sue for peace. This would have undoubtedly been the death-blow to the Alliance, as the German princes would have withdrawn their contingents, and northern Italy would have fallen at once into French hands.

CHAPTER 3

The Campaign of 1704

Encouraged by his successes in the previous year, Louis XIV. conceived a most masterly scheme for the ensuing campaign and strained the resources of his empire to the uttermost to enable him to carry out his ideas on a suitable scale. The decisive blow was to be struck in the valley of the Danube. Tallard, advancing from the Rhine, was to join Marsin and the Elector of Bavaria in carrying the war into the heart of Austria, and taking advantage of the diversion caused by the rebellion in Hungary, the French commander was to advance on Vienna and force the emperor to sue for peace.

Vendôme, meanwhile was to drive the Imperialists from northern Italy, subdue the Tyrol, and finally co-operate with the main Franco-Bavarian Army in the valley of the Danube. Villeroi was to remain on the defensive in the Netherlands and to prevent the Allies sending reinforcements to the aid of the Imperial forces in Germany, the Duke of Berwick with a large army was to stamp finally all resistance in Spain, and Villars was to suppress the insurrection in the Cevennes. Such was the scheme, Napoleonic in its scope, for the employment of the armies of France in the ensuing campaign, and it appeared certain that Louis' bold strategy must achieve the most far-reaching results even if it failed to bring the war to a triumphant conclusion.

From a military standpoint, the Empire was undoubtedly the predominant partner in the 'Grand Alliance,' and if the emperor could be forced to come to terms, the Duke of Savoy and the minor German princes must of necessity follow his lead. Louis XIV. could then concentrate an overwhelming force against the Dutch and their British allies in the Low Countries, and force the former to sue for peace on any terms he might choose to grant. The great Confederacy, organised with such pains by William III., appeared to be tottering to its fall, but it was destined to be saved, and the carefully thought-out schemes of

Louis XIV. brought to naught, by the Duke of Marlborough's remarkable diplomatic and military ability. Realising that the decisive issue of the campaign would be fought out on the Danube, and weary of the purposeless operations in the cramped, fortress-studded 'terrain' of the Netherlands, where, owing to the continual interference of the Dutch field deputies, decisive results were impossible, the duke determined to transfer the greater portion of the Allied Army to join Eugene in the valley of the Danube.

This daring scheme was not communicated in all its details either to the British government or to the States General, only Eugene and the able Dutch statesman, Heinsius, on whose loyal co-operation the duke could implicitly rely, being taken into his confidence. He intimated to the States General that he proposed to undertake a campaign in the valley of the Moselle, and wrung from them a most reluctant consent by threatening to withdraw all the troops paid by Great Britain unless they fell in with his views.

Overkirk was to remain in the Low Countries with a small force to counter Villeroi, and, by the exercise of the greatest patience and tact, Marlborough eventually succeeded in persuading the King of Prussia and the rulers of the other German states to place their contingents in such a position as would enable them to take part in the forthcoming operations.

In order to entail as little hardship as possible on the troops, the most careful preparations for the 'great march' were made, the route was minutely reconnoitred, the stages mapped out beforehand, and supply depots established at suitable points. Fifty battalions and 90 squadrons, among whom were 16,000 British troops, were assembled on the Maas, in the vicinity of Roermond, under the duke's brother, General Charles Churchill, and during its march the army was to be joined by the Prussian, German and Danish contingents. The troops quitted their cantonments on the 19th of May, and moved towards Bonn, at which town they were to be joined by Marlborough, who had been temporarily detained at The Hague making final arrangements for the campaign. He had barely started to join the army when he received an urgent message from Overkirk, informing him that Villeroi had crossed the Meuse at Namur and was advancing towards Huy; while almost at the same moment, Lewis of Baden begged for reinforcements, as he feared that Tallard meditated an attack on his entrenched lines at Stolhofen.

Realising that Villeroi would not seriously invade Holland while he imagined his opponent to be moving towards the valley of the Moselle, and that Tallard's real object was to effect a junction with the Franco-Bavarian Army on the Danube, Marlborough managed to reassure his allies.

By his visit to Bonn and the fact that he had sent his baggage and artillery up the Rhine to Mainz, the duke strengthened his opponents' belief that he was about to commence a campaign in the valley of the Moselle, and he confirmed their suspicions by pressing forward with his cavalry to Mainz. He still further mystified them by ordering the Landgrave of Hesse to bring his artillery to Mannheim, and thoroughly alarmed Villeroi and Tallard by ordering the construction of a bridge over the Rhine at Philipsburg. Marlborough then crossed the Main, and accompanied by his cavalry, pushed forward to the Neckar, which he crossed at Ladenburg on the 3rd of June.

Halting for a couple of days to rest his troops and arrange for the movements of some reinforcements, which were marching up from the Rhine, the duke then resumed his march southward, and reached Mondelsheim a week later. He was joined by Eugene, who had ridden across from his army to meet him and who was much struck by the appearance and equipment of the British cavalry, which he pronounced the best appointed that he had ever seen, and whose splendid condition, he was convinced, promised well for the coming campaign.

Three days later, the Margrave Lewis of Baden arrived in the Allied camp to confer with his brother commanders; his presence, however, appeared likely to cause considerable friction, as though he was a brave and moderately capable general, he was slow and extremely cautious, as well as most punctilious with regard to his rank. It had been arranged that the duke should co-operate with Eugene in the valley of the Danube, while the Margrave conducted the operations on the Rhine, where his territorial influence would be of considerable value. But this arrangement did not suit Lewis of Baden, who insisted on Eugene returning to the Rhine, while, as senior general, he laid claim to the command of the Allied armies, and it needed all Marlborough's great diplomatic skill to induce him to accept command on alternate days.

Though this was a most undesirable arrangement, it was probably the best that could have been made under the circumstances, and it resulted in allaying all jealousies, while the duke, by his tact and charm of manner, succeeded in getting a large share of the direction of affairs into his own hands. It was eventually settled that Eugene, reinforced by a division from the valley of the Danube, should remain on the Rhine watching Tallard, who was still in Alsace with some 40,000 men, while the main body of the Allies should crush the Franco-Bavarian force under the Elector and Marsin. A fresh difficulty now arose, for the States General were again becoming alarmed as to Villeroi's intentions; but Marlborough, recognising that the decisive issue of the campaign would be fought out in the valley of the Danube, managed to pacify them by collecting a flotilla of boats on the Upper Rhine, and promising to return to Holland if a serious invasion took place.

He then resumed his march, and in spite of the wretched state of the roads and the continual rain, passed through the difficult defile of Geislingen and effected his junction with the Imperial Army a few miles north of Ulm on the 22nd of June. The whole force then marched eastward to Gingen to await the arrival of the artillery and the bulk of the infantry under General Churchill, who had been delayed by the difficulties of the road; while the Elector and Marsin took up their position round Dillingen, on the Danube between Ulm and Donauworth, whence they could operate on either bank of the river.

During the march of the Allies from the Meuse, every possible provision had been made for the comfort of the men, while the discipline of the troops and the fact that all supplies were scrupulously paid for, astonished the inhabitants of the countries through which they passed. About the middle of May, Tallard had made a brilliant dash through the Black Forest and handed over to the Elector, who had moved westward to meet him, a strong reinforcement of over 7,000 men and a huge convoy of supplies. As soon as his task was safely completed, the French marshal had returned to the Rhine, as the objective of Marlborough's march was still uncertain and it was considered probable that he intended to operate in the valley of the Moselle or to invade Alsace.

Lewis of Baden had then chased the Elector out of the Black Forest and eastward down the valley of the Danube, and having driven the Franco-Bavarian Army away from their allies on the Rhine, the Margrave remained near Ulm to await the arrival of Marlborough's force.

By the junction of their armies on the Danube, the Allied leaders had successfully accomplished the first part of their scheme, and they were in a position to choose whether they would at once destroy the hostile field army or capture Donauworth and open up an alternative line of communication. Undoubtedly Napoleon would have first crushed the Franco-Bavarian Army, before it could possibly receive re-

Sketch Map Illustrating
MARLBOROUGH'S MARCH TO
THE DANUBE
MAY–JUNE 1704

WESTPHALIA

HOLLAND

SPANISH NETHERLANDS

F R A N C E

LORRAINE

THE PALATINATE

WURTEMBERG

BAVARIA

ROERMOND

BESBACH

BONN

COBLENTZ

MAINZ

LADENBURG

FRANKFORT

THIONVILLE

STRASBURG

ULM

AUGSBURG

INGOLSTADT

R. RHINE

R. DANUBE

MARLBOROUGH'S ROUTE ------

SCALE

inforcements from the Rhine, and then have carried out the remainder of his plan at leisure, but though Marlborough was far in advance of his age as a strategist, he was to a certain extent bound by the prevailing methods of waging war and the idea that the enemy's fortresses, not their field armies, were the true objective. Even had the duke adopted the former course, Lewis of Baden would have certainly opposed it, probably to the extent of refusing to co-operate, and there was much to be said in favour of the immediate capture of Donauworth.

Situated on the Danube, near its junction with the Lech, the city was undoubtedly the 'gate of Bavaria,' and its possession would afford the Allies an excellent advanced base, enable them to act at will on either bank of the river and open up a fresh line of communication with Nordlingen and Nuremberg. It was decided to make a dash at Donauworth and seize the town before the Franco-Bavarian Army could interfere, but the advance was delayed by the dilatory movements of the Duke of Wirtemberg, who was on his way to join the main body with the Danish cavalry. Foreseeing his opponent's intention, the Elector sent forward a detachment of 12,000 men under D'Arco to occupy the heights of Schellenberg, which commanded the town, and prepared to follow him with the remainder of his force.

The duke was most anxious to seize the position before D'Arco could be reinforced, but Lewis of Baden, whose turn it was to command the Allied Army, was so impressed by its strength that he refused to risk an immediate assault. Next day, however, it was Marlborough's turn, and before dawn Cadogan, the quartermaster-general, pushed forward with the pioneers and bridging train, escorted by a detachment of cavalry, and was shortly followed by the advance guard, some 10,000 strong, and the artillery. Driving the hostile pickets from Obermorgan soon after eight o'clock, he commenced to lay out the camp, while Marlborough, riding forward with the cavalry escort, carefully reconnoitred the enemy's position.

Their camp was pitched on the flat top of the Schellenberg, a hill on the left bank of the Danube, just east of the town, on which some old entrenchments already existed, and on these the garrison were working with feverish activity. A small half-ruined fort, in which some guns had been mounted, commanded the line of approach from the north-west, on which side the works were also protected by a small stream, which ran through a narrow ravine, past the eastern wall of the town into the Danube. On the right, which rested on the river, and in the centre, the entrenchments had been nearly completed, and even

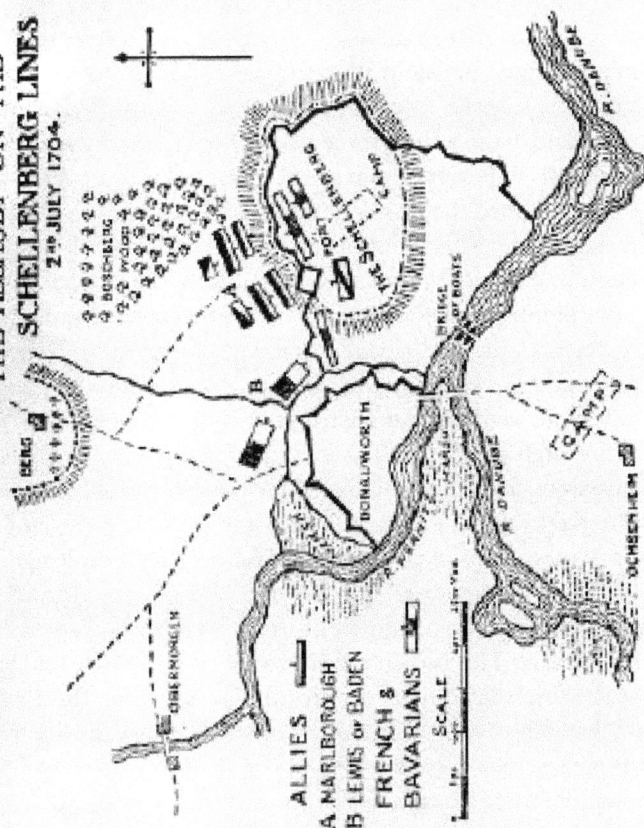

THE ASSAULT ON THE
SCHELLENBERG LINES.
2ⁿᵈ JULY 1704.

R. DANUBE

FORT SCHELLENBERG

THE SCHELLENBERG CAMP

BOSCHBERG

WOOD

BERG

B

DONALWORTH

BRIDGE OF BOATS

R. DANUBE

CAMP

OCHSENHEIM

OBERMDSELN

ALLIES ———
A MARLBOROUGH
B LEWIS OF BADEN
FRENCH &
BAVARIANS ▭▭▭

SCALE

now the position appeared so formidable, that the duke realised that every additional hour the garrison were allowed to strengthen their defences, would cost the Allies several hundred men.

South of the Danube, near Ochsenheim, a large-camp had been marked out and the space on either side was already occupied by 'cavalry, clearly indicating that reinforcements might be expected almost immediately. The roads were so bad that the Allies' advance guard only reached the bridge over the Wernitz at noon, and they then halted to allow the main body to close up; while the cavalry were sent forward into the woods to make fascines.

While waiting for his troops to arrive, Marlborough received a despatch from Eugene informing him that Villeroi was at Strasburg, and that Tallard with a large force was about to commence his march through the Black Forest to join the Elector, and this unwelcome intelligence strengthened the duke's determination to capture Donauworth as soon as possible. Meanwhile D'Arco, hearing of the Allies' advance, had ridden out to reconnoitre, but seeing only the cavalry patrols and noting the preparations for pitching camp, he came to the conclusion that no attack would be delivered that day. However, on his return, he pressed forward the work on the defences, and devoutly hoped that the expected reinforcements would arrive during the night.

Marlborough detailed 6,000 infantry for the attack, of whom five battalions were British, (1st Guards, 1st Royals—two battalions, 23rd and 37th Regts. Fortescue's *History of the British Army*), and the remainder Dutch, the cavalry were to follow the assaulting column, while eight battalions were to move forward in support and to prolong the line if necessary, and eight more were to be kept in hand to form the reserve. The infantry were to carry fascines to enable them to cross the ditch in front of the hostile works, while the British and German batteries were to come into action from the high ground round Berg to cover the advance.

The whole force was under the command of General Goor, a brave and experienced Dutch officer, and Marlborough, accompanying the troops up to the edge of the Boschberg wood, which extended almost up to the centre of the hostile position, gave the order to advance at six o'clock. The infantry moved forward in four lines, the British battalions being on the left, close to the wood, while the cavalry followed in two lines in close support; the first line was commanded by Brigadier-General Ferguson, and the whole was preceded by a 'forlorn hope' composed of volunteers from the Grenadier Guards under

Lord Maudant and Colonel Munden.

As the infantry moved forward against the left centre of the hostile works, they were exposed to a furious fire from the guns in the entrenchments and on the walls of the town. But though many of the British regiments were largely composed of young soldiers taking part in their first battle, they advanced with the greatest steadiness, and in spite of their heavy losses, arrived within a hundred yards of the entrenchments without having fired a shot. The hail of grape and musketry now began to tell on the crowded ranks with deadly effect, but closing up the gaps in their line, the staunch infantry pressed steadily forward. General Goor and many of the officers fell, and the column staggered for a moment, but quickly recovering itself, again surged forward.

By an unfortunate mistake the men threw their fascines into a shallow ravine some yards in front of the hostile works, and when they reached the ditch, they were seriously delayed and suffered heavily. Seeing that the assailants showed signs of wavering under the deadly fire, D'Arco ordered some French and Bavarian battalions to make a counter-attack, but the Guards, though most of their officers had fallen, stood as firm as a rock and beat back their opponents with heavy loss. The whole line then dashed forward and strove desperately to storm the entrenchments, but the garrison, fighting with dogged courage behind their breastworks, drove them back into the ditch after a sanguinary hand to hand combat. Appalled by the slaughter, some of the young soldiers from the regiments in support began to drift back into the wood, but they were driven forward into the fight by Lumley's cavalry, who had closed up to support their hard-pressed comrades.

For over an hour the furious struggle continued. D'Arco drawing more and more troops from his left, managed to hold his own though the dauntless infantry swarmed over the entrenchments three times, but only to be hurled back by their stubborn opponents. Lumley moved the whole of his first line of cavalry into the fight to support the infantry, and a counter attack was beaten back with crushing loss, but still the Allies could not gain a foothold in the works. At this moment the Imperialists, who had advanced under the walls of Donauworth against the extreme left of the position, scaled the almost deserted entrenchments, and cheering lustily, suddenly fell on their opponents' flank. The latter held their ground doggedly, but with a supreme effort the dauntless British and Dutch infantry, among whom the Scots Greys were fighting on foot, hurled themselves against the parapet and drove the garrison from the works they had so stoutly held.

The resistance suddenly collapsed, the French and Bavarian infantry flying in wild panic towards the pontoon bridges over the river, while the Scots Greys, hastily remounting, joined the remainder of the cavalry, which Marlborough at once launched in pursuit. Hundreds of fugitives, half mad with terror, were cut down or driven into the Wernitz, while to add to the horror of the scene, the pontoon bridges over the Danube gave way under the strain of the disorganised crowd endeavouring to force its way across. Hundreds of panic-stricken wretches were precipitated into the rapidly flowing river, and barely 3,000 stragglers succeeded in reaching the Elector's camp at Dillingen.

Many senior officers, including the Prince of Bevern, Generals Goor and Stirum, had fallen in the desperate assaults, while 1,500 of the Allies lay dead in front of the entrenchments, and the wounded amounted to another 3,500. Though the action had lasted for little more than an hour and a half, it had been a most sanguinary struggle, and the French and Bavarians had offered such a desperate resistance, that it was only the appearance of the Imperialists on their flank which had decided the issue of the day.

At the conclusion of the engagement the rain poured down in torrents, and after doing everything possible for the comfort of the wounded, Marlborough, leaving a strong garrison to hold the captured works, returned to the camp on the Wernitz. Though he had entered the position almost without resistance, Lewis of Baden, with characteristic perversity, insisted in claiming the victory as his own, on the grounds that he actually set foot in the entrenchments before the Duke of Marlborough. The latter had undoubtedly taken a great risk in attacking the formidable position with a force only equal to the garrison, but his daring was justified by the result, as well as by the enormous value of the town to the Allies.

Louis XIV. endeavoured to minimise the disaster by styling it 'a successful retreat,' but the fact remained that the duke had succeeded in his object, and that the hitherto invincible French troops had been driven from their strong position with appalling loss. Donauworth was abandoned and set on fire, but the Allies entered the town before much damage had been done, and the Elector, thrown into a state of wild panic by the news of the disaster, set fire to his magazines, evacuated his entrenched camp at Dillingen, and retired in haste to a position under the walls of Augsburg.

Marlborough followed up his victory with vigour; crossing the

Danube and Lech, he captured the small fortress of Rain, which protected the passage over the latter river, and went into camp at Mittelstellen, whence he issued an ultimatum to the Elector, giving him the choice of abandoning the French alliance or exposing his country to the horrors of a military execution. While these stirring events had been in progress on the Danube a most important development had occurred on the Rhine. Tallard had made up his mind on the 1st of July to advance through the Black Forest with some 40,000 men to join the Elector, and as Eugene was too weak to attack him during the march, the brilliant Austrian general was forced to resort to a ruse.

Advancing unmolested through the Black Forest, the French marshal laid siege to Villingen, a fortress which was situated on his line of communication from the Rhine to the Danube, but on the 18th of July he received a letter from Marsin informing him of the disaster at Schellenberg, the invasion of Bavaria, and begging him to hasten his march regardless of obstacles, as the Elector was contemplating suing for peace unless he was supported at once. Eugene meanwhile had carried out a most brilliant manoeuvre; marching northward as far as Turbingen on the Neckar, he apparently intended to return to his original position on the Rhine, but selecting a picked force of 15,000 men, a large proportion of whom were excellent cavalry, he suddenly struck due east towards the Danube, moving parallel to, but north of, his opponent's line of march.

As the Elector had refused to abandon his alliance with France, Marlborough, much as he disliked inflicting suffering on the unoffending inhabitants, had been forced to give Bavaria over to the horrors of a military execution. Burning villages and destroying crops, the Allies raided up to the gates of Munich, but were unable to capture the town as they were without heavy artillery, though they thoroughly succeeded in bringing home to the wretched inhabitants of Bavaria the peril of allying themselves with France. Meanwhile Tallard, on the receipt of a second letter from Marsin begging him to join the Elector without delay, had raised the siege of Villingen and resumed his march.

Though his men were almost starving and his horses dying in hundreds from want of proper forage, he resolutely pushed forward, reaching Ulm at the end of July, and successfully effecting his junction with the Elector under the walls of Augsburg on the 4th of August. His arrival entirely altered the situation, for the Allies were now slightly inferior to their opponents, and their only line of retreat through Donauworth to Nordlingen and Nuremberg was seriously threatened, while the peasants, maddened by the misery they had endured, were already menacing their communications.

The Franco-Bavarian Army moved northward towards their original position at Dillingen, and the Allies, forced to comply by the danger to their communications, moved towards the Danube, making for the crossing at Neuburg. The situation underwent another startling change on the 8th of August, for on that day Eugene arrived at Hochstädt, on the Danube, some twelve miles west of Donauworth, and rode over to the Allied camp to confer with Marlborough. The Margrave of Baden was persuaded to undertake the siege of Ingolstadt, a strong fortress lower down the Danube, and his departure with a force of 16,000 men freed Marlborough and Eugene from the presence of an unwelcome colleague, whose extreme caution acted as a drag on their brilliant strategy.

The Franco-Bavarian Army had meanwhile crossed to the northern bank of the Danube at Dillingen and advanced towards Eugene's detachment, which had taken up its position behind the Kessel, a small stream flowing into the river some six miles west of Donauworth, and the only problem to be solved was whether the Allies could concentrate before Tallard attacked the isolated force. Requesting Eugene to fall back to the Schellenberg position, if necessary, Marlborough made a splendid forced march, and crossing the Danube in two columns at Merxheim and Donauworth, succeeded in joining his colleague late on the evening of the 11th of August.

The Allies were now in a strong position on the northern bank of the Danube, covering Donauworth and their communications through Nordlingen to Nuremberg, and had the choice of either attacking their opponents or falling back towards their base at the latter town. As the opposing forces were almost equal in strength, Marlborough was strongly in favour of fighting a decisive battle, which should settle the fate of the campaign and once for all break the French power in the valley of the Danube, and Eugene unhesitatingly concurred in the bold scheme. Tallard had advanced through Hochstädt and taken up a strong position behind the Nebel, with his right resting on the Danube at Blenheim; the Elector was now most eager to fight, but the French marshal considered it most probable that the Allies would retreat northward towards their base.

CHAPTER 4

The Campaign of 1704 (Continued)

THE BATTLE OF BLENHEIM—13TH OF AUGUST 1704.

The great battle which was to crown Marlborough's brilliant strategy by a decisive victory, and once and for all free Austria from the menace of invasion, took place some three miles east of Hochstädt, on the undulating plain, which was bounded on the south by the Danube, and on the north by a range of wooded hills, running parallel to, and about three miles distant from, the river.

The Nebel, a shallow, sluggish stream, rising in the hills near Schwenenbach, flowed between low marshy banks in a south-easterly direction past the villages of Oberglau, Weilheim, Unterglau to Blenheim, where it joined the Danube. Midway between the two latter villages, the main road from Donauworth to Ulm crossed the stream over a stone bridge, and bending southward to Hochstädt, followed the northern bank of the Danube to Dillingen.

The Franco-Bavarian Army was encamped on the rising ground about three-quarters of a mile west of the Nebel. Tallard was on the right, with his outer flank resting on the village of Blenheim, which had been put in a state of defence, and was strengthened by a formidable stockade. His centre was astride the main road, and his left opposite the village of Unterglau, from which point Marsin and the Elector carried on the line, the bulk of the former's troops being round Oberglau, while the Bavarians were on the extreme left, between the village and the wooded hills. In point of numbers there was little difference between the rival armies, the Allies numbering 52,000, and their opponents about two thousand more, but the French had a great superiority in artillery, having 90 guns against their adversaries' 60.

There was, however, no comparison in the abilities of the rival leaders, Marlborough and Eugene were the two most brilliant com-

43

THE BATTLE OF BLENHEIM
13ᵗʰ AUGUST 1704.

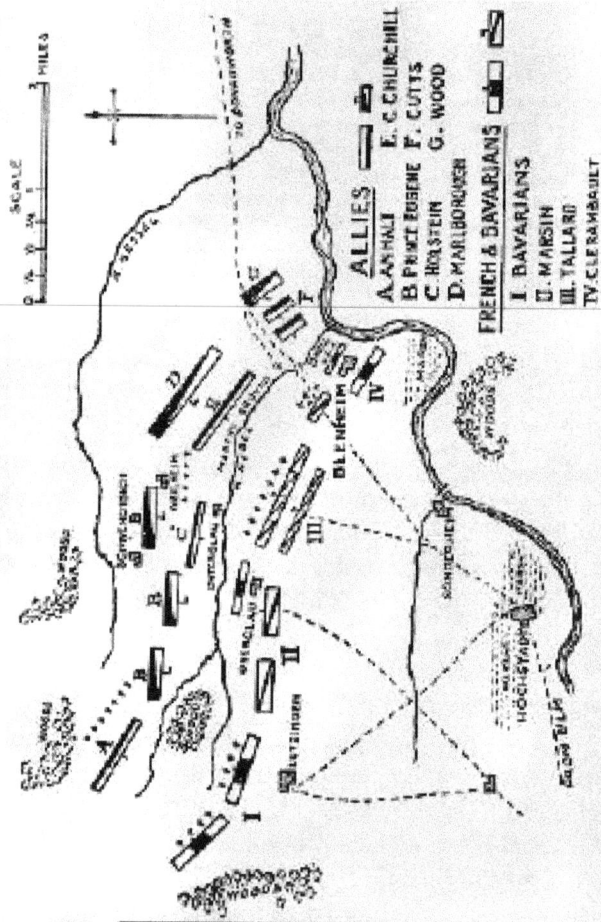

SCALE

3 MILES

ALLIES

A. ANHALT   E. C. CHURCHILL
B. PRINCE EUGENE   F. CUTTS
C. HOLSTEIN   G. WOOD
D. MARLBOROUGH

FRENCH & BAVARIANS

I. BAVARIANS
II. MARSIN
III. TALLARD
IV. CLERAMBAULT

R. SEDEL

BLENHEIM

SONDERHEIM

OBERGLAU

UNTERGLAU

HÖCHSTADT

manders of their time and though this was the first occasion on which they had acted together, their movements were marked by that mutual understanding and perfect confidence which was so noticeable in all their subsequent undertakings, and which made them such ideal colleagues on the field of battle.

On the other hand, Tallard, though an able strategist, was no great tactician, while the Elector, though personally brave, had no claim to be considered a general, and Marsin possessed very little military ability. Except at Blenheim the Franco-Bavarian Army had made no attempt to strengthen its position, as Tallard thought it most unlikely that the Allies would risk an engagement, and he merely intended to remain in position to block their retreat westward along the northern bank of the Danube.

Marlborough and Eugene had carefully reconnoitred the hostile camp on the 12th of August, and at dawn next morning the Allied Army advanced from their bivouac, some five miles east of the Nebel, in nine columns, every man in the cosmopolitan host, which was composed of British, Dutch, Austrians, Prussians, Danes and Germans, being full of enthusiasm and supremely confident in the ability of their leaders. The Allied commanders rode forward to the village of Werdel, whence the whole of the enemy's position lay spread out before them, and Marlborough at once noticed the faulty manner in which his opponent had drawn up his troops.

Holding the village of Blenheim were the regiments of Navarre, Artois and Guelders, while the hedges and enclosures on their left were held by the Zurlaben regiment, with the Montreux regiment stationed immediately in rear of the village in reserve. In all, Clairambault had some 8,000 infantry and 1,500 dismounted dragoons crowded into Blenheim, which he had been ordered to hold to the last, while eight squadrons of mounted *gens d'armes* were drawn up on the left of the village, prepared to fall on the Allies as they struggled across the Nebel. The open space, some two miles in extent, between Blenheim and Oberglau was held by ten squadrons of cavalry, supported by a similar number of squadrons and nine battalions of infantry in the second line. For some not very obvious reason, Tallard had posted the whole of his reserve, consisting of eleven battalions of infantry, slightly in rear of Blenheim, to which he had already allotted a disproportionately strong garrison.

The Elector and Marsin had also posted the whole of their cavalry along their front, Oberglau was strongly held, and the Champagne,

Bourbonnois and Irish brigades were drawn up in behind the village, while on the left flank, eighteen Bavarian battalions were stationed in front of Lutzingen. The Franco-Bavarian leaders had made two very obvious mistakes: they had left a space of about half a mile between their front and the Nebel, on which the Allies could deploy, and the broad extent of open ground between Blenheim and Oberglau, through which the main road from Donauworth ran, was held almost entirely by cavalry.

Marlborough quickly formed his plans: he intended to make his main attack on Blenheim, the key of the hostile position, and as soon as the village was captured, roll up the enemy's line and cut off their retreat to Ulm. An attack was also to be made against the hostile centre astride the main road, while Eugene with his own corps, was to keep the opposing left, in front of Lutzingen, fully occupied. Shortly after seven o'clock the columns of the Allied Army approached the Nebel and deployed on the eastern bank under the distant fire of the hostile artillery, while some staff officers trotted forward to locate the fords, and five temporary bridges were hastily constructed over the stream.

The French Army was already drawn up, and their advanced posts had withdrawn from Unterglau, setting fire to the village as they retired, when Tallard, realising the danger of the weakly held gap between the villages of Blenheim and Oberglau, requested Marsin to post his reserve in rear of the centre, but the latter was unable to comply as he had already used them to prolong his line to the left. Owing to the greater distance which Eugene had to traverse to reach his position opposite the hostile left, a long wait was necessary, and during the interval Divine Service was celebrated at the head of every regiment.

On the extreme left of the Allied line, opposite Blenheim, a strong force of infantry, half of which was British, was drawn up in four lines under the command of Lord Cutts, who had been entrusted with the task of capturing the village. On their right, extending across the main road and almost up to the village of Unterglau, the main body of the Allied Army was formed in four lines, the first and last being composed of infantry, and the two intermediate lines of cavalry. Eugene's infantry were posted in front of Weilheim, and his cavalry on the extreme flank between Schwenenbach and the lower spurs of the wooded hills, while the bulk of the artillery had taken up their position in rear of his line, on the high ground between the two villages, to cover his advance.

Marlborough waited impatiently until his right should have got into position, but they had been considerably delayed, as it was found that the enemy's left extended much farther than had been anticipated, but about half-past twelve an *aide-de-camp* galloped up to report that Eugene was about to advance, and shortly afterwards his tidings were confirmed by the roar of the Allied batteries, which had come into action on the right. Shortly after 1 o'clock, Lord Cutts advanced against Blenheim with his division formed in four lines: the first line was composed of the Guards, 10th, 21st, 23rd and 24th Regiments under Row; the second of Hessians; the third of the 1st (the Royal Scots), 8th, 16th and 20th Regiments under Ferguson, and the fourth of Hanoverians, while Lumley commanded a force of British cavalry, which moved up on the right of the infantry.

The first two lines, crossing the marshy stream under the fire of the French guns, seized the partially burnt mill and reformed under the shelter of a slight rise in the ground. Leaving the Hessians under cover, Row, who had given his men orders to take the village with the bayonet, advanced on foot at the head of his brigade, which moved forward across the open space of under two hundred yards in perfect order. When they had arrived within thirty yards of the edge of the village they were met by a deadly volley, which caused enormous loss, but closing the gaps in their ranks they pressed forward, and it was not until Row had driven his sword into the palisade that the men received the order to fire. Forcing their muskets between the tree trunks they strove desperately to close with their opponents, but no troops, however courageous, could hold their ground in face of the deadly fire poured into their ranks from behind the palisades; the gallant Row fell, mortally wounded, and in the space of a few minutes a third of his staunch brigade had fallen.

As the survivors wavered and commenced to retire, they were thrown into confusion by a furious charge of some squadrons of *gens d'armes*, who had galloped round the northern edge of the village. The Hessians, however, gallantly covered the retreat of their comrades, recaptured a colour belonging to the 21st Regiment which had been lost in the *mêlée*, and drove back their opponents. Lord Cutts, seeing that a second charge was imminent, requested Lumley to bring forward his cavalry to protect the threatened flank, and the latter immediately ordered five squadrons to cross the Nebel. Though they had only just struggled through the marshy stream and had barely formed up, they drove back eight squadrons of *gens d'armes*, who had charged down the slope, and pursued them as far as the village, but disordered by their success, and galled by the fire of the French infantry, they were compelled to retreat.

They were pursued by the hostile cavalry, but the Hessians, swinging back their right with admirable steadiness, drove the *gens d'armes* from the field with deadly volleys delivered at point-blank range. In spite of the heavy fire of the hostile artillery, the Earl of Orkney led forward the second line, composed of Ferguson's and Hulsen's brigades, and the staunch infantry, undismayed by their losses, struggling through the marsh bordering the stream, advanced with perfect steadiness against the village. Three times they hurled themselves against the palisades with the most reckless gallantry, but each time they were driven back by the murderous fire of the infantry and dismounted dragoons holding the village.

Seeing that Blenheim was too strongly held to be taken by assault, Marlborough quickly decided to change his plan and make his decisive attack against the hostile centre; he ordered Cutts, who would have continued to hurl his men against the village until they had been annihilated, to withdraw to the cover of the crest of the ridge and remain opposite the hostile position, so as to prevent reinforcements being sent to the centre. Meanwhile General Charles Churchill had commenced his advance, part of his infantry struggling across the marsh bordering the Nebel by means of boards and fascines, while the remainder, marching through the blazing village of Unterglau, crossed the bridge, and the whole force deployed on the far side of the stream.

On their left, the bulk of the Allied squadrons had crossed the Nebel, but had not yet completed their formation, when they were fiercely charged by the French cavalry and thrown into confusion. Marlborough quickly brought some Danish and Hanoverian squadrons to their aid, and the steady fire of the infantry eventually forced the opposing horsemen to retreat; but had the French second line charged, the Allies must have been driven back into the marshy ground bordering the stream. To give room for his cavalry to deploy, Marlborough ordered the Prince of Holstein-Beck, with eleven Hanoverian battalions, to capture the strongly held village of Oberglau, but the men had hardly struggled across the marshy stream ere they were assailed by a vigorous counterstroke.

Charging down the slope from the village, the Irish brigade, supported by several battalions of French infantry, fell on the Hanoverians with the utmost fury, driving them back across the stream and capturing their leader, who had been mortally wounded while gallantly endeavouring to rally his men. Marlborough, however, was at hand, and sending a request to Eugene for reinforcements, he led forward Bernsdorf's Danish brigade to repair the disaster. Though Eugene had himself been driven back across the Nebel, and was at that moment engaged in reforming his line, he sent the Austrian *cuirassiers*, without a moment's hesitation, to support his colleague.

Galloping to the critical point, they suddenly fell on the French flank and threw their opponents into confusion, while the Allied infantry, pressing vigorously forward, drove them back to the village. Marlborough had now succeeded in firmly establishing his whole line on the western bank of the Nebel, and shortly after 5 o'clock prepared to lead his massed cavalry against his opponent's centre. Realising the imminence of the danger, Tallard ordered up his reserve from their position in rear of Blenheim, and requested Marsin to send some reinforcements. The latter, however, was engaged in a desperate struggle with Eugene's troops, and was unable to spare any men, while the message never reached Blenheim. Ordering his batteries east of the Nebel to cease fire and his trumpets to sound the charge, Marlborough swept up the gentle slope at the head of nearly 8,000 sabres.

For a few minutes they were checked by the accurate fire of the hostile infantry and artillery, but quickly rallying his men, who were now closely supported by some Hanoverian battalions, the duke charged forward in irresistible might at the head of his formidable array of horsemen. Though mostly young soldiers, the French infantry stood their ground with the most determined gallantry, and their deadly fire emptied many of their opponents' saddles, but their own cavalry, after a half-hearted attempt to charge, fired a few scattered volleys from their carbines, and, turning about, galloped from the field in hopeless rout.

The heroic infantry were ridden down and cut to pieces, while Marsin's squadrons, seeing their flank uncovered, fell back, and, after a desperate struggle among the burning cottages, Lord Clare's regiment was driven from the village of Oberglau, which they had so gallantly defended. Owing to the long detour they had been forced to make, it was not until nearly 2 o'clock that the right wing of the Allies came into action, the Prince of Anhalt then led eighteen Prussian and Danish battalions across the Nebel against the extreme left of the Bavarian position.

Suffering from the hostile artillery posted some distance in front of Lutzingen, they were unable to make much headway until their own batteries had taken up a position in front of the wood, southwest of Schwenenbach, to cover their advance. Then, pressing forward gallantly, they succeeded in capturing the battery which had caused them such heavy loss, while the Imperial cavalry, fording the stream on their left, deployed and drove back the first line of the opposing horsemen. Their success was short-lived, however, for the Bavarians, fighting under the eye of their Elector, quickly rallied, driving back the Imperial squadrons, recapturing the battery, and after a furious struggle, forced the staunch Prussian infantry to fall back. Anhalt threw himself into the thick of the fight, and rallying his shaken battalions, led them back to the shelter of the wood, while Eugene, sword in hand, led two successive charges, but without gaining any ground.

Both sides now halted for a short breathing space; the Elector, with excellent judgment, advanced his line close up to the Nebel, and riding down the ranks, encouraged his men to renew their exertions, while Anhalt, reforming his battalions, extended them northward in order to outflank his opponent's line. As soon as he was in position Eugene again charged at the head of his cavalry, but discouraged by their previous want of success they put little heart into their work. In disgust he left them to George of Hanover and the Duke of Wirtemberg, galloping off to put himself at the head of his staunch infantry, who were gradually fighting their way forward in the teeth of a dogged resistance. Inspirited by the presence of their leader, who as usual recklessly exposed himself in the thickest of the fight, they drove back their opponents as far as the village of Lutzingen.

It was now past 5 o'clock; the crisis of the battle was at hand, and Marlborough had already launched his decisive stroke against his opponent's centre. Eugene witnessed the overthrow of the French cavalry from the high ground north of Lutzingen, and promptly sending the only two squadrons that he had at hand to join in the pursuit, he forced his way towards the village at the head of his dauntless infantry. Marsin had already given the order to retreat, and the whole left wing of the Franco-Bavarian Army fell back in good order to Dillingen, setting fire to Lutzingen as they retired, and abandoning their comrades in Blenheim to their fate.

Eugene urged his men forward in pursuit, but his infantry were desperately weary after their prolonged and deadly struggle, while the firm array of the retreating French and Bavarian battalions, rendered futile any attempt by the cavalry to carry out the pursuit unsupported. In the centre, the rout had been complete, and Marlborough, ordering

Hompesch to swing forward to his right, sent the Prussian squadrons thundering in pursuit of the masses of fugitives streaming towards the temporary bridge at Sonderheim, and along the road to Hochstädt.

Hundreds of wretched fugitives were driven into the Danube or entangled in the morass bordering the Hochstädt road were cut down by the Prussian troopers, while Tallard himself with his entire staff was captured by a Hessian squadron near Sonderheim, as he was endeavouring to make his way to Blenheim to bring up his infantry reserve. Collecting his cavalry, Marlborough was about to let them loose on the hostile left wing, which was retiring in excellent order, but the rapidly approaching darkness, which was intensified by the pall of smoke hanging over the battlefield, made it almost impossible to distinguish friend from foe. Under these circumstances he decided to stay the pursuit and confine himself to the destruction of his opponent's right, now hopelessly surrounded in Blenheim.

The unfortunate French troops holding the village, who had witnessed the rout of their centre, realised that they had been abandoned to their fate, but though their commander, de Clairambault, had fled and been drowned endeavouring to escape across the Danube, they prepared to make a desperate attempt to cut their way out of the trap in which they found themselves. However, a couple of British battalions had taken up their positions in rear of the village, and when the garrison attempted to break out in two columns, they were driven back by a fierce charge delivered by some squadrons of the Scots Greys and Irish Dragoons. General Churchill, moving his infantry to his left, now took up a position in rear of the village, completely blocking the only avenue of escape, while Orkney's men made another desperate attempt to storm the palisades, but the garrison, fighting with the courage of despair, made a dogged resistance, defending the churchyard in particular with the most obstinate gallantry.

The village had already caught fire in several places, and Churchill, bringing up his artillery to close range, was about to attack in overwhelming force when the French drums beat the '*parley*.' Churchill, however, insisted on an unconditional surrender, and as resistance was obviously hopeless, and could only result in further useless loss of life, the luckless garrison laid down their arms. The regiment of Navarre, heart-broken at their cruel fate, burnt their colours and buried their muskets, while the officers, breaking their swords, to spare themselves the shame of handing them to their conquerors, could only repeat in sorrowful accents: 'What will the king say?'

Nearly 12,000 unwounded prisoners laid down their arms, as the incompetent de Clairambault had called the whole of the reserve into the village instead of sending them to the aid of their hard-pressed comrades in the centre.

The victory was overwhelmingly complete, the French and Bavarians had lost nearly 40,000 men, of whom 12,000 were killed, 14,000 captured, and the remainder wounded or missing. A marshal of France and several generals were among the prisoners, while nearly the whole of the artillery, baggage and equipment of the defeated army fell into the victors' hands.

The Allies' casualties amounted to some 4,500 killed and 7,500 wounded, among the former being the Prince of Holstein-Beck, Brigadier-General Row, Colonel Dormer, commanding the Guards, and several other distinguished officers. The stupendous results of the victory are excellently summarised by Alison, as follows:

"The decisive blow struck at Blenheim resounded through every part of Europe, it at once destroyed the vast fabric of power which it had taken Louis XIV., aided by the talents of Turenne and the genius of Vauban, so long to construct.'

The part played by the cavalry in the great battle had been unusually large, and it was in this arm that the great superiority of the Allies lay; not only were their mounted troops nearly twice as numerous as those of their opponents, but they were of the most excellent quality, while Tallard's squadrons had been weakened by the poor condition of their horses and the numbers they had lost during their arduous march. Marlborough was renowned for his brilliant handling of his cavalry on the field of battle, and the manner in which he used them, as a mobile reserve to rapidly reinforce any threatened point, had much to do with his subsequent successes. The promptitude with which he changed his plan of attack, when he found that he was unable to capture Blenheim, and the vigour with which he carried out his scheme of breaking the hostile centre, are equally worthy of admiration.

In fact, it is impossible not to contrast the cool, serene and confident manner in which the Allied commanders directed the battle with the want of control displayed by their opponents. Tallard never recovered from the faulty manner in which he had drawn up his troops, and at the crisis of the battle his cavalry failed him badly, while his superiority in artillery was to a great extent wasted by the fact that his guns were dispersed along the whole front of his line. The number of wounded and prisoners in the Allied camp, as well as the serious shortage of ammunition and supplies, prevented Marlborough undertaking a vigorous strategic pursuit; consequently, the Elector and Marsin, making their way in safety through the Black Forest, joined Villeroi, and the united armies, crossing the Rhine at Kehl, went into cantonments in the neighbourhood of Strasburg.

Bavaria was compelled to disband her army and declare herself neutral, while the strong fortress of Ulm, into which the Elector had thrown a garrison as he retired, surrendered at once to the Allies. Marlborough, who had now accomplished his task on the Danube, decided to invade France *via* the valley of the Moselle, and sent Eugene to besiege Landau, which had been greatly strengthened since its recapture by the French.

Winter quarters had not yet been decided upon, and it was determined that the armies should separate. At the end of October, Marlborough marched to reduce the fortresses of Treves and Trarbach, the former town, situated on the Moselle, being necessary to the Allies for their contemplated invasion of France. This dispersion of their forces was of course dangerous, but the French, still stupefied by their disastrous defeat, were not in the least likely to undertake a vigorous offensive. After a difficult and tedious march, the Allied Army arrived before Treves, which at once capitulated, but Trarbach gave a considerable amount of trouble before it surrendered to the Prince of Hesse.

Marlborough had meanwhile repaired to Berlin, in the hope of inducing the King of Prussia to send substantial reinforcements to the Duke of Savoy, who was with difficulty holding his ground against Vendôme in Northern Italy. The campaign came to an end with the fall of Landau, and, thanks to Marlborough's brilliant strategy, it had proved most successful; Germany had been freed from all fear of invasion, the French power in the valley of the Danube broken, Bavaria had been forced to become neutral, and the armies of Louis XIV. thrown on the defensive. Landing in England in December, the great Duke had a magnificent reception, Blenheim Palace and the royal manor of Woodstock were presented to him, while his officers and men were not forgotten; three months' pay was given as a gratuity to all those present at the great battle, while if wounded they received double the amount.

A most important event had occurred in Spain, though at the time it excited very little notice: on the 4th of August the fortress of Gibraltar had been captured by a landing party from the fleet under the

Prince of Hesse-Darmstadt and taken possession of by Admiral Rook. Altogether the year had been a singularly successful one for the Grand Alliance, all Louis' schemes had ended in failure, and henceforward he was always more or less on the defensive, struggling desperately to defend his own frontiers.

CHAPTER 5

The Campaign of 1705-1706

Had it not been for the obstruction of the British, Dutch and Imperial cabinets, the scheme formed by Marlborough and Eugene for the ensuing campaign must have been attended with the most triumphant success, and would in all probability have brought the war to a speedy conclusion. The Allied Army, 90,000 strong, was to assemble in the valley of the Moselle, based on Treves and Trarbach, and was subsequently to invade Lorraine in two columns. Marlborough was to operate in the valley of the Moselle, while Lewis of Baden was to advance down the valley of the Saar, the united armies were then to endeavour to capture Saarlouis before their opponents were ready to take the field.

Thus, the Allies would carry the war into the enemy's country, avoiding the numberless fortresses in the Low Countries and on the northern frontier of France, which tended to reduce all military operations to a series of sieges or blockades. But the very magnitude of the successes obtained during the previous campaign militated against the carrying out of the scheme which promised such decisive results, for it was the imminent danger of invasion which had alone galvanised the emperor and the German princes into action, and this peril had been removed by the victory of Blenheim. Harassed by the rebellion in Hungary, and crippled by illness, Leopold was incapable of energetic action, and with the removal of the pressing danger, the German princes had relapsed into their habitual torpor.

Though the British government had sanctioned the increase of their contingent, they had taken no steps to bring the promised reinforcements into the field, while the Dutch were totally unprepared to commence the campaign. On the other hand, the recent disasters had acted as a tonic to the French nation, while Louis XIV. had made the greatest exertions during the previous winter to repair the losses of his armies and to enable them to take the field in sufficient strength to ensure the defence of his frontiers.

In Flanders, Villeroi was to assume the offensive at the head of 75,000 men. Villars, who had succeeded in pacifying the insurgents in the Cevennes, was to block the Allies' most probable line of advance, and Marsin with some 30,000 men was to operate in the valley of the Upper Rhine.

Returning to Holland early in April, Marlborough eventually succeeded in persuading the Dutch authorities to agree to the proposed invasion of France, but unfortunately Eugene, with whom he hoped to co-operate, was ordered to northern Italy to check Vendôme, who had made considerable progress in that quarter during the preceding campaign.

When Marlborough was at last able to assume command of the army on the Moselle, he found that, thanks to the want of energy of the emperor and the German princes, his force only amounted to about 30,000 men.

Eventually Lewis of Baden, who was too sick to take the field in person, sent a few wretchedly equipped battalions; while, to make matters worse, one of the chief commissariat officers deserted, after having embezzled the money entrusted to him to purchase supplies. Though bitterly disappointed by these unforeseen difficulties, Marlborough commenced operations on the 3rd of June—by which date some of the promised contingents had arrived—with a force a little over 40,000 strong. Though Villars was considerably stronger numerically, he had received positive orders to avoid an engagement, consequently the French marshal fell back to a strong position near Sirreck, which effectually covered Luxembourg, Thionville and Saarlouis.

The position was so well chosen that Marlborough with his inferior force dared not risk an attack, and was constrained to remain in observation in the valley of the Saar, awaiting reinforcements from Germany ere he could commence the siege of Saarlouis. Meanwhile Villeroi, assuming the offensive in the Low Countries with 60,000 men, had advanced rapidly to the Meuse, captured Huy, occupied the town of Liege, and besieged the citadel.

Overkirk, who had been entrusted with the defence of Holland, finding himself too weak to keep the field in face of the formidable hostile force, had been compelled to retreat to the entrenched lines round Maestricht. The French were evidently about to carry out a vigorous offensive campaign, and as the promised reinforcements failed to arrive, Marlborough found it necessary to abandon his projected invasion of France. When once his decision had been made, he acted with his usual promptitude, and in spite of the hopeless inefficiency of the transport, the Allies silently evacuated their camp after dark on the 17th June, and disregarding the pouring rain marched with such rapidity throughout the night, that their rear-guard was out of sight before dawn next morning.

The retreat was so skilfully carried out, that until he saw the deserted camp on the following day, Villars had no idea of his opponent's movement, and entirely lost touch of his army. Hoping to fall on Villeroi, ere the latter was aware that he had left the valley of the Moselle, Marlborough pushed forward by forced marches to join Overkirk, but the French marshal, hearing of the Allies' movements, hastily abandoned his attempt to capture the citadel of Liege and fell back to his entrenched lines on the Meuse.

The Allies effected their junction on the 2nd of July, and at once proceeded to invest Huy, which capitulated after a few days' siege; but this minor success was promptly discounted, for d'Aubach, who had been left with a strong detachment to guard the supplies collected with such difficulty at Treves and Saarbruck, burnt his magazines and fled at the approach of a small hostile force. To make up for the time he had been forced to waste in the valley of the Moselle, owing to the failure of his allies to send their promised contingents, Marlborough determined to strike vigorously at Villeroi, who lay in fancied security behind his formidable lines, stretching from Namur along the Mehaigne, Little Geete, Great Geete and the Demer to Antwerp.

These lines, which had taken three years to complete, had been constructed with the greatest care; streams had been dammed to form inundations, redoubts covered the most vulnerable points, and the whole of the defences were armed with numerous guns of large calibre and garrisoned by 70,000 men.

Marlborough, however, was no slavish adherent to the then generally accepted theory of the impregnability of fortified lines, and thoroughly realised that, in spite of his opponent's numerical superiority, it was impossible that he could be equally strong at all points.

He decided, therefore, to deceive Villeroi as to the real point of attack by feints along his whole front, and then to mass his troops suddenly and break through his opponent's line before the latter could concentrate to oppose him. The point selected for attack was near Tirlemont, on the Little Geete, where the lines were especially formidable.

Crossing the Mehaigne on the 17th of July, Overkirk marched towards Namur, and Villeroi, at once falling into the trap, concentrated his forces to oppose him some twelve miles from the real point of attack. As soon as darkness had fallen, Marlborough moved from his camp preceded by the advance guard under Cadogan, who was accompanied by a thousand workmen with waggons carrying bridging materials, while during the night Overkirk, having successfully imposed on Villeroi, turned about and followed the main body.

The thick fog, however, which covered the Allies' movements caused their guides to lose their way, and the vanguard did not reach the castle of Wanghé, which formed a *tête du pont* at the entrance to the lines, until after daylight. The small garrison, consisting of some thirty men, was promptly chased across the bridge by the grenadiers, who hacked down the palisades with their axes and entered the main position at the heels of the fugitives.

So full of enthusiasm were the troops that they waded breast high through the river and scaled the entrenchments before the bridges had been completed; they were followed by the cavalry who quickly filed across the hastily constructed bridges, and the whole force was successfully concentrated within the hostile lines. But the alarm had been given, and the Marquis d'Allegre, collecting every available man within reach, hastened to the spot with some 9,000 cavalry and infantry. Putting himself at the head of the Allied squadrons, Marlborough charged sword in hand, and after a desperate *mêlée*, in which the Marquis d'Allegre was captured and the Duke himself barely escaped being cut down by a French dragoon, the opposing horsemen were driven from the field and their infantry routed.

Overkirk, whose men had marched hard all night, joined the main body, and shortly afterwards Villeroi, who had remained at Meerdorp during the hours of darkness anxiously expecting an attack, appeared with a strong force of cavalry, but finding the Allies drawn up inside the lines, the French general promptly retired, sending orders to his detachments to fall back across the Dyle and rendezvous at Louvain.

Marlborough wished to take up the pursuit at once, but the Dutch generals stubbornly refused to move; the Allied cavalry, however, striking across country, caught up the French rear-guard and hustled them across the Dyle, capturing over a thousand prisoners. Luckily for his army, Villeroi had caused bridges to be constructed beforehand. These were now broken down, and Marlborough was forced to suspend operations for a day or two as the recent heavy rains had rendered the river impassable; but even when the weather cleared, it was some time before he could persuade the procrastinating Dutch deputies to consent to an attempt to force the line of the Dyle.

Two detachments under Wirtemberg and Heukelom, moving off late in the evening of the 29th of July, secured the passage during the night, and by dawn next morning the Dutch, with the British in close support, were in position to commence their crossing. The Dutch generals, however, refused to advance, and when the duke rode up to ascertain the cause of the delay, Slangenberg burst into a torrent of violent remonstrance, and finally recalled Heukelom's detachment.

By this time the hostile troops had concentrated in considerable force, and the enterprise, at first so brilliantly successful, ended in failure owing to the deliberate obstruction and insubordination of the Dutch generals. Though bitterly disappointed, Marlborough glossed over their glaring disobedience of orders in his despatches, and set himself to obtain his object in a different way.

After halting a few days to enable him to fill up his commissariat waggons, he moved off to his left to turn the line of the Dyle. On arriving at Genappe he turned northward towards the forest of Soignies and finally went into camp—near Braine L'Alleud, close to the future battlefield of Waterloo. By his rapid march he had placed himself between his opponent's army and France, forcing Villeroi either to fight a pitched battle or abandon Brussels, and as he carried supplies for six days in his waggons, the fact that he had cut himself adrift from his communications was of minor importance.

As Villeroi had been joined by Marsin, who had Groene a large reinforcement with him from the army of the Rhine, the French general determined to risk a decisive battle and took up a position behind the Issche with his right resting on the forest of Soignies.

Deciding to force the line of the river at once, Marlborough detached his brother, Charles Churchill, with 12,000 infantry to work through the forest and turn the French right, while he himself marched at daybreak on the 18th of August to attack the enemy's position. He was forced to halt, however, to await the arrival of his artillery, as Slangenberg, in direct defiance of the duke's order, had blocked the road by placing his baggage in the centre of the column, and it was not until noon that the guns arrived on the scene.

Marlborough then requested the deputies to sanction an attack, but Slangenberg protested in the most insubordinate language that 'it was simply murder and massacre,' and by the time the generals and deputies had finished wrangling, the French had reinforced their position, and the opportunity had been lost. The fruits of the duke's brilliant strategy had been once again wasted by the obstruction of Slangenberg and the deputies who, by deliberately wrecking their ally's plans, enabled the French to extricate themselves from a most critical position.

During the day the enemy strongly entrenched their position, and as the Dutch still obstinately refused to attack, even Marlborough's exemplary patience gave out, and he retired in disgust to his former position. Enraged by Slangenberg's open insubordination and the deputies' continual obstruction, he threatened to withdraw the British contingent altogether, and this at last brought the States General to their senses. The offending general was deprived of his command and the deputies censured, but the summer was now over and nothing remained to be done except to level the enemy's lines between the Demer and the Mehaigne before putting the Allied Army into winter quarters.

In spite of the high hopes of success with which it had been commenced, the campaign of 1705 had ended in a complete fiasco. France had, to a great extent, recovered from the disasters of the previous year, and even to the incapable statesmen who directed the Allies' policy, the cause of the failure was perfectly clear. The failure of Austria and the German princes to supply the stipulated number of troops had rendered Marlborough's brilliant scheme for the invasion of France impossible, while his remarkable strategic and tactical abilities were powerless to achieve success, as his carefully laid plans were continually thwarted by the insubordination of the Dutch generals and the pig-headed opposition of their deputies.

During the ensuing winter the duke visited the courts of Vienna, Berlin and Hanover, in the hope of persuading the Allies to agree on some definite course of action, but their interests were too divergent, and Marlborough returned to England without having achieved any definite success. Disgusted with his selfish and incapable allies, he determined to abandon the Netherlands and transfer his army to northern Italy, join Eugene in crushing Vendôme, and then invade France from the south, where he was sure of receiving some support from the Protestants of Languedoc. However, he was again doomed to disappointment, for the Prussian, Hanoverian and Danish governments refused to sanction the employment of their contingents in Italy, while the successes gained by Villars on the Upper Rhine alarmed the States

General, and caused them to refuse to allow any of their troops to serve out of the Netherlands.

Marlborough's promising schemes were once again ruined by his fatuous allies, and reluctantly abandoning his enterprise, he was forced to content himself with sending 10,000 men to reinforce Eugene.

The States General, badly frightened by his threat of withdrawing the British contingent, now proposed to allow him to choose the deputies to accompany the army, or to give them secret instructions to comply with his commands, and with this makeshift arrangement he was obliged to rest content. After his heart-breaking experience of the previous year, however, he was most pessimistic as to the results of the campaign, and set out at the beginning of May to join the army assembled round Liege, as he himself expressed it, 'With a heavy heart and no prospect of doing anything considerable.' But his depression was quickly banished by an unlooked-for blunder on the part of his opponent, who, with some 62,000 men was lying in cantonments round Louvain covered by the lines of the Dyle.

Though Villeroi had received distinct orders not to commence operations until he had been joined by Marsin, who was on his way from the Rhine to reinforce him, the French leader formed the entirely erroneous idea that the Allies had not yet completed their concentration.

Hearing that they were advancing towards Namur, he moved out of his entrenched lines with the object of crushing them in detail; but as a matter of fact, the Allied force, in splendid condition after its winter's rest, was fully prepared to take the field, and most anxious to meet the foe. Concentrating his army at Bilsen, near Maestricht, Marlborough moved southward towards Borchleon at the end of May. Before he could commence operations, however, he had to arrange for the payment of the Danish auxiliaries in the Dutch service, as they refused to take part in the campaign until they had received their arrears of pay; this difficulty was speedily settled, and the gallant Danes, after a magnificent forced march, joined the army just in time to take part in the general advance.

Shortly after 1 a.m. on the morning of Whit-Sunday, the 23rd of May, Cadogan, the Quartermaster-General of the Allied Army, rode forward from Borchleon with an escort of 600 men to lay out a camp for the main body near the village of Ramillies, situated some two miles from the bridge over the River Mehaigne, on the road from Louvain to Namur.

Pushing forward through the misty rain which enveloped the low-lying plains of Brabant, the vanguard had arrived within five or six miles of their destination, when from the hill of Meedorp, Cadogan noticed that the heights above Ramillies were occupied by the enemy's troops.

He immediately reported the fact to Marlborough who, accompanied by Overkirk, at once rode forward to reconnoitre. Shortly after 10 a.m., the sun shone out brilliantly, the mist rolled away, and the whole French Army, over 60,000 strong, appeared moving into position on the heights above Ramillies. As the main body of the Allies was toiling laboriously along the muddy roads, with their guns sinking up to their axle-trees every few hundred yards, Marlborough halted the heads of his columns to allow the men to close up. Meanwhile Villeroi, whose patrols had warned him of his opponent's approach, was rapidly forming his line of battle in a position which he had seen the hump-backed Duke of Luxemburg, one of the ablest of the French leaders, deliberately reject some ten years previously. (Fortescue's *History of the British Army.*)

Believing that the Allies were moving against Namur, Villeroi determined to check their advance on the plateau enclosed between the head waters of the Great and Little Geete and the River Mehaigne, and which, though only rising slightly above the surrounding country, formed the highest point in the level plains of Brabant. His position formed a rough crescent some four miles in extent, as the villages of L'Autre Eglise and Taviers on the extreme left and right flank respectively were some distance in advance of Ramillies and Offuz, in the centre of the line. The bulk of the cavalry was drawn up on the open down between Taviers and Ramillies, though a strong detachment of mounted troops was stationed in rear of the left section of the line, the villages were held by strong bodies of infantry, and the greater portion of the artillery was massed in front of the centre of the position. Franquinaise, about a mile in front of Taviers, was held as an advance post, and the cottages and hedges round the village were lined by skirmishers.

At first sight the position appeared a remarkably strong one, the flanks well secured, the right resting on Taviers and the Mehaigne, and the left protected by the marshy ground round L'Autre Eglise, while the villages of Ramillies and Offuz, lying about a mile apart, formed a strong *point d'appui* in the centre. But Marlborough, with his unerring tactical *coup d'œil*, at once recognised the weak points of the position and the faulty disposition of his opponent's troops. The left wing, behind the marsh at the source of the Little Geete, was immovable, and could be safely ignored, the key of the position, the high ground round the tomb of Ottomond, was occupied by mounted troops almost entirely unsupported by infantry, while the right wing at Taviers was to a great extent isolated; but more important still, the whole line was concave, which would enable the Allied general to mass his troops at a given point more rapidly than his opponent could.

The duke, who thoroughly realised the enormous advantage of concentrating superior numbers at the critical point, intended to feint at his opponent's left and, if possible, force him to strengthen that flank, then to make the decisive attack against the hostile right and centre.

The batteries came into action soon after 1 o'clock, but it was not until more than an hour later that the main body of the Allied Army, marching in eight columns, reached the field and deployed on the line Bonef-Foulz. They were to a certain extent hidden from view by the high ground south of the latter village, and the whole extent of the front was under two and a half miles. Foulz was occupied, and heavy columns of infantry advanced against the hostile position round L'Autre Eglise, the result being as Marlborough had intended, that his opponent, seriously alarmed by the threat against his flank hastened thither in person, and even withdrew troops from his right and centre to reinforce what he imagined to be the critical point. Ascending the slope, the first line of the Allies deployed on the crest opposite their opponents' left, and their artillery opened a heavy fire, while the remainder of the infantry, forming column of route, moved off under cover of the rising ground to take up their appointed positions opposite the French right and centre.

While Marlborough's feint had been so successful in riveting Villeroi's attention to his left, the battle had commenced in earnest on the opposite flank, where Wertmüller's four Dutch battalions had already succeeded in driving their opponents out of the village of Franquinaise. Then, regardless of the biting fire of the hostile skirmishers lining the hedges and ditches, they pressed eagerly forward to close with the strong body of French infantry drawn up in front of Taviers. Realising that he had been completely outgeneralled, Villeroi hastily sent reinforcements to his isolated right wing, and 14 squadrons of dragoons, arriving in the nick of time, managed to dismount and join their infantry in the fierce struggle raging round the village.

The Duke of Wirtemberg, bringing up his Danish hussars unobserved along the bank of the Mehaigne, suddenly fell on the extreme right of the hostile line, and driving the dismounted dragoons and infantry from the field in confusion, followed up his success by cutting to pieces a couple of Swiss battalions, who were advancing to their support. The Dutch infantry, encouraged by his success, carried the village at the point of the bayonet in gallant style, but were checked by the Musketeers of the Guard, the pick of the French Household Cavalry, who had advanced to support their hard-pressed infantry.

However, Overkirk, with his Dutch and German squadrons was close at hand, and ordering his trumpets to sound the charge, he dashed at the Musketeers and threw their first line into confusion. The second line, however, stood firm, and seizing their opportunity, fell on their opponents before they could reform their ranks after their charge, and drove them back into some marshy ground some distance in rear. Marlborough's quick eye at once noted the overthrow of the Allied cavalry and, calling up every available squadron from the right and centre, he hastened to the point of danger. In his eagerness to reach his hard-pressed left wing, Marlborough recklessly exposed himself, and narrowly escaped capture by a party of French dragoons. His horse was shot under him, and as he was mounting another a cannon ball carried off the head of Colonel Bingham, his military secretary, who was holding his stirrup.

The duke managed, however to extricate himself from the confused *mêlée* and was quickly joined by Murray and Argyle, who had hastened to the spot with a strong body of fresh troops. Putting himself at the head of these reinforcements, Marlborough led them in a desperate charge against the Musketeers, who were driven from the field after a short but fiercely contested struggle. Following up their success, the Allied cavalry swept irresistibly forward on to the high ground south-west of Ramillies, driving the French Household cavalry, infantry and dragoons before them as far as the tomb of Ottomond.

While the battle had been raging fiercely round Taviers, Schultz, deploying his German battalions, had launched his attack against the strongly held village of Ramillies which formed the centre of the French line.

A formidable array of guns had been massed in front of the village, and the scarlet coats of the regiments of Lord Clare, Lee and Dorrington, appearing among the houses and gardens betokened the presence of the famous Irish brigade, and foreshadowed a desperate

SKETCH MAP OF THE BATTLE OF RAMILLIES
23ᴿᴰ MAY 1706.

resistance. Advancing with twelve battalions in column of companies in the first line, followed by a strong reserve, the Allies came under a deadly fire from the hostile guns as they approached the village, but though great gaps were torn in their ranks, the well-trained infantry steadily continued their advance.

After a fierce struggle in which both sides lost heavily, they succeeded in establishing themselves in the cottages and gardens on the outskirts of the village, but for some time were unable to make any further progress. Their supports closed up, and surging forward through the dense canopy of smoke, they forced their way into the village, and after a desperate hand-to-hand fight, in which Lord Clare's Irish greatly distinguished themselves, they drove out their opponents. With their ranks still somewhat disordered by their fierce struggle among the houses and gardens, the Allies endeavoured to follow their adversaries up the slope west of Ramillies, but were checked by Count Maffei, who charged them vigorously at the head of the Elector of Cologne's Guards. At the same moment the French Horse Guards, coming up at the gallop, struck fiercely at their flank, and reeling under the shock, the gallant infantry, after a desperate effort to hold their ground, were hurled back to the village in confusion.

Help, however, was close at hand, for Marlborough, fresh from his success at Taviers, wheeled his squadrons to the right, and falling suddenly on the flank of the victorious French troops, threw them into hopeless confusion. Count Maffei was captured and the Allied infantry, which had been rallied after their repulse, bursting from the village with exultant cheers completed the victory by driving their opponents up the slope in rear of Ramillies, after a furious struggle with some troops who had been sent by Villeroi to their support.

By half-past six the French right and centre had been crowded into a confused mass on to the plateau round the tomb of Ottomond, but they were picked troops, and though hopelessly outnumbered by Marlborough's brilliant generalship, they continued to offer a dogged resistance.

The Allies had also fallen into unavoidable disorder, horse and foot were hopelessly mingled together in the open space between Ramillies and the tomb of Ottomond, and while Marlborough was endeavouring to restore order, his opponent made one last bid for victory. Holding L'Autre Eglise and Offuz, Villeroi attempted to form a fresh right wing, extending from the latter village to Geest Toromont on the Great Geete, and almost at right angles to his original line of bat-

Progress of the Battle.

The Attack on the French Right and Centre.

A. 2·30 PM

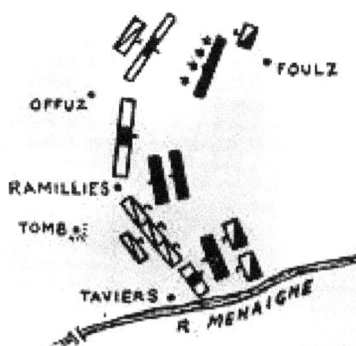

OFFUZ

FOULZ

RAMILLIES

TOMB

TAVIERS

R. MEHAIGNE

The Rout of the French

B. 6·PM

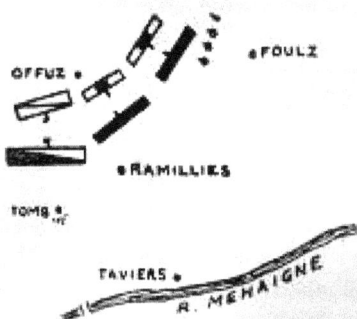

OFFUZ

FOULZ

RAMILLIES

TOMB

TAVIERS

R. MEHAIGNE

tle. But he had been so eager to get his troops into position in the morning, that he had ignored all thought of retreat, and had allowed the whole of his vast collection of transport and baggage to remain close in rear of the centre of his line.

This oversight was destined to cost him dear and ruin his last possible chance of saving the battle, for his cavalry, moving from the left of the position, were thrown into complete disorder by the mass of carts and waggons through which they had to make their way, and the confusion spread rapidly among the rest of the troops on the plateau.

Promptly remedying the disorder in the ranks of the Allies, Marlborough had massed the bulk of his mounted troops on the plateau just north of the tomb of Ottomond, and seeing that the moment to complete his victory had arrived, he determined to use every available man to drive home his advantage.

The British battalions which since the commencement of the action had remained in observation of the enemy's left, behind the long line of the Allies' guns in action on the high ground south of Foulz, had become heartily weary of their role of spectators. For nearly four hours they had remained idle, eagerly awaiting the order to advance, and at last their chance had arrived. Rapidly descending the slope, they struggled through the marsh bordering the Little Geete, forded the river and bursting into Offuz with a triumphant cheer, drove their demoralised opponents headlong from the village.

Striving gallantly to cover the retreat, the *Regiment du Roi* lost their 'King's Colour,' and were cut to pieces by a furious charge delivered by Lord John Hay at the head of his Scots Greys. Meanwhile Marlborough, seeing that the critical moment had arrived, ordered his trumpets and bugles to sound the charge, and at the head of his massed squadrons, swept forward in irresistible might to complete his victory. The Elector of Bavaria made a brave but futile effort to cover the retreat of the infantry from L'Autre Eglise by advancing with his *cuirassiers*, but his men were ridden down by Wood's squadrons, and he himself narrowly escaped capture. Seeing themselves left without support, the French infantry, casting away their arms, fled in wild panic towards the Louvain road, hotly pursued by the Allied troopers, while on the opposite flank some squadrons attempting to charge, were driven into the marshes bordering the Mehaigne and cut to pieces by the Danish hussars.

Meanwhile Marlborough, at the head of his formidable force of cavalry, swept over the field like a whirlwind, scattering the isolated bodies of horse and foot which hopelessly endeavoured to check his advance.

Several battalions, which had commenced their retreat earlier in the afternoon, were retiring in excellent order, but the Allied cavalry, pressing their pursuit with relentless vigour, caught them up, and charging through their ranks, sabred the wretched fugitives almost without resistance.

Darkness brought no respite to the stricken army, for Marlborough was determined to give them no chance of rallying and urged on the pursuit throughout the night, only halting his wearied infantry at dawn after they had covered fifteen miles and were within sight of the spires of Louvain, while Orkney's troopers only drew rein after they had hunted the wretched fugitives up to the very gates of the city.

The Allies who had brought just under 60,000 men into the field, paid a by no means excessive price for their brilliant and decisive victory, as their casualties amounted to some 1,100 killed and 2,500 wounded.

The French losses, however, had been much heavier, amounting in all to 8,000 of whom about 4,000 had been killed in the battle and during the pursuit, while the remainder had been wounded; moreover 50 guns, 80 stand of colours and all their baggage fell into the hands of the victors.

Ramillies was a typical 'encounter battle,' in which neither commander had time for a prolonged reconnaissance, and the promptitude with which Marlborough made his plans and the skill with which he took advantage of his opponent's mistakes, stamped him as a leader of the highest ability.

Posting the British contingent and the greater part of his artillery on the high ground south of Foulz, he held the French left to its position, and thus, though slightly weaker than his opponent, was able to mass superior numbers against the hostile right and centre. The skill with which he used his large force of mounted troops as a mobile reserve, and several times brought them into action at the critical moment, is also most remarkable; in fact the battle was a great personal triumph for the Allied commander.

In spite of the fact that the French were not finally overthrown until late in the evening, and that his men were wearied by a long march to the field of battle, the vigour with which he carried out the tactical pursuit was phenomenal. The marching power displayed by the Allies at the commencement of the campaign was also most remarkable, for starting at dawn on the 23rd of May, they covered a distance of fifteen miles, took part in a fiercely contested action, and then completed a forced march of another fifteen miles before daybreak on the 24th, in spite of the fact that the roads were ankle-deep in mud. Villeroi and the Elector of Bavaria, panic-stricken by their defeat, determined to abandon Louvain, and the Walloons in the French service were so impressed by the result of the battle, and the hurried flight from the city, that no less than 7,000 deserted, some joining the Allies, but the majority returning to their homes.

The French Army fell back in a hopeless state of disorganisation and finally took up its position behind the Scheldt, while Marlborough, leaving a small detachment to hold Louvain, marched on Brussels, which at once surrendered. Mechlin opened its gates to the Allies, and the population of Brabant, which had no particular love for the French rule, willingly furnished supplies. After a halt of a couple of days at Brussels, Marlborough advanced to Ghent, and the Elector, who was lying near the latter city with part of the beaten army, hastily retired, while Villeroi, seized with panic, abandoned the line of the Scheldt and fell back to the French frontier. Ghent and Bruges surrendered without resistance, Oudenarde expelled its French garrison, while the great fortress of Antwerp, which was held by a mixed force of French and Walloons, capitulated on condition that the former were allowed to join Villeroi. In less than three weeks from the commencement of the campaign, Marlborough had gained possession of by far the larger half of the Spanish Netherlands, and driven the French Army, in hopeless confusion, behind their own frontier.

Overkirk with a large force besieged Ostend, while a British squadron blockaded the town, and aided by the fire of the warships, the siege made such progress that, after an unsuccessful sortie, de la Motte was forced to surrender. Menin, situated in the low-lying country, which could be flooded at will, was next invested, and in spite of the delay caused by the inundations, was carried by assault towards the end of August, when a large number of prisoners, fifty heavy guns and an immense quantity of stores fell into the hands of the Allies. Vendôme, who had been hurriedly brought from Piedmont to check Marlborough's progress, managed to collect a considerable force which, augmented by strong reinforcements drawn from the Rhine, amounted to nearly 90,000 men. Though the covering force under Marlborough, exclusive of the detachments engaged in siege operations, numbered only some 50,000 strong, the French troops were so dispirited by their recent disasters, that even the able and courageous Vendôme dared not risk a pitched battle.

He was forced to witness the reduction of the Flemish fortresses, and eventually retired behind the Lys and the Deule, to a position covering the great barrier city of Lille, which he imagined would be his opponent's next objective. Marlborough, however, determined to take advantage of the drought to lay siege to Dendermonde, a strong fortress situated at the junction of the Scheldt and Dender, and which from the ease with which the surrounding country could be flooded, was impregnable except in the very driest weather. Ath, a small but exceedingly important fortress, situated at the junction of the roads from Lille and Valenciennes to Brussels, was next besieged by Overkirk, Marlborough meanwhile driving back Vendôme, who had advanced to its relief.

The Allied commander was most anxious to capture Mons, one of the most important fortresses guarding the French frontier, before the end of the campaign, but the Dutch stolidly refused to supply the necessary stores and ammunition, so the great Duke was most reluctantly forced to abandon his project. In the hope of tempting Vendôme to risk a battle, he advanced towards the French lines, but as his opponent was obviously determined not to fight until he had restored the morale of his thoroughly disorganised army, Marlborough ordered Overkirk to place the Allies in winter quarters. The results of the brilliant campaign, which by the way had been gained at very little cost to the Allies, had been stupendous; Villeroi's army had not only been decisively defeated, but had been so completely disorganised that it was unable to keep the field, while Flanders, with its innumerable fortresses and inexhaustible supplies of food and forage, had been wrested from the French.

Moreover, the brilliant success of the operations in the Netherlands had produced a marvellous effect in every part of the theatre of war; on the Rhine, Villars had been checked in his victorious career, and with his army reduced by the large drafts he was forced to send to the Low Countries, had been too weak to carry out his plan of assuming a vigorous offensive in the heart of Germany. In northern Italy, the withdrawal of Vendôme to oppose Marlborough in the Netherlands was the signal for Eugene to assume the offensive, and completely outgeneralling his opponents, he relieved Turin, routed the French, and regained practically the whole of Piedmont for the Emperor.

Altogether the year 1706 had been a most glorious one for the

'Grand Alliance,' and if only the confederates could be persuaded to make use of their resources, and give their two great leaders a free hand, it seemed that Louis XIV. would be hard put to it to defend his own frontiers in the ensuing campaign.

CHAPTER 6

The Campaign of 1707–1708

During the winter following the campaign of 1706, the position of France appeared almost hopeless; her commerce had been ruined, agriculture crippled by the ceaseless drain of her manhood caused by the five years of war, the treasury was practically bankrupt, and even the proud spirit of Louis XIV. humbled. Overtures for peace were made, but refused by the Allies, who considered the terms unsatisfactory, and preferred to continue the war rather than patch up a hollow truce which would give France breathing time and a chance to reorganise her resources. The extraordinary successes obtained during the preceding campaign were almost responsible for the breaking up of the Alliance, for the confederates, imagining that France was hopelessly crippled, commenced to quarrel among themselves over the partition of the Spanish possessions.

The Dutch were determined to obtain the Flemish fortresses as a bulwark against future French aggression, though they rightly belonged to the Empire; and Louis XIV., well aware of this fact, entered into secret negotiations with the States General in the hope of detaching Holland from her allies.

In recognition of his valuable services, the emperor offered Marlborough the viceroyalty of the Spanish Netherlands, but though the British government cordially approved of the arrangement, the Dutch bitterly opposed it, and rather than risk wrecking the Alliance, the Duke refused the appointment which carried with it a salary of £60,000 *per annum*. The conquered territory was eventually administered by a mixed tribunal, which, however, by its misgovernment drove the important cities of Ghent and Bruges to revolt in the following year. A violent quarrel also broke out between the emperor and the Duke of Savoy, both of whom laid claim to the Spanish possessions in northern Italy; the former wished to use the Allied forces to capture Naples, while the latter demanded that the Imperial troops should be employed to consolidate and protect his own dominions. So bitter did the quarrel become that the emperor entered into a compact with Louis XIV. guaranteeing the neutrality of northern Italy, in order to carry out his designs with a free hand.

The situation was further complicated by the arrival of Charles XII. of Sweden and his victorious army at Dresden, which seriously alarmed the Emperor and German princes. Louis XIV. did his utmost to bring the Swedish monarch into the field as an ally of France, and only the wonderful tact and great diplomatic ability of Marlborough, who visited Dresden during the spring, averted the threatened alliance which would have been the deathblow to the confederate's cause. Marlborough and Eugene had intended to follow up the advantages gained in the previous campaign by assuming a vigorous offensive, and had arranged to carry the war into the enemy's country by invading France from both Flanders and Piedmont. However, Vendôme had opened the campaign early in May by advancing with a force just under 80,000 strong, and taken up a position near Sombref, menacing Brussels.

Marlborough at once collecting some 65,000 men, marched to Soignies, and everything pointed to a decisive battle at the commencement of the campaign; but though they had already sanctioned an engagement, the deputies, acting on an order received from the States General, changed their minds and absolutely refused to allow the Dutch troops to take part in the attack. Thoroughly disgusted with his allies, but too weak to carry out his scheme without their support, the duke was reluctantly forced to adopt a purely defensive role, while Vendôme, who had no intention of risking a battle except on the most favourable terms, set himself carefully to strengthen his position.

As Marlborough could not, and Vendôme would not, risk a decisive battle, the rival armies remained stationary, the leaders carefully watching each other, and each hoping that his opponent, by making a false move, would offer a favourable opportunity for attack.

A fresh quarrel had meanwhile broken out between the Emperor and the King of Sweden, which forced the duke to proceed to the latter's camp and taxed his abilities to the uttermost to adjust; in fact, it was not until the end of summer that a definite agreement between the two monarchs was concluded, and danger of Swedish intervention removed.

In the hope of achieving some decisive success in the Netherlands before winter put an end to the campaign, Marlborough re-commenced operations in the beginning of August by crossing the Dyle and advancing to Genappe, intending to attack the French Army encamped at Gembloux.

His opponent, however, promptly fell back towards Mons, and though closely followed by the Allies, Vendôme making a rapid forced march, succeeded in reaching his entrenched camp under the guns of the city without molestation, though his army was much exhausted by its exertions, and dispirited at its hasty retreat before the Allies. Heavy rains now set in, rendering all movement impossible for nearly a fort-night, and though Marlborough had not succeeded in defeating his opponent, the latter's hasty retreat had clearly shown that the French Army was unwilling to hazard the result of a battle.

As soon as the weather cleared, the Allies advanced to Ath on their way to Mons, but as their opponents had meanwhile fallen back to the line of the Scheldt, they followed them and took up a position at Helchin, menacing the enemy's line of retreat. The French then en-tirely abandoned the Scheldt and retired to their strongly-entrenched camp under the guns of Lille, and as the Allies' heavy artillery was far in rear, and the commencement of the autumnal rains threatened to put a stop to all military operations, Marlborough decided to put the army into winter quarters at once.

The campaign of 1707, at the commencement of which the Allies had seemed certain to complete their triumphs of the previous year, had ended in a series of disasters in every part of the vast theatre of war.

In Spain their defeat at Almanza had crushed their hopes for ever, while Eugene's incursion into southern France and attempt to cap-ture Toulon had ended in a most disastrous failure. On the Rhine, the Imperialists had been driven from their lines at Stolhofen, which had been supposed to be impregnable, and after ravaging the Palatinate with fire and sword in revenge for the treatment meted out to Bavaria three years before, Villars had marched his victorious army into the valley of the Danube.

In the Netherlands the campaign had dragged to a close without any definite result being obtained. Marlborough had been forced to forgo his only chance of gaining a decisive victory by the fatuous op-position of the deputies, and Vendôme could congratulate himself on having kept the field throughout the summer without having been compelled to risk a pitched battle.

The intrigues of the great Duke's political enemies were already beginning to bear fruit in England, and the States General, fully aware that his fall would be the prelude to the collapse of the Grand Alliance, were seriously thinking of making terms with the French monarch, ere they were left to oppose him single-handed. When Marlborough returned to England in November, a violent outcry was raised both in and out of Parliament; he was held responsible for the disaster at Almanza, for Eugene's failure before Toulon, and for the victories of the French arms in Germany, as well as for the want of success of the Allies in the Netherlands.

The truth was that the country, whose hopes of an advantageous peace had been raised by the brilliant triumphs of the campaign of 1706, was bitterly disappointed by the heavy expenditure rendered necessary by the continuance of the war, as well as with the selfish conduct of the emperor, and doubtful policy of the States General.

Harley and St. John skilfully fanned the flame; many of the Whigs plainly showed their dissatisfaction, and the national discontent became so obvious that Marlborough and Godolphin threatened to resign.

Elated by his successes in the late campaign, and fully cognisant of the state of affairs in England, Louis XIV. made the most energetic preparations for the resumption of the campaign in the Netherlands. Vendôme, who, much to his annoyance, was joined by the Duke of Burgundy, found himself at the head of a force consisting of just under 100,000 men, while the Duke of Berwick, fresh from his triumphs in the Spanish peninsula, was brought in to command the army of the Lower Rhine, some 35,000 strong.

Marlborough was most anxious to obtain an early and decisive success in order to silence, for a time at all events, the campaign of calumny organised by his political opponents in England, and meeting Eugene at The Hague in April, he elaborated a scheme which promised the most far-reaching results. France was to be simultaneously invaded by the Allied Army from Brabant and by the Imperial forces moving down the valley of the Moselle, the united armies were then to move against Vendôme, and force him to accept battle, while the Elector of Hanover was to hold the Duke of Berwick to his position on the Rhine.

However, the duke's carefully thought-out scheme met with the usual opposition, for George of Hanover, who was jealous of Eugene, was dissatisfied with the role allotted to him, and the States General threatened to conclude a separate peace with the French monarch; moreover, the great Flemish cities, irritated by the misgovernment of the mixed tribunals, were seething with discontent, as the Allies were shortly destined to discover. Concentrating his army south of the River Haine, Vendôme, whose orders were to assume the offensive, but to avoid risking a general action as far as possible, advanced at the end of May towards the forest of Soignies, whence he could threaten Brussels and the other important cities of southern Brabant.

Marlborough at once concentrated a force of over 70,000 men at Hal, and sent an urgent message to Eugene, requesting him to join him as soon as possible, but as usual, the contingents furnished by the German princes were late, and Eugene was forced to await their arrival at the rendezvous before commencing his march to join his colleague.

The French then moved to their right to threaten Louvain, but Marlborough anticipated them by making a forced march to the Dyle. A considerable period of inaction followed, and then Vendôme, who had been busily engaged in negotiating with the malcontents in the Flemish cities, suddenly broke up his camp and moved rapidly towards Hal. Bruges and Ghent, the latter city containing the Allies' park of heavy artillery, opened their gates to the French detachments and Vendôme scored the first trick of the campaign. Marlborough marched at once to bring his opponent to action, but the latter rapidly transferred his army across the Senne and Dender, finally taking up his position at Alost whence he could cover the siege of the citadel of Ghent, threaten Brussels, and interrupt the Allies' communications.

By his successful *coup* he had secured the command of the Bruges-Ostend canal and also obtained possession of the line of the Scheldt and Lys. He was aware that Oudenarde was in a bad state of defence and feebly garrisoned, so to complete his triumph, he determined to capture that important fortress by a *coup de main*. In face of this pressing danger, Marlborough acted with the greatest promptitude, taking post at Assche to cover Brussels, which had been thrown into a state of wild panic by the French successes, and ordering Lord Chandos to collect every available man from the neighbouring garrisons and throw himself into Oudenarde.

Consequently, when Vendôme appeared before the town, he found that it was too strongly held to be taken by assault, and determining to proceed with its reduction in due form, he ordered up his heavy guns from Tournai and prepared to take up a position at Lessines to cover the siege.

Marlborough was so worried by the untoward course of events that he fell into a violent fever, but in spite of his physician's orders refused to leave the army, and fortunately was able to count on the invaluable assistance of the gallant Overkirk, on whose loyalty in the critical state of affairs he could absolutely rely. Meanwhile Eugene, whose force was at last complete, was advancing by rapid marches towards the decisive point, but finding that his army could not possibly arrive in time, he pushed forward at the head of his cavalry as far as Maestricht, and as even they would be unable to join the Allies before the expected battle, he rode forward with a small escort and reached the camp on the 7th of July. The arrival of his brilliant colleague, even without his army, was a great delight to Marlborough, who had determined to attack the French at once, and Eugene thoroughly approved of the plan, which was to strike at the enemy's communications and forestall them by seizing the position at Lessines; thus, the Allies would interpose between their opponents and France, and also compel them to fight with their backs to the Scheldt.

Before dawn on the 9th of July, the Allied Army, amounting to 80,000 men, moved from their camp and followed Cadogan, who with a strong advance guard had pushed forward to construct bridges over the Dender and seize the position at Lessines. Halting at noon, the army resumed its advance after a few hours' rest, and, thanks to the wonderful marching powers of the troops, succeeded in occupying the position just as the enemy's vedettes appeared in sight. Vendôme, who was bitterly chagrined at having been outmanoeuvred and outmarched, now determined to fall back to the Scheldt, which he intended to cross at Gavre, some six miles below Oudenarde.

Marlborough at once followed, determined to raise the siege, and if possible, force his opponent to accept battle while his army was disordered by its retreat across the Scheldt. At daybreak on the 11th of July, Cadogan pushed forward with a large force of cavalry supported by a body of infantry, in all some 11,000 strong, and throwing six temporary bridges across the river immediately below Oudenarde, took up his position about a mile north of the town.

The ground on which the battle was about to take place was enclosed between the Scheldt, the Nörken rivulet and the high ground to the westward. on which the village of Oycke was situated. The undulating 'terrain' was studded with villages and cut up by banks and hedges forming the boundaries of the highly cultivated fields, while

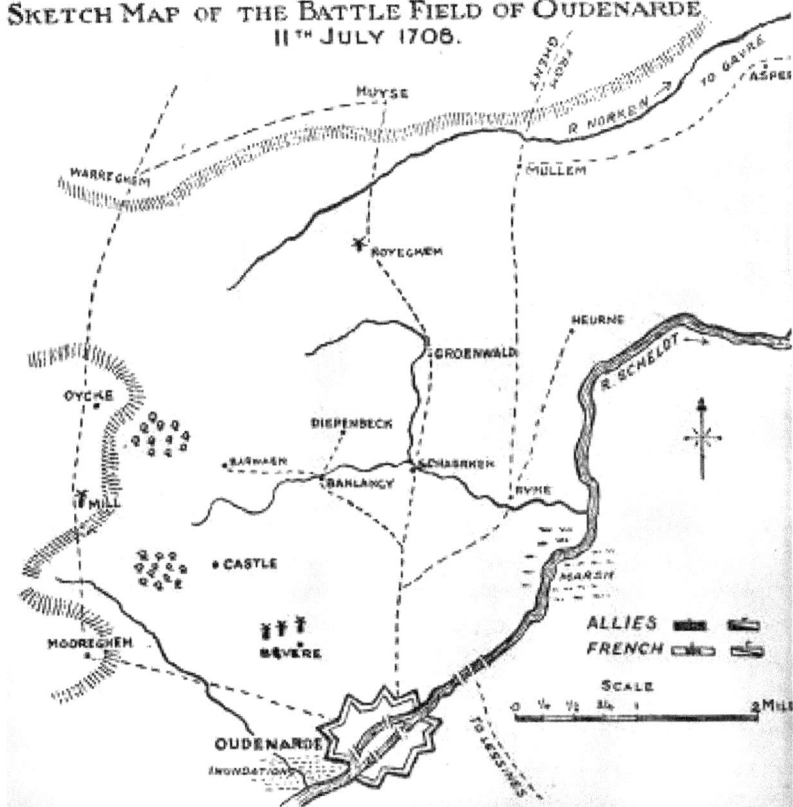

SKETCH MAP OF THE BATTLE FIELD OF OUDENARDE
11TH JULY 1708.

two small streams, uniting near the village of Schaerken, flowed past Eyne into the Scheldt.

Shortly after 11 a.m. the French advance guard under the Marquis de Biron, which had crossed the Scheldt at Gavre and was marching, with its foragers scouring the country, entirely unaware of the proximity of the enemy, suddenly became aware of the presence of their opponents on the northern bank of the river. Immediately reporting the fact to his chief, de Biron advanced to the village of Eyne and perceived the whole of Cadogan's infantry drawn up some distance to the southward, while a strong body of Prussian cavalry, which had been led forward at the gallop by Marlborough in person, was already crossing the bridges over the Scheldt.

Riding forward to reconnoitre, Vendôme saw that the bulk of his opponent's army was still some considerable distance from the river, and he at once decided to oppose the crossing by occupying the villages of Heurne, Eyne, Bevere and Mooreghem in force. The Duke of Burgundy, however, decided to take up a position considerably farther to the rear, extending from Asper to Warreghem on the heights of Huyse, and promptly countermanded Vendôme's orders.

The friction already existing between the two French commanders was naturally intensified by Burgundy's interference, and in the ensuing confusion seven battalions and some squadrons of cavalry took up their position at Eyne, while the remainder of the army, some 85,000 strong, formed upon the high ground in rear of the Nörken rivulet.

Cadogan opened the action by sending Sabine's infantry brigade across the stream to make a frontal attack on Eyne and followed with the other two brigades in support, while the cavalry, crossing higher up, took up their position in rear of the village to cut off their opponent's retreat. Sabine's brigade, composed of the 8th, 18th, 23rd and the 27th Regiments, pressed home their attack with vigour, but their opponents, disheartened by the hopeless position in which they found themselves, offered but a feeble resistance, and three battalions were speedily captured, while the other four were broken and dispersed.

The French squadrons stationed in rear of the village, already demoralised by the overthrow of their infantry, made a short stand, but were speedily routed and driven back across the Nörken by the Allied cavalry, among whom was Prince George of Hanover, fighting with his usual gallantry. This minor disaster convinced the French commanders that a battle had now become inevitable; and the misunderstanding between them rapidly increased. The Duke of Burgundy

PROGRESS OF THE BATTLE

CADOGAN'S ATTACK ON EYNE.

A.
3.p.m.

HUYSE

OYCKE

R.SCHELDT

OUDENARDE

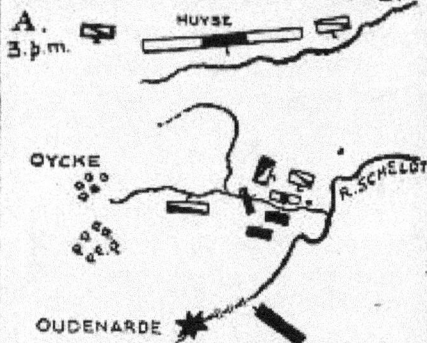

THE FRENCH ATTACK

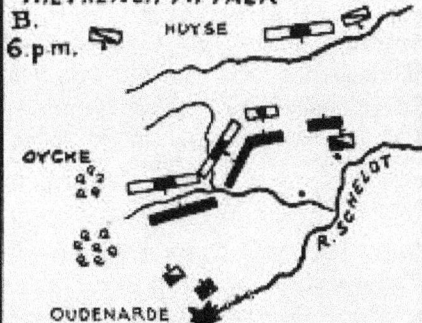

B.
6.p.m.

HUYSE

OYCKE

R.SCHELDT

OUDENARDE

ROUT OF THE FRENCH RIGHT WING.

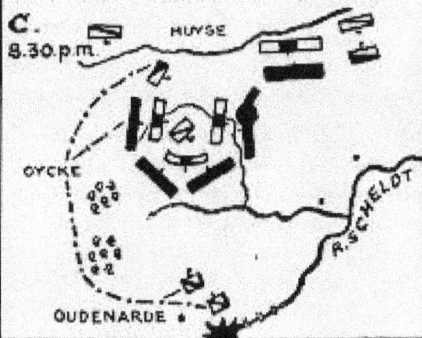

C.
8.30.p.m.

HUYSE

OYCKE

R.SCHELDT

OUDENARDE

wished to continue the march towards Ghent, but Vendôme justly pointed out that it was too late, as the heads of the hostile columns were already crossing the river. The former then maintained that he had only halted at Vendôme's express wish; but the latter retorted that he had intended to dispute the crossing, not to take a position two miles in rear of the river.

Eventually the Duke of Burgundy decided to await attack in his position on the heights of Huyse and ordered sixteen squadrons to advance, but immediately countermanded the order. The French horsemen, however, daunted by the sight of the Prussian cavalry drawn up behind the stream near Diepenbeck, had already retired to the open ground in the neighbourhood of the mill of Royeghem. While these purposeless manoeuvres were taking place the Allies' columns were toiling forward towards the Scheldt and some of the infantry had already crossed the river.

Shortly after 4 o'clock the Duke of Burgundy, becoming impatient, ordered forward the right wing and part of the centre, and Vendôme instructed the left wing to join in the advance; but Burgundy again interfered and ordered them to halt and entrench their position.

Carefully watching his opponent's hesitating movements, Marlborough clearly foresaw that the full force of the French attack would fall on the extreme left of the Allies' line and took prompt measures to reinforce the threatened flank. Two Prussian regiments from Cadogan's force were pushed forward to hold the villages of Groenwald and Herlhem, and twelve more battalions were hurried to their support, while Argyle, who had just crossed the Scheldt, was ordered to place his twenty battalions in support round the village of Schaerken. The British and Prussian squadrons were stationed in the second line, the former on the high ground south of Bevere and the latter near Heurne, and nothing more could be done until the remainder of the Allied troops reached the field of battle.

Promptly as Marlborough had made his dispositions to resist the threatened onslaught, the storm burst before his men could reach their allotted positions. Crossing the Nörken and advancing rapidly, but in perfect order, thirty battalions, composed of the flower of the French infantry, furiously attacked the two regiments holding Herlhem and Groenwald, but though hopelessly outnumbered and driven from the former village, the gallant Prussians clung desperately to the banks and hedges until the remainder of Cadogan's battalions arrived to support them. Argyle's men followed and prolonged the line as far south as the village of Shaerken, and a fiercely contested hand-to-hand contest raged among the hedges and enclosures.

Pressing forward with the greatest gallantry and *élan*, the French infantry, extending to their right, continually outflanked their opponents, and after a sharp struggle seized the villages of Barwaen and Banlancy.

Realising the critical position of affairs in this quarter of the field, Marlborough handed over the command of the right wing to Eugene and, ordering Count Lottum to support him with twenty battalions, he himself hastened to the point of danger. Encouraged by their great leader's presence, the staunch Dutch and Hanoverian battalions strove desperately to check their opponent's advance, and after a furious struggle, in which butt and bayonet were vigorously plied by both sides, the dogged courage of the Allied infantry triumphed. Gallantly though the French fought, they were slowly but surely driven back. Banlancy and Barwaen were recaptured and, still fighting fiercely, they were forced back to the plateau round the village of Diepenbeck, but here, turning on their opponents, they offered such a dogged resistance that they succeeded in temporarily checking the advance of the Allies.

On the right, meanwhile, Eugene, supported by Lottum, had pressed forward vigorously and overthrown his opponent's first line, while General Natzmar, seizing a favourable opportunity and charging home furiously at the head of his Prussian cuirassiers, had broken through their second line and penetrated as far as the chapel of Royeghem. He was brought to a standstill, however, by the deadly fire of the French infantry lining the banks and hedges, and, leaving half his gallant *cuirassiers* dead or wounded on the ground, was forced to retreat, hotly pursued by the French Household cavalry, who in their turn were driven back in confusion by the deadly volleys of Lottum's infantry.

Marlborough, however, had already launched his decisive stroke, for, noting that the high ground round the village of Oycke, on his opponent's extreme right, had been left unoccupied, he ordered Overkirk with the reserve cavalry, supported by twenty Danish and Dutch battalions, to seize the important position. Though in his sixty-seventh year and sick unto death, the gallant Dutch general carried out his important task with all the dash and vigour of a young man. Leading the Danish cavalry in person, and followed by the infantry at the double, he drove the French from the woods round the castle of Bevere, and as soon as he had occupied the high ground on which the village of Oycke was situated, he swung forward his left and bore down on his opponent's flank.

The French right, formed up in a semicircle on the plateau round Diepenbeck and struggling desperately to make head against the vigorous attack of the Allied infantry, was now entirely isolated and their line of retreat to their former position on the heights of Huyse seriously threatened. At once perceiving the result of Overkirk's successful turning movement, Marlborough ordered him to continue his advance as far as the mill of Royeghem, so as to block entirely his opponent's retreat by closing the road through Mullem. The Prince of Orange and General Oxenstein carried out their task with great success, and the isolated French right was almost completely surrounded as the Allies, pressing relentlessly forward on both flanks, crowded their opponents into a confused mass on to the plateau between Diepenbeck and Royeghem.

Seven regiments of cavalry made a desperate charge to check their advance, but were ridden down and captured, while the Danish hussars cut to pieces the mounted *gendarmerie*, the finest body of horsemen in the French Army. In a last desperate effort to extricate the hard-pressed right, Vendôme led forward the infantry from the left of the position, but, thrown into confusion by the numerous banks and hedges, they could make no impression on the British battalions and eventually fell back under cover of the gathering darkness.

Entirely surrounding the isolated French right, the wings of the Allied Army commenced to fire into each other in the dim light, and consequently Eugene and Orange were ordered to halt their men, and a considerable number of the troops composing the hostile centre were thus enabled to escape.

Eugene ordered his drummers to beat the French 'Assembly,' while the Huguenots serving in his ranks shouted out the titles of the regiments known to be present, and by this means hundreds of dazed fugitives were attracted and quietly laid down their arms. A large number also escaped westward, past the castle of Bevere, but the bulk of the gallant infantry which had formed the right wing of the French Army lay dead or wounded on the field.

Undismayed by the disaster, Vendôme, with his habitual cool courage, set himself to form a rear-guard of his least shaken troops, but the bulk of the army fled in wild panic towards Ghent, and it was only the darkness coupled with the exhaustion of the Allies that saved the

French from complete annihilation. The disastrous policy of appointing a prince, with nothing but his royal birth to recommend him, and a brilliant professional soldier to the joint command of an army was never more clearly exemplified than at Oudenarde, for had Vendôme been allowed to carry out his original intention of taking up a position to oppose the crossing immediately in rear of the river, the result of the battle must have been very different.

Gallantly though the French fought, they were hopelessly handicapped by the incompetence of the Duke of Burgundy. His interference caused the disaster to the detachment at Eyne, and his vacillating tactics were entirely responsible for the employment of only a portion of his force in the attack on the Allies' left, which ended in the utter rout of the French Army.

That Marlborough ran a great risk of being defeated in detail before the bulk of his army could complete the crossing of the Scheldt cannot be denied, but the duke was aware of the difference of opinion existing between the commanders of the hostile army, and was willing to take any reasonable chance of obtaining an immediate and decisive success, which was absolutely essential both from a military and a political standpoint.

On the field of battle, he handled his troops with remarkable skill and promptitude, taking full advantage of his opponent's blunders and finally crushing the unsupported French wing by a powerful and vigorously executed turning movement. His bold strategy was thoroughly justified, for the victory was most complete, his opponents losing 6,000 killed and wounded, 9,000 prisoners, while at least 5,000 more deserted immediately after the battle.

Marlborough's staunch troops had performed a most remarkable feat of arms, having marched nearly fifty miles between 2 a.m. on the 9th and 2 p.m. on the 11th of July, and won a brilliant victory at the cost of about 5,000 men killed and wounded. Owing to the late hour at which the battle had commenced, and the physical exhaustion of the Allies, consequent on their long-forced march to the Scheldt, a vigorous pursuit was impossible, but at daylight next morning Marlborough despatched 40 squadrons towards Ghent to harass the fugitives. Count Lottum also marched next day with 35 squadrons and 40 battalions to seize the enemy's lines at Ypres, and succeeded in capturing them together with some 5,000 prisoners just as Berwick, marching in desperate haste from the valley of the Moselle with a force of 20,000 men, arrived to reinforce the garrison.

By hampering Vendôme—who, with the exception of Villars, was by far the most able general in the French service—by giving him the incompetent Duke of Burgundy as a colleague, Louis XIV. had neutralised the advantages obtained in a previous campaign and placed his army, operating in the most important section of the theatre of war, at a great disadvantage.

Marlborough's great victory came at a most opportune moment, as it silenced, for the time at least, his calumniators in England, and undoubtedly saved the Grand Alliance, which was in grave danger of falling to pieces.

CHAPTER 7

The Campaign of 1708 (Continued)

After his defeat at Oudenarde, Vendôme concentrated his army in the large entrenched camp he had previously constructed behind the great canal in the neighbourhood of Ghent, and, undismayed by the result of the battle, set himself to restore the morale of his troops.

By his brilliant march across his opponent's communications, Marlborough had forced him into the western portion of Spanish Flanders and compelled him to leave the greater part of the French frontier uncovered.

Quick to grasp the strategic situation, the duke wished to make the most of his opportunity by invading France as soon as he had been joined by Eugene's army, and to cooperate with General Erle who had landed with a small British expedition on the coast of Normandy. To avoid loss of time he intended to mask the strong fortified city of Lille by a detachment, but his scheme was bitterly opposed by the States General, and even Eugene considered the advance too hazardous until the important fortress had been taken and secured as a base for further operations. This great frontier stronghold, which had been put into a more thorough state of repair by Vauban, regardless of expense, was considered to be so formidable that Vendôme never imagined that Marlborough would attempt to invest it, more especially as the powerful French Army, stationed near Ghent, denied the use of the Scheldt and the Lys with their network of canals to the Allies.

The capable French commander, however, had no intention of remaining quiescent behind his entrenchments, but proposed to keep the Dutch authorities in a continual state of alarm by frequent incursions into Brabant, while he covered the recently acquired cities of Bruges and Ghent and prevented the Allies using the rivers and canals to bring up their siege material.

Though he thoroughly realised the vast difficulties of the under-

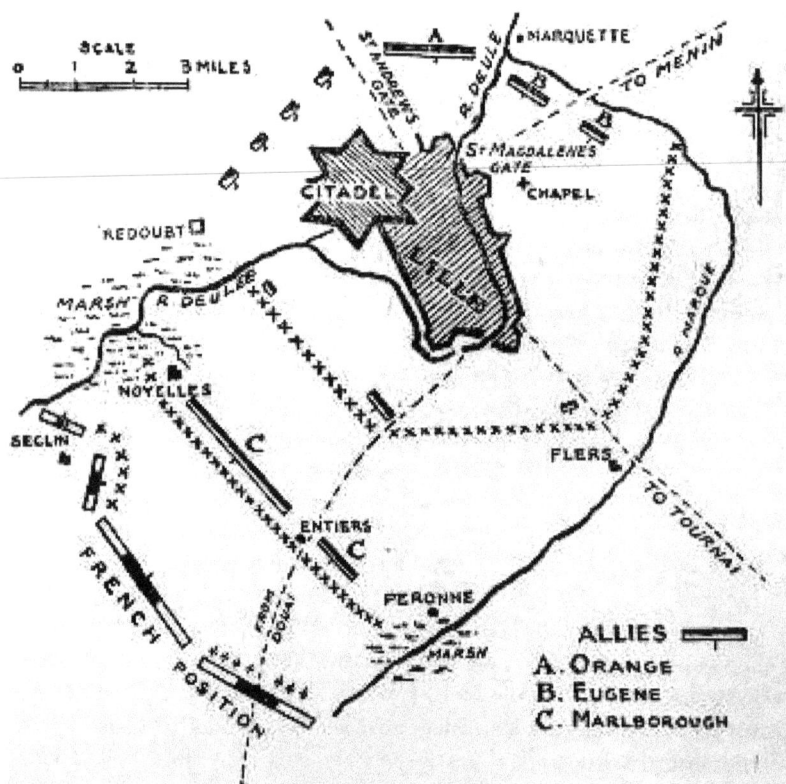

THE SIEGE OF LILLE

AND

THE POSITION OF THE COVERING FORCE AUG – SEP. 1708.

SCALE

0   1   2   3 MILES

A ● MARQUETTE

ST ANDREW'S GATE

TO MENIN

R DEULE

B

ST MAGDALENE'S GATE

✝ CHAPEL

CITADEL

LILLE

REDOUBT ▢

MARSH   R. DEULE

○ MARQUE

NOYELLES

SECLIN

C

FLERS

ENTIERS

C

TO TOURNAI

FROM DOUAI

PERONNE

FRENCH POSITION

MARSH

ALLIES ━━━
A. ORANGE
B. EUGENE
C. MARLBOROUGH

taking, Marlborough determined to lay siege to Lille, the more so as he hoped that Vendôme might be tempted to leave his entrenchments and fight a pitched battle rather than permit the investment of the fortress. The most elaborate preparations were made for the forthcoming siege and, as the enemy commanded the waterways of Brabant, some 16,000 horses were collected at Brussels to transport the enormous mass of material by road to the Allies' camp. The huge convoy, which covered over fifteen miles of road, was escorted by Eugene with 90 squadrons and 50 battalions from Brussels to the camp at Helchin, where it arrived safely on the 12th of August.

Marlborough had meanwhile stationed his army at Menin, and so carefully had his measures been taken that neither Vendôme from Ghent nor Berwick from Douai were able to interfere with the march of the convoy. The French, however, had been extremely active in western Flanders: they had captured some small forts at the mouth of the Scheldt and in the neighbourhood of Ostend, and though these minor successes were without the least permanent result, they nevertheless caused the Dutch government considerable uneasiness. Towards the end of July, Marlborough had detached a strong force of cavalry, supported by a body of infantry, to levy contributions and collect supplies in Artois, and by bringing home to the inhabitants the horrors of war, show them that their barrier of fortresses was by no means impassable. The commander, Count Tilly, was most successful, and after ten days' hard marching, during which he had burnt the suburbs of Arras, spread terror throughout northern France and bitterly wounded the pride of Louis XIV., he returned unmolested to the Allied camp.

At his own special request, Marshal Boufflers had been entrusted with the defence of Lille, and, throwing himself into the town with some reinforcements which brought up the strength of the garrison to some 15,000 men, he at once commenced vigorous preparations to strengthen the already formidable defences. The inhabitants as well as the garrison were set to work to construct earthworks, clear the field of fire and to honeycomb the approaches with mines, while a large body of troops encamped on the glacis to keep the Allies from interfering with the working parties.

The siege which was now about to commence promised to be one of the most memorable of modern times, for not only was the fortress immensely strong, but the defences were in an excellent state of repair, and the large garrison was commanded by the veteran Boufflers, who was beloved by his men and had been associated with the triumphs obtained by the French arms under Turenne, Conde and Luxemburg. Moreover, two powerful armies under Vendôme and Berwick, which, united, were superior to the Allied force in point of numbers, lay within a comparatively short distance of the city, and both commanders were equally determined to do all in their power to hinder the operations of the besiegers.

The investment was undertaken by Eugene with a force of about 40,000 strong, while Marlborough with the covering army remained in an excellently chosen position at Helchin, whence he could deal with any attempt by Vendôme or Berwick, who had now moved up the French frontier to within eighteen miles of Lille, to interfere with the large convoys constantly arriving from Brussels. Six bridges were thrown over the Scheldt and formidable lines of circumvallation, consisting of a ditch and parapet, which were to extend over the whole nine miles between Deule and the Marque, were commenced.

The commencement of the siege was marked by an act of the greatest daring on the part of Sergeant Littler of the Grenadier Guards, who swam across the Marque to a block-house garrisoned by the enemy on the far bank of the river and let down the drawbridge. The gallant non-commissioned officer escaped unhurt and was deservedly rewarded for his exploit by being promoted to the rank of Ensign. On the 23rd of August, Eugene opened his trenches against the north-east face of the town and constructed his batteries opposite the St. Andrew's and St. Madalene gates, the points against which he intended to make his decisive attack. The northern half of the line of investment was allotted to the Dutch troops under the Prince of Orange, who had succeeded Overkirk, as the latter was too ill to keep the field, and the southern to the Imperialists under Eugene's own command.

The second parallel was quickly completed and fifty heavy guns, placed in position during the night, opened a destructive fire on the chapel, near the Madalene Gate, which had been turned into a redoubt. On the same evening the Allies carried it by assault, but the work was recaptured by a sudden attack delivered by 400 volunteers from the French garrison, who drove out the small Dutch detachment, destroyed the building and retreated to the town before the Prince of Orange could arrive with reinforcements.

Next day the Allies succeeded in capturing the fortified mill in front of the St. Andrew's Gate after a fiercely contested struggle, but were forced to abandon their position by the murderous fire from the ramparts of the town. Becoming seriously alarmed at the progress made by the besiegers, Vendôme determined to effect his junction with the Duke of Berwick, but, as the Allies blocked the direct route, the French Armies were forced to make a circuitous march to the rendezvous in the neighbourhood of Lessines, which they reached without mishap on the last day of August.

Marlborough had decided not to oppose the movement, as he was confident that his opponents would not dare to attack him from the east, and if they endeavoured to relieve the fortress from the south-west, as he expected, they would be unable to harass his convoys, and, being nearer Lille than his adversaries, he could forestall them at any given point.

As Marlborough had anticipated, the French marshals advanced with their united armies, some 110,000 strong, between the Deule and the Marque, but the British general anticipated them and with a force amounting to about 70,000 men took up a position between the two rivers, with his right at Noyelles and his left at Peronne. He had barely drawn up his troops ere Vendôme appeared at the head of his formidable army, and a battle which would not only decide the fate of the fortress and the campaign, but possibly also of the war itself, appeared inevitable.

However, the evils attending a divided command made themselves felt. Vendôme and Berwick were both exceptionally able generals, but their mutual jealousy rendered co-operation impossible, and though the former wished to attack immediately, the latter pointed out that it was first of all necessary to cut paths through the densely cultivated country in front of the Allies' position. As they could come to no agreement, they referred the matter to Versailles, and Louis XIV. despatched his Minister for War, M. Chamilliard, to explain his views and to urge the marshals to attack at once.

While his opponents were wasting time, Marlborough had so strengthened his position that he was able to send back a large detachment that he had originally brought up from the trenches before Lille.

Vendôme, Berwick and Chamilliard reconnoitred their opponent's position on the 10th of September, but were so impressed by its strength that they unanimously decided against making an attack and again sent to Versailles for instructions. Finding that Vendôme would not advance, Marlborough and Eugene wished to assume the offensive, but as usual the deputies were afraid to take the bolder course, though the defeat of the hostile field army would have caused the fall of Lille and insured the success of the campaign.

A few days later the French Army retreated across the Scheldt, taking up a carefully selected position which threatened Brussels, Oudenarde and Menin, and so judiciously had Vendôme distributed his troops, that he could concentrate his whole force at any point within six hours.

Marlborough was becoming uneasy, as his opponent's position threatened the roads which the convoys must traverse, and in spite of Eugene's energy in urging on the construction of the trenches, at which 16,000 labourers impressed from the surrounding country were constantly at work, little real progress had been made with the siege. A desperate assault had been made on the breaches near the St. Andrew's Gate by a storming party of 800 grenadiers followed by 2,000 workmen, while De Mey advanced on their left with 3,000 men and Brigadier-General Sabine with 2,000 British followed in support.

But the engineers had been in error as to the practicability of the breach, the French, supported by a murderous fire from the ramparts, defended the palisades with desperate courage, and when at last the storming party forced their way into the outworks, many of them were destroyed by the explosion of a mine. However, the supports pressed forward with undaunted gallantry, in spite of their heavy losses, and eventually managed to effect a lodgement in the covered way, but at the cost of no less than 4,000 killed and wounded. Three days later the garrison made a vigorous sortie and regained part of the captured position, but were again driven back into the city on the following day. After the retreat of the relieving army the siege was pressed with renewed vigour, another assault was determined on and Marlborough sent 5,000 British troops to take part in the attack.

Just before dark on the 21st of September the storming columns, headed by the British contingent, advanced against the whole north-eastern face of the town. Regardless of the murderous discharges of grape and musketry from the ramparts, the assailants stormed the breach three times, only to be hurled back with fearful loss. Eugene made one last desperate bid for success, leading a fourth assault in person with his usual reckless gallantry and calling on the men to remember Blenheim, Ramillies and Oudenarde.

His hat was carried away by a cannon-ball and he was shortly afterwards wounded in the forehead, but after a sanguinary struggle of over two hours' duration the Allies succeeded in establishing themselves in the outwork, though at a cost of 5,000 killed and wounded, of whom no less than 3,000 were British. Eugene's wound forced Marlborough to undertake the direction of the siege as well as to command the covering army, and only his extraordinary ability and indefatigable energy enabled him to carry on both duties simultaneously. Two days later he ordered a renewed assault, when, in spite of the explosion of a mine which caused fearful havoc among the Allies, they succeeded in establishing themselves in a considerably stronger position.

Boufflers managed to inform Vendôme that the garrison were running short of ammunition, and during the night of the 28th of September 2,500 French dragoons under the Chevalier de Luxemburg made a desperate effort to break through the besiegers' lines. Each man carried sixty pounds of gunpowder in a bag fastened to his saddle and mounted a sprig of green, the emblem of the Allies, in his headdress. On their arrival at the gates of the lines of circumvallation, an officer who could speak Dutch gave out that they were German dragoons bringing supplies for the besiegers.

Some 1,800 had passed through in safety, when the officer commanding the guard heard the order to 'close up' given in French, and at once suspecting a ruse, he called upon them to halt, and as they attempted to gallop through the gate, he ordered his men to open fire. Some sixty bags of powder exploded, blowing the troopers carrying them to bits, but over 1,000 of the gallant dragoons, galloping through the Allies' camp, reached the town with their precious but dangerous burdens.

The difficulty of obtaining ammunition and stores while the enemy held Bruges, Ghent, Ypres and Tournai, caused Marlborough considerable annoyance, and he resolved to open up a fresh line of communication from Ostend to the camp, in spite of the danger involved by this course.

At his request the expedition under Erle, which had achieved nothing by its descent on the coast of Normandy, had been diverted to Ostend and had arrived at that port with a large supply of stores and ammunition.

General Erle, who was a most capable officer, soon organised a base at Ostend and seized the passages over the Nieuport canal at Leffinghem and Oudenbourg. The safe arrival of the convoy was of the most vital importance to the Allies, and Marlborough took the most elaborate measures to secure it from molestation during its march. Twelve battalions and 20 squadrons were sent to Ostend to act as escort; Webb with 12 battalions was stationed at Thourout, about a third of the way between Ostend and the Allied camp, and Cadogan was posted at Roulers, with a strong force of cavalry, to help the convoy along. Webb sent a couple of battalions to Oudenbourg to keep watch towards Bruges, where de la Motte was lying with some 25,000 men, and also sent out strong patrols in every direction to give timely notice of the enemy's approach. The convoy set out from Ostend on the evening of the 27th of September, consisting of 700 carts laden with ammunition and supplies and escorted by a detachment of 6,000 men.

Count Lottum, who with 150 horsemen had been sent to meet the convoy, which had safely crossed the canal at Leffinghem and was advancing towards Thourout, returned at noon, reporting that he had seen the advance guard of a strong hostile force some miles north of Wynendael.

Collecting every available man, Webb immediately pushed forward and drew up his small force in two lines across a gap in the woods which bordered the road near the castle of Wynendael, while Lottum with his horsemen skirmished with the enemy to delay their advance. On one side of the clearing through which the French must of necessity advance a few companies of grenadiers and a Prussian battalion had been stationed, while on the opposite side a Hanoverian battalion was posted. As soon as these arrangements had been completed. Lottum's horsemen fell back behind the infantry and the French guns commenced a desultory cannonade which, though it lasted for a couple of hours, did little damage, as Webb had ordered his men to lie down.

About 5 o'clock in the afternoon de la Motte sent his infantry forward in four lines, supported by his cavalry in a similar formation; the troops, expecting to meet with but little opposition, advanced in perfect order and entered the clearing with their flanks almost touching the undergrowth on either side. They had approached within less than a hundred yards of their opponents concealed in the woods when a deadly fire was suddenly poured in from both flanks, and the astonished infantry, shrinking from the hail of lead, threw the centre of the line into hopeless confusion. To support his men in driving home their attack, de la Motte brought up his cavalry, but by this time his whole force, surrounded on three sides by a circle of fire, had fallen into complete disorder. Impeded by their own infantry, the cavalry were unable to charge, while the wounded horses, maddened by the pain, kicked and plunged to such an extent that they broke up every vestige of formation.

However, their great numerical superiority enabled them to break through the two foremost lines of their opponents, but they were brought to a standstill by the third line, composed of some battalions which had most opportunely arrived just as the attack had commenced. Blinded by the swirling smoke and mown down by the deadly hail of bullets rained on them from every side, the unfortunate French infantry shrank back, and not even the blows and curses of their officers could urge them to make another effort.

Seeing that the moment had come to complete their rout, Webb gave the signal to advance, and the Allies, moving forward as steadily as if on parade and halting every few paces to pour deadly volleys into the struggling mass of their opponents, drove them from the field in irretrievable confusion.

Cadogan, hastening to the sound of the guns with some squadrons, wished to continue the pursuit, but Webb wisely contented himself with the repulse of his assailants, who had lost over 4,000 men, while the Allies' casualties amounted to about 900. Under cover of the action the convoy passed unmolested in rear of the wood and eventually reached Menin without the loss of a single horse or waggon.

Though the forces engaged at Wynendael were comparatively small, Webb having about 8,000 men on the field and de la Motte some 22,000 men and 9 guns, the results of the brilliant little victory were most important, for had the French succeeded in capturing or destroying the convoy, the Allies would have been forced to abandon the siege of Lille; but with their magazines replenished by the stores of ammunition brought up from Ostend the surrender of the fortress was only a matter of time.

At the beginning of October another assault was delivered against a redoubt on the counterscarp; about midday a Scottish sergeant, followed by a dozen grenadiers, scaled the parapet and, finding the garrison asleep, leapt into the work; the supports promptly followed, but the assailants suffered so heavily from the murderous fire from the ramparts that they commenced to give way and were only prevented from abandoning their position by the gallantry of a Prussian colonel who refused to quit his post, though wounded in four places. Reinforcements, however, quickly arrived, bringing with them materials for erecting cover, and after a desperate struggle the assailants succeeded in establishing themselves in the counterscarp opposite the main breach. Determined to leave no stone unturned to hinder the

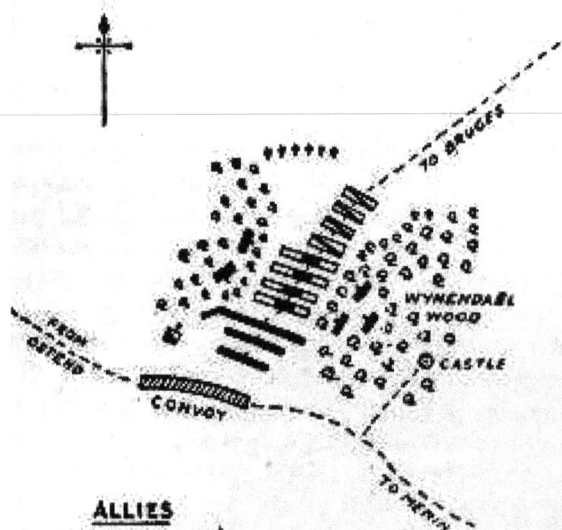

SKETCH PLAN OF THE ACTION
AT
WYNENDAEL
28TH SEPT. 1708

TO BRUGES

WYNENDAEL
WOOD

CASTLE

FROM
OSTEND

CONVOY

TO THERIN

ALLIES
INFANTRY
CAVALRY

FRENCH
INFANTRY
CAVALRY

siege, Vendôme opened the sluices, hoping, by flooding the low-lying country, to prevent the Allies drawing supplies from Ostend. But Marlborough dealt with the difficulty with his usual promptitude, organising a service of flat-bottomed boats to convey the stores from Ostend to Leffinghem, and high, two-wheeled carts to convey them thence along the inundated causeways to the camp. Cadogan superintended the operations with his wonted energy and skill, and so successfully was the service carried out that the Allies suffered comparatively little inconvenience.

Foiled in his endeavour to prevent supplies reaching his opponent, Vendôme next seized Nieuport and the important post of Leffinghem on the canal, thus entirely blocking the road from Ostend to Lille; but his success came too late to save the latter fortress. With sixty heavy guns and thirty mortars continually battering the walls, the defences began to crumble away, and as the garrison had suffered enormously, Boufflers had no option but to demand a parley. Eugene signed the capitulation on the 23rd of November without reading the text, remarking that, after Boufflers' heroic defence, the latter could ask no terms which he would be unwilling to grant.

The cavalry, some 3,000 strong, were allowed to escort the wives of the officers and men of the French garrison to Tournai, while Boufflers and the remainder of his gallant force, now reduced to barely 5,000 men, shut themselves up in the citadel to withstand a second siege.

The Allies sent foraging parties far and wide into northern France, obtaining supplies in plenty, and spreading consternation throughout Artois.

Owing to the Elector of Hanover's incompetence, the Elector of Bavaria had been allowed to quit the Rhine and bring reinforcements to the main French Army; and in the hope of creating a diversion, Vendôme sent the latter with 15,000 men to seize Brussels by a *coup de main*, while he himself remained on the Scheldt, blocking the Allies' direct route to the city.

Marlborough proceeded to deal with the problem in his usually masterly manner. Sending his field artillery to Menin, he proceeded to fix his headquarters at Courtrai and gave out that he was about to place his army in winter quarters. His plan was to lull his opponent into a state of fancied security and then make a sudden dash at the long line of entrenchments the French had constructed on the Scheldt, and break through before Vendôme could concentrate his forces to oppose him. Consequently, he secretly assembled his army on the Lys, and early on the 26th of November two detachments under Cadogan and Lottum advanced to the Scheldt with orders to construct pontoon bridges across the river both above and below Oudenarde.

The main body followed during the night and crossed the river next morning under cover of a dense fog, without having been discovered by the hostile patrols; a few squadrons of dragoons were dispersed and the initial stage of the duke's scheme had been crowned with complete success. Vendôme, who was at Tournai, hearing a rumour of his opponent's advance, wished to concentrate at once and march to meet him, but by the time he and Berwick could agree on a plan of action the Allies had forced the laboriously constructed lines and were in full march to the relief of Brussels.

The Elector of Bavaria meanwhile had appeared before the city and summoned the governor to surrender, but though the latter had barely 5,000 men to defend the extensive fortifications, he returned a defiant answer.

Two days later the Elector attempted to storm the defences of the city, and though the garrison resisted desperately throughout the night, the French eventually succeeded in establishing themselves on the glacis.

During the morning, however, the news of the approach of the Allied Army arrived, and the Elector, abandoning his guns and wounded, retreated in haste, while Marlborough entered the city in triumph. The communications with Brussels being reopened, the siege of the citadel of Lille was pressed with the greatest vigour, and it was obvious that even Boufflers and his staunch garrison could not hold out much longer. Ammunition and food were almost exhausted, and the gallant marshal had received an autograph letter from Louis XIV. congratulating him on his heroic defence, and ordering him to surrender to avoid further useless sacrifice of life.

Under these circumstances the French beat a 'parley,' and Boufflers marched out of the citadel on the 11th of December with 4,500 men, all that remained of the original garrison. All Europe had watched with absorbing interest this most remarkable siege, in which Marlborough and Eugene had set themselves to capture one of the strongest fortresses in France, defended by a capable general and 15,000 excellent troops, while Vendôme and Berwick lay near at hand with a numerically superior army and used every endeavour to hinder the besiegers. The Allies had triumphed in spite of every difficulty, but at a cost to themselves of nearly 20,000 men, over 12,000 of whom had been killed or wounded, while fully 7,000 more had died from sickness and exposure. The honours, however, were shared by Boufflers and his gallant men, who for nearly four months had opposed a most desperate resistance to every attack and had lost more than half their numbers in their heroic defence.

As soon as Lille had fallen, Marlborough, with his mind still fixed on the invasion of France, determined to recapture Bruges and Ghent before the close of the campaign. Meanwhile the differences between the two French commanders had reached such an acute stage that Berwick had been ordered to return to the Rhine, and Chamilliard had arrived at Vendôme's headquarters with an order from Louis XIV. to put the army into winter quarters at once and to undertake no further operations.

A week after the surrender of Lille, Marlborough, suddenly concentrating his forces, appeared before Ghent, and Count Lottum was entrusted with the direction of the siege, while Eugene, with the troops who had had such an arduous time in the trenches, formed the covering army. The siege was pressed with the utmost vigour, and though de la Motte, who had been ordered to hold out to the last, had no less than 18,000 men in the city, his courage failed him, and after a half-hearted sortie he surrendered on the 1st of January 1709. Bruges opened its gates to the Allies, while the small forts of Leffinghem and Plass Endael, blocking the road to Ostend, were abandoned by their garrisons.

A severe frost now set in, and Marlborough placed his army in winter quarters after a campaign which had been carried on much later than usual and which, in spite of the reverses which had marked its commencement, had ended in the most glorious triumphs. Vendôme, one of the ablest French marshals, had been heavily defeated at Oudenarde; Lille, the great barrier stronghold, hitherto deemed impregnable, had been captured, in spite of the heroic defence of the garrison and the ceaseless efforts of a powerful French Army to relieve it; Bruges and Ghent had been recovered and the hostile armies driven back to their own frontiers.

The Allies, however, had suffered a great loss by the death of gallant Marshall Overkirk, at the age of sixty-seven. The veteran commander, who had taken part in no less than thirty campaigns, was a natural cousin of William of Orange, who had always had the highest opinion of his ability.

Though not a great general in the broader sense of the word, he was a thoroughly capable and reliable soldier, who always carried out his orders with the most conspicuous ability, and was beloved by his men on account of his dauntless courage. The brilliant way in which he handled his command both at Ramillies and at Oudenarde had contributed in a marked degree to the success of the Allies, and above all he was absolutely disinterested and loyal, in fact he was the one Dutch general on whom Marlborough could unhesitatingly rely.

On the Rhine, owing to the small forces engaged, nothing 'of importance had taken place, while in northern Italy the bitter quarrel between the Emperor and the Duke of Savoy had completely paralysed the Allies' operations. But in spite of the great duke's brilliant successes in the Netherlands the intrigues of his political opponents in England were gaining ground and his staunch ally, Godolphin, was hard put to it to retain his position.

CHAPTER 8

The Campaign of 1709

Well aware of the differences existing between chief members of the coalition, Louis XIV. used every endeavour to open negotiations with them separately. Holland still coveted Ghent and Bruges, in addition to as much of the Spanish Netherlands as she could filch from Austria, while the quarrel between the Emperor and the Duke of Savoy had reached such a pitch that combined operations in northern Italy were no longer possible.

Prussia and Hanover had also become weary of the long-drawn-out war, and as the Grand Alliance showed unmistakable signs of breaking up, Marlborough earnestly desired peace, provided suitable terms could be arranged, and used his best endeavours to induce the States General to consent to reasonable conditions. The Allies, however, grown arrogant with success, demanded that, Louis XIV. should surrender the whole of the Spanish possessions, and if necessary, use force to drag his grandson from the throne of Spain. England stipulated that the Stuarts should be banished and the fortifications of the great naval base at Dunkirk destroyed, while Holland demanded the fortified cities of Dendermonde, Ghent, Ypres, Menin, Lille, Valenciennes, Tournai and Mauberge, which would have left France crippled and helpless.

The situation of the latter country was indeed pitiable: famine stalked through the land during the bitter winter of 1708-9, the treasury was empty, and owing to the naval supremacy of Great Britain in the Mediterranean, supplies could only be obtained with the greatest difficulty. It seemed that France must agree to any terms, however ruinous; but the conditions of the ultimatum delivered by the Allies were such as no great nation could accept, so Louis XIV., who throughout his long life had never been wanting in courage, issued a stirring proclamation to his people and determined to fight to the last rather than agree to the humiliating conditions of peace. The nation nobly seconded his efforts, and with the prospect of invasion all classes threw themselves with enthusiasm into the preparations for the defence of their country, and crowds of recruits flocked to join the colours in Flanders, where Villars had been appointed to command the armies of France.

During the spring, the marshal, always popular with the army an account of his courage and ability, had done wonders for his starving and disheartened troops: under his energetic care the mob of famished skeletons had developed into a splendid fighting force, full of enthusiasm and eager to try conclusions with their foes. Reinforced by strong drafts from the Rhine, Villars found himself at the head of a powerful army of some 90,000 men, animated with the courage of despair and determined to shed the last drop of their blood in the defence of their country. Early in May he had taken up a strong position between Douai and Bethune, which barred the Allies' probable line of advance into France, and set himself to render it impregnable. Redoubts were erected at frequent intervals, the approaches were obstructed and narrowed by inundations, and the whole front of the position covered by a deep ditch and line of entrenchments.

After immense difficulty Marlborough induced the British Government to send 10,000 additional troops to the Low Countries, though they had at one time contemplated withdrawing seven veteran regiments from the main theatre of operations to support the hopeless cause of the Allies in Spain. Holland had also taken an additional 4,000 Wurtembergers into her pay for the coming campaign, but the other powers obstinately refused to increase their contingents. When negotiations were finally broken off, in June, Marlborough, finding himself at the head of nearly 110,000 men, determined, if he could not induce Villars to leave his entrenchments and fight a pitched battle in the open, to reduce the important fortress of Tournai, which was situated on the direct road from Brussels to Lille.

On the 23rd of June the Allies commenced their forward movement, Eugene with the right wing crossing the Deule below Lille, while the left, composed of the British and Dutch contingents, crossed the Marque, and the whole army concentrated on the Upper Deule. Villars did exactly what Marlborough had expected, calling in his detachments and drawing large reinforcements from the garrison of Tournai and the other fortress to repel what he imagined to be the threatened assault on his lines. Marlborough and Eugene reconnoitred the enemy's entrenchments, but finding them much too strong to attack, the duke, who had compelled his opponent to concentrate, carried out a most brilliant manoeuvre, first advancing towards the French lines and then, during the night, changing direction and marching in dead silence towards Tournai.

By 7 o'clock the next morning the Allies surrounded the town, taking the weakened garrison completely by surprise and capturing several of their foraging parties. Marlborough's scheme had been a triumphant success, for not only had he invested Tournai without opposition, but he had also forced his opponent to play into his hands, by inducing him to withdraw half of the garrison. Eugene commanded the covering army, which was to prevent Villars interfering with the reduction of the fortress, while General Lumley conducted the siege operations; the heavy artillery was brought up the Scheldt from Ghent, and the trenches were opened on the 7th of July.

The siege was vigorously pressed and the besiegers established themselves on the covered way, but found their further progress checked by the water in the ditch; however, the ditch was eventually drained and the heavy batteries, established at close range, battered the defences with considerable effect. The Duke of Argyle, at the head of his Highlanders, gallantly stormed an outwork named the 'Seven Fountains,' which gave the Allies possession of the counterscarp, and as de Surville saw no prospect of relief, he surrendered the town and retired into the citadel with the garrison.

Hoping that the siege would keep the Allies occupied throughout the remainder of the summer, Villars had made no attempt to relieve the town, but had laboured unceasingly at the construction of fresh lines of entrenchments extending from Douai to the Scheldt, near Conde, which he hoped would prevent his opponents advancing into France. The entire space surrounding the citadel of Tournai had been honeycombed with mines, and as the Allies were lamentably deficient in engineers, they were at a great disadvantage in the subterranean warfare which ensued, and were, to a certain extent, paralysed by the continual explosions and terrors of the underground combats. A vigorous sortie was repulsed and an important outwork captured, beneath which, however, a mine exploded, blowing a number of the assailants to pieces, while next night a desperate combat took place in the bowels of the earth, which resulted in the defeat of the garrison.

Ten days later a large number of the besiegers were destroyed by the explosion of a mine, and another party crushed beneath a falling bastion; but in spite of these accumulated disasters, which proved most trying to the men's nerves, the dogged determination of the Allies triumphed over every obstacle. After nearly two months' siege, de Surville was forced to surrender and the important fortress fell into the hands of the Allies, but at the cost of nearly 5,000 men, who had been killed or had died of sickness during the siege. As a mark of his appreciation of their gallant defence, Marlborough allowed the garrison, which had been reduced to barely 3,000 men, to march out with the honours of war. The duke at once decided to capture the important city of Mons, one of the last of the great frontier fortresses remaining in French hands, and ordered Orkney with a detachment to surprise the fort at St. Chislain, which covered the passage over the Haine, but finding it strongly held and the garrison on the alert, the latter decided not to risk an attack.

The Prince of Hesse-Cassel meanwhile, marching with extraordinary rapidity, had crossed the river at Oubourg, some five miles east of Mons, before the French were aware of his approach. Marlborough, promptly following up his success, seized the plateau of Jemappes and established his headquarters at the Abbey of Belain, cutting off Mons completely from Valenciennes and the interior of France. The effect of these brilliant manoeuvres was prodigious, as it entirely destroyed popular confidence in the elaborate and laboriously constructed lines of entrenchments, which had been twice forced by the Allies without loss.

While Marlborough had been carrying out these brilliant manoeuvres, Villars, uncertain where the blow would fall, had remained inactive, but directly he was informed of Hesse-Cassel's success, he concentrated his forces and moved to meet his opponent. As Mons was only held by some 5,000 men and was badly off for supplies, the French marshal was faced by the alternative of fighting a pitched battle or allowing the important frontier stronghold to fall into the hands of the Allies.

He naturally chose the former alternative, and on the 4th of September his cavalry came into contact with Hesse-Cassel's detachment, but believing that his opponents had already concentrated, Villars forbore to attack and missed his opportunity of crushing the isolated hostile corps. Advancing to within ten miles of Mons, he took up his position in rear of the two great gaps in the belt of dense forest which stretched across the elevated plateau between the Hon and the Trouille. He had acted with great decision and rapidity and chosen his ground so well that the Allies would be forced to attack him before they could commence the investment of the fortress. On the afternoon of the 7th of September, the advanced troops of the opposing armies came in contact, and leaving a force drawn from Eugene's command to observe Mons, the Allies bivouacked on the high ground some five miles from the hostile position.

Villars, who had carefully reconnoitred the ground on which he meant to offer battle, had taken up his position in rear of the more easterly of the two gaps in the belt of the forest, between the woods of Taisnieres and Lanieres, between the roads from Bavay and Mauberge to Mons.

After carefully reconnoitring the hostile position, Marlborough and Eugene wished to attack at once before Villars could render it more formidable, but as usual the pig-headed deputies objected to the obvious and reasonable course, declaring that the position was too strong and the risk of defeat too great. Eventually a middle course was adopted, the Dutch consenting to an attack as soon as the rear-guard, which was on the march from Tournai, should have arrived and the fort of St. Chislain, which commanded the passage over the Haine, should have been taken.

Hearing that a decisive battle was imminent, the veteran Marshal Boufflers, though so crippled by gout that he had to be helped into his travelling carriage, begged to be allowed to serve under Villars, despite the fact that the latter was junior to him in rank. Boufflers, whose undaunted courage had endeared him to the army, was received in camp by a *feu de joi* and such an outburst of cheering that the Allies, imagining that the French were about to advance to the attack, stood to arms.

The rival forces, assembled for the greatest and most fiercely contested battle of the whole war, were singularly equal in numbers, Villars having about 95,000 men in position while the Allies mustered to some two thousand less, but were slightly superior to their opponents in artillery.

The army, which under Villars' able leadership had entirely regained its morale after the disasters of the previous campaign, numbered many of the great nobles as well as the pick of the French troops in its ranks. About to fight behind their solidly constructed earthworks, under leaders in whom they had implicit confidence, they eagerly looked forward to the coming battle, which would obviously settle the issue of the campaign and possibly of the war, and were fully prepared to shed the last drop of their blood in the defence of their

MALPLAQUET
11TH SEPTEMBER 1709.

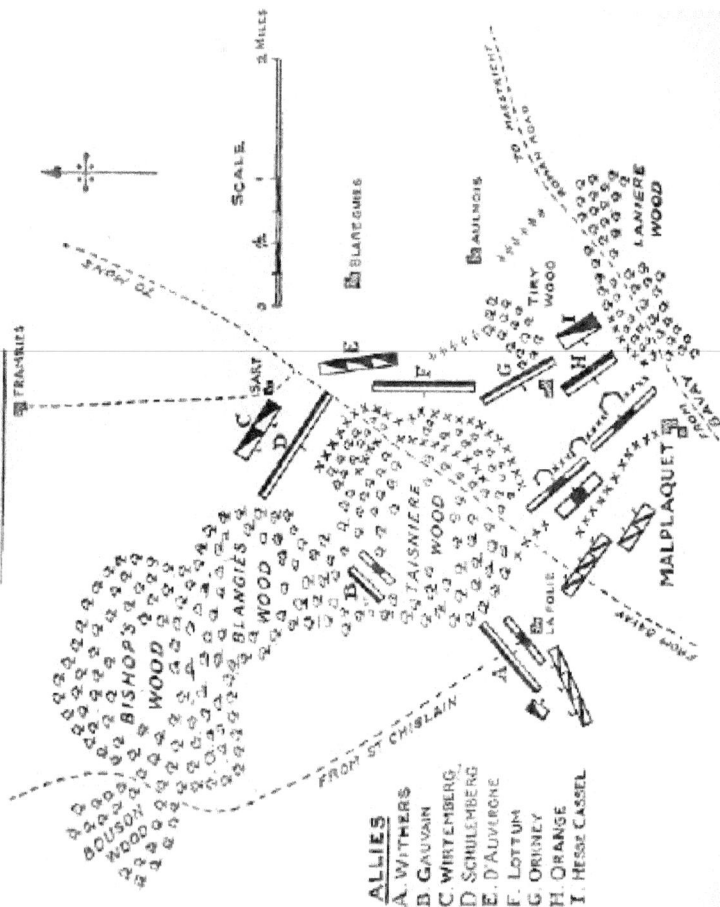

SCALE

TO MONS

FRAMERIES

SART

BISHOP'S WOOD

BOUSON WOOD

BLANGIES WOOD

FROM ST GHISLAIN

TAISNIERE WOOD

SLAREGNIES

AULNOIS

TIRY WOOD

TO MAESTRICHT

ROMAN ROAD

LANIERE WOOD

FROM BAVAY

MALPLAQUET

LA FOLIE

FROM QUÉVY

ALLIES
A. WITHERS
B. GAUVAIN
C. WIRTEMBERG
D. SCHULEMBERG
E. D'AUVERGNE
F. LOTTUM
G. ORKNEY
H. ORANGE
I. HESSE CASSEL

country. The Allies, though composed of many different nationalities, were equally eager to fight; they were veteran troops welded together by their long series of victories and with unbounded trust in their brilliant leaders, under whom they had never known defeat.

Villars had laboured unceasingly to render his position secure and had used the respite given him by the obstinacy of the deputies to the greatest advantage, indeed the latter were to a great extent responsible for the enormous losses sustained by the Allies. The entrenchments, on which one half of the army worked while the other half remained under arms, were so solidly constructed that they resembled permanent fortifications rather than field works. From the wood of Lanieres, on the right, the edge of which had been protected by abatis and entanglements, a triple line of trenches with a high parapet extended to a large redoubt, beyond which a series of small redans covered the open ground up to the outskirts of the wood of Taisnieres. The eastern and northeastern front of the latter wood was defended by abatis and formidable entrenchments, while the position was still further strengthened by a second line of trenches running from the village of Malplaquet through the Taisnieres wood, a powerful battery had been constructed in rear of the centre, and guns placed at intervals behind the parapets of all the works.

Marlborough, who with Eugene had several times reconnoitred the hostile position, considered it so strong that he ordered Withers, who was marching from Tournai with nineteen battalions and ten squadrons to join the main army, to move via St. Chislain and through the woods in rear of the French position, so as to fall on their extreme left and rear round the farm of La Folie. He was to co-operate with the main attack, which was to be made on the north-eastern salient of the Taisnieres wood, while subsidiary attacks were to be made against the right, and later against the centre, of the hostile position.

Schulemberg with forty battalions and Lottum with twenty-two battalions were to carry out the main attack against the northern and eastern front of the wood, while the Prince of Orange was to assail the French right with forty battalions, and Orkney, in the centre, was to keep up connection between the two wings. The night preceding the battle found the Allies drawn up from Aulnois to Framries, opposite the centre and extreme left of their opponent's position, their troops massed in two main groups opposite the points which they were destined to attack.

The men, lying down fully accoutred in the ranks, snatched a brief rest, standing to arms at 3 a.m. on the morning of the 11th of September, and when Divine Service had been held at the head of each regiment, the whole marched in perfect order and profound silence to their allotted positions under cover of a thick mist. The artillery followed, taking up a central position on the right of the wood of Tiry, whence they could closely support their infantry by bringing an effective fire to bear on the enemy's line of entrenchments.

The cavalry formed the second line and were divided into four groups: on the right came the Duke of Wirtemberg with the Austrians; next the British and Hanoverians; then D'Auvergne's Dutch cavalry, with Hesse-Cassel's twenty-one squadrons on the extreme left, in rear of Orange's division.

Owing to the fact that the French entrenchments in the gap were a considerable distance in rear of their flanks, posted on the outskirts of the woods, Marlborough adopted a most unusual but extremely suitable formation for his attack. His force advanced in two independent masses against the left and right of his opponent's position, the line of batteries near the wood of Tiry and Lord Orkney's fifteen battalions of British troops, some distance in rear, forming the only connection between the widely separated wings. The duke's intention was first of all to drive his opponents from the woods on either flank, then roll up their line from the left, and finally, drawing troops from either wing, to storm the line of entrenchments which covered the gap, some 2,000 yards in extent, between the woods.

As soon as their outposts reported that the Allies had commenced their advance the French Army stood to arms, the working parties, who were still labouring energetically at the entrenchments, threw down their tools and, eagerly donning their equipment, took their place in the ranks.

Boufflers had been given the post of honour on the right, and as Villars, mounting his horse shortly before 7 o'clock, rode round the left and centre of his position, he was greeted by an enthusiastic outburst of cheering from his gallant troops. At 7.30 a.m. the sun shone out brilliantly, dispersing the thick white mist, and a furious artillery duel commenced, during which the Allies advanced in echelon, left in front, to the attack.

The Prince of Orange, on the extreme left, halted just out of range of the hostile guns and was ordered not to move forward with his Dutch and mixed division until the main attack had been in progress for half-an-hour. In spite of the deadly fire from the French guns,

Lottum's battalions advanced in perfect order and then, changing direction half right, struggled across a marshy brook and pressed vigorously forward against the eastern front of the Taisnieres wood. Orkney meanwhile, who had followed Lottum, kept straight on and, occupying the ground his colleague had vacated, halted just out of range of the artillery, opposite the hostile centre.

Meanwhile Schulemberg's battalions, led by Eugene in person, had forced their way through the outskirts of the wood, regardless of the fire of the hostile guns, to within fifty yards of the entrenchments, but a sudden outbreak of musketry struck them with such deadly effect that the whole line staggered back in confusion for over two hundred yards.

Resting their muskets on the parapets, the masses of French infantry holding the trenches fired with murderous effect into the crowded ranks of the Imperialists, who were so shaken by their losses that Eugene, who as usual was recklessly exposing himself in the thick of the fight, had the greatest difficulty in bringing them forward for a second attack.

Gauvain, marching up from Mons, had meanwhile penetrated into the heart of the wood unobserved and gained touch with the extreme right of Schulemberg's line, but even with his aid the Austrians were unable to drive back the Marines and the Picardy regiment, who clung to their position with desperate gallantry. However, Lottum's staunch infantry, supported by a British brigade, pressed doggedly forward in spite of their losses and drove their opponents from the edge of the wood, while the advance of D'Auvergne's cavalry forced Villars, who was about to make a vigorous counterstroke, to withdraw his troops.

Still struggling forward, Lottum's infantry hurled themselves at the entrenchments with such fury that they drove the 'Regiment du Roi' from its position at the point of the bayonet and, amid deafening cheers, stormed a redoubt. Villars, however, had been carefully watching the progress of the battle, and he now led forward a brigade from the reserve, and after a furious struggle drove the gallant infantry from the captured redoubt. Marlborough, who was close at hand, had noted their repulse, and putting himself at the head of D'Auvergne's squadrons, fully 3,000 strong, he charged furiously through the gaps in the entrenchments and, supported by the staunch infantry, drove his opponents back into the wood.

Withers, who had meanwhile advanced unobserved by the tracks through the wood of Blangies, was beginning to make his presence felt, and was gradually driving back the extreme left of the French line, round La Folie.

Chafing at his enforced inaction, the Prince of Orange launched his attack the minute the stipulated half-hour had elapsed. Hamilton with the Highland brigade was to drive back the French right in the wood of Lanieres, while nine Dutch battalions under Oxenstein and Spaar were to assault the entrenchments outside the wood, and ten battalions advancing on the right of the wood of Tiry were to capture the powerful battery on the Malplaquet road. Seven Dutch battalions under Pallant, which had originally been intended as a reserve, were almost immediately drawn into the fight, and the cavalry and artillery under the Prince of Hesse-Cassel moved up in close support of their infantry.

The Highlanders, led by the young Marquis of Tullibardine, dashed forward with such fury that in spite of a deadly fire they burst into the first line of entrenchments and pushing on without a check captured the second line. On their right, meanwhile, the Prince of Orange was advancing between the edge of the forest and the wood of Tiry: his horse was shot under him, but, sword in hand, he led forward his Dutch battalions against the entrenchments. The murderous discharges of grape and musketry tore great gaps in their ranks, and the gallant Oxenstein fell mortally wounded; but, regardless of their losses, the Dutch Blue Guards carried the hostile works at the point of the bayonet, after a furious struggle. Bringing up his second line, Boufflers launched a vigorous counterstroke to recover the entrenchments, while a battery in the wood of Lanieres, taking the Allies in flank, did enormous execution among the Dutch and Highlanders.

The gallant Tullibardine died a soldier's death, defending the redoubt his men had so heroically captured; Spaar was killed in the trenches, and Hamilton carried, desperately wounded, from the field. Human flesh and blood could stand no more, and the Allied infantry staggered back, leaving the ground thickly strewn with their dead and wounded. Orange heroically rallied his division and, seizing the colours of Mey's regiment, advanced almost alone to the entrenchments, shouting in a voice heard clear above the din of the battle: 'Follow me, my friends, here is your post!' His gallant troops responded nobly to his call and again hurled themselves against the hostile works, but in vain; the French second line had now closed up, and the parapet was lined by a bristling hedge of bayonets, five or six deep, while the hail of the bullets issuing from the cloud of smoke which shrouded the works, mowed down the assailants in hundreds.

The brigade of Navarre, issuing from the entrenchments, made a vigorous counterstroke and were promptly followed by the Horse Grenadiers, sent by Boufflers to their support. But the Dutch, sullenly retreating, were still full of fight, and turning on their opponents they checked them by their steady volleys, while Hesse-Cassel, charging furiously to cover the retreat of the hard-pressed infantry, drove the French back to their entrenchments. Orange could do no more, his reserves were exhausted, as he had used the whole of his forty battalions in his desperate assaults on the formidable works, bristling with guns and held by nearly double his force.

Hearing of the disastrous repulse, Marlborough, who had up till then been with Lottum's infantry, galloped across to his hard-pressed left and was almost immediately followed by Eugene. Reinforced by four Hanoverian battalions, drawn from the reserve, Orange again hurled his devoted infantry against the enemy, and even succeeded in capturing the first line of the entrenchments; but Boufflers led forward his reserve and the Allies were again driven back with fearful loss. The Hanoverians lost nearly all their officers, and Orange's divisions were so crippled by their enormous casualties, nearly 9,000 men having fallen in the three desperate assaults, that Marlborough ordered the left wing to withdraw out of range and merely observe their opponent's position.

It seems probable that Orange altogether exceeded his orders by making repeated onslaughts on the formidable line of trenches, but undoubtedly his desperate assaults held the whole of the French right wing to its position, prevented Boufflers from complying with Villars' urgent and repeated requests for reinforcements and forced the latter to dangerously weaken his centre.

While Boufflers was successfully holding his own on the right, Villars was becoming anxious about the fate of the opposite flank, which was hard put to it to hold its ground against the combined efforts of Schulemberg, Lottum and Withers. Withdrawing the Irish and two other brigades from the centre, he assumed a vigorous offensive, driving back Schulemberg's and Lottum's men for a considerable distance. Then, turning on Withers, he led a furious bayonet charge on foot and was severely wounded in the knee, but in spite of the pain, he called for a chair and continued to direct the battle until he became unconscious from loss of blood.

Quick to notice that his opponent had withdrawn a large body of troops from the centre, Marlborough at once seized the opportunity of dealing him a shattering blow, and ordered Orkney to advance against the weakly held entrenchments, while he withdrew some of the least-shaken troops from the left to support the attack. Leading his men forward in one long line, Orkney gallantly advanced against the entrenchments held by the Bavarians and the Cologne Guards, who had been left unsupported by the withdrawal of the troops to the left, and after a brief but fierce struggle, drove them from their position.

D'Auvergne's cavalry galloped through the intervals between the redans, and the artillery from the great central battery near the wood of Tiry, ordered forward by Marlborough himself, came up at the trot and took up its position within the hostile lines. The captured guns were slewed round and a deadly fire poured on the splendid array of French cavalry drawn up in rear of the position and occupying a frontage of nearly a mile in length. Meanwhile the gallant Lottum had fallen, desperately wounded, but Argyle, leading his own regiment, two battalions of the Guards and the Royal Scots, against the entrenchments, had pressed his attack with such vigour that his opponents were forced to abandon the edge of the wood.

After a gallant resistance the marines and the Picardy regiment at last fell back, but, supported by the Champagne regiment, they turned on their assailants and a furious struggle took place in the heart of the wood, every inch of ground, tree and stone being the object of a desperate hand-to-hand combat. At the same time Schulemberg's men, led by Eugene in person, were forcing their way through the thick undergrowth, half blinded by the dense cloud of sulphurous smoke which hung low amongst the trees, but gradually driving back their opponents in spite of their furious resistance, and Withers was doggedly fighting his way forward past La Folie.

Shortly before 1 o'clock the French infantry had been driven entirely out of the forest, and just about the same time Orkney had succeeded in capturing the entrenchments on their right, but though they had lost heavily they were by no means demoralised, and forming a fresh line some distance in rear of the wood they calmly awaited their opponent's onset. After their long hours of desperate fighting, at the edge of and in the heart of the dense forest, Schulemberg's and Lottum's men had fallen into hopeless confusion, and it was some considerable time before their ranks could be reorganised.

Meanwhile Boufflers, who had assumed command when Villars was carried unconscious from the field, realised that the state of his army was most critical, his left had been driven back and his centre broken, but his right still held their ground, and his magnificent force of cavalry was as yet intact. He determined to use them in making one desperate bid to restore his line of battle, and collecting some 2,000 sabres, the pick of the Household cavalry, he furiously charged D'Auvergne's squadrons, which were in the act of deploying after their passage through the gaps between the redans. The Dutch cavalry were driven back in confusion, but Orkney, with great judgment, had posted his infantry on the reverse slopes of the captured entrenchments and their steady volleys forced Boufflers to retire with half his saddles empty.

However, he promptly rallied his men, and bringing a strong body of infantry from his extreme right to support them, he again charged D'Auvergne's squadrons who had meanwhile rallied under cover of their infantry. A furious *mêlée* ensued: Marlborough charged with the British and Hanoverian cavalry against his opponent's right, only to be driven back by a desperate onslaught of the French Horse Guards. The fate of the combat hung in the balance until the whole of the Imperial cavalry, galloping round the British right, fell like an avalanche on the French flank, and Boufflers' gallant squadrons were at last forced to fall back. His infantry was melting away under the fire of the Allied guns when a sudden hoarse roar of triumph, heard high above the din of battle, announced that Orange's invincible troops had driven the weakened garrison from the entrenchments, before which, earlier in the day, they had poured their blood without result.

Nothing was now left for the French but retreat; but the respite gained by the most desperate cavalry action of the whole war had been used to advantage, and massive columns of infantry under D'Artagan and Puysegur were already leaving the field. While they fell back in perfect order and admirable steadiness, the indefatigable Boufflers covered their retreat by repeated charges delivered by his least-shaken squadrons. The Allied horsemen, weary with their exertions, were in no condition to pursue the unbroken French columns, while their infantry was too crippled by their appalling losses; consequently, the beaten army moved off the field unmolested, shortly after 3 o'clock.

The battle, which had been the most sanguinary and desperately contested of the whole war, ended in a bare victory for the Allies, who had forced their opponents to abandon their entrenched position, but at the most appalling cost to themselves, for their casualties amounted to over 20,000 men, killed and wounded. The French losses were considerably less, not exceeding 14,000, which is to a great extent accounted for by the fact that they fought behind formidable entrenchments of an unusually solid profile, and that the Allies were too shaken by their losses to attempt a pursuit. Practically no prisoners or trophies were taken, for in the desperate hand-to-hand fighting in the Taisnieres wood little quarter was asked or given, and even the bulk of the French artillery was successfully withdrawn, only some dozen guns falling into the hands of the victors.

The losses among the senior officers were unusually severe. Generals Lottum, Spaar, Wick and the Marquis of Tullibardine were killed, and Eugene, Hamilton and Webb wounded, while the French had to mourn the loss of the brave Steckemberg, who was killed in opposing one of Orange's furious assaults.

With his usual humanity, Marlborough did everything possible to relieve the sufferings of the troops, regardless of nationality, and proposed a suspension of hostilities to collect the wounded and bury the dead, to which Villars willingly agreed. The victory was in many ways barren of result: the enemy's field army had been beaten but not destroyed, and fighting behind their formidable entrenchments, the French infantry had developed a most unexpected power of resistance; but the main cause of the indecisive nature of the engagement had been the splendid stand made by the cavalry, which enabled the rest of the army to retreat at leisure. Marlborough had shown all his habitual control of the battle by the promptness with which he seized his opportunity of breaking through his opponent's centre and the manner in which he made use of his cavalry.

The Allies lost no time in commencing the siege of Mons, for, in spite of the heavy rains, the trenches were opened at the end of September, when the duke took up his quarters at Belain, while Eugene was at Quarregnon, and the actual operations for the reduction of the fortress were carried on by the Prince of Orange. After his defeat Boufflers had fallen back to Quesnoi, some twenty miles south of Mons, and though he remained in observation, he was unable to interfere with the siege, as the Allies had selected an extremely strong position and his own army was destitute of supplies. His wretched men were forced to live on roots and herbs, while Berwick, who had been hastily summoned from Dauphine to report on the situation, thoroughly agreed with him that any attempt to relieve Mons was impossible.

The siege was pushed forward with the greatest vigour; a lodgement was effected on the covered way, the outworks were stormed, and as there was no hope of relief and the weak garrison had been reduced to less than half its original strength, the governor surrendered at the end of October. With the fall of Mons, the Allies went into winter quarters round Ghent, Bruges, Brussels and on the Meuse, while their opponents remained round Quesnoi and Valenciennes, and Berwick, with some 20,000 men, settled down for the winter on the Sambre, round Mauberge. From the Allies' point of view, the campaign had been disappointing, for though the formidable lines of La Bassée had been forced, Villars' army defeated, and the important barrier fortresses of Tournai and Mons had been captured, the war still seemed likely to drag on for years.

The great struggle taking place on the French frontier had reduced the operations in the remaining theatres of war to a minor importance, and they had been so mismanaged, owing to the quarrels between the Allies and the incompetence of their leaders, that no definite results had been obtained. The emperor had several times repeated his offer of the viceroyalty of the Spanish Netherlands, but owing to the determined opposition of the States General to the scheme, Marlborough had felt himself bound to refuse. He had the greatest difficulty in reconciling the conflicting interests of Great Britain, Holland and the Empire, while the defeat of Charles of Sweden, at Pultowa, was within an ace of wrecking the coalition.

Prussia and Denmark entered into an alliance with Russia to divide the Swedish dominions, and all Marlborough's great diplomatic abilities were needed to prevent the two former powers severing their connection with the Grand Alliance. His task was even more difficult in Great Britain, for the country was weary of the apparently interminable strain of the long war, and his political opponents used every means in their power to belittle his successes and blacken his character.

CHAPTER 9

The Campaign of 1710-1711

A conference was held at Gertruydensberg in the spring of 1710, but the firm determination of the Emperor to obtain the whole of the Spanish Netherlands and of the States General to demand the surrender of the fortresses of northern France to Holland as a condition of peace, rendered all hope of agreement impossible. Once again Marlborough and Eugene evolved a scheme which promised to bring the war to a speedy conclusion : to obtain a secure base, connected with Amsterdam by the Scheldt, Douai was to be captured; then Arras, the last of the great fortified cities barring the road to the interior of France, was to be reduced, and, finally, Calais and Abbeville were to be taken by a combined naval and military expedition, after which the Allies were to advance on Paris and force Louis XIV. to accede to their terms. The town of Douai, lying between the Haine and the Scarpe, was strongly fortified, and was, moreover, protected by the formidable lines of La Bassée, which had been most carefully constructed by Villars and were held by Marshal Montesquieu with some 20,000 men.

The Allied commanders, meeting at Tournai at the end of April, determined to strike before their opponent could concentrate his forces to oppose them; consequently, Marlborough ordered the Duke of Wirtemberg with 15,000 men to march at once *via* the bridge at Tessin to Vendin, while Eugene sent Count Fels with a similar force to Auby. The main body followed in two columns. The crossing over the Deule at Vendin was seized without opposition, and though Eugene was checked at Auby, he crossed at Courriers without loss, and the Allied Army concentrated at the end of April at Lens, in rear of the hostile lines. Hopelessly outnumbered, Montesquieu fell back to Vitry, while Cadogan, moving to Rache, completed the investment of Douai, the whole scheme, which included the forcing of the formidable French lines, having been carried out with brilliant success and

116

without the loss of a man.

Entirely outmanoeuvred by his opponent, Villars, who had no intention of risking a battle to prevent the investment of Douai, occupied himself by still further strengthening the lines protecting Arras and rendering them absolutely impregnable. The siege of Douai promised to be a long and arduous one, for the Scarpe flowing round the walls made the approaches most difficult, and the garrison, some 8,000 strong, was commanded by the Marquis Albergotti, a most capable officer. The investment was completed at the beginning of May, but two days later the garrison made a vigorous sortie, doing considerable damage to the trenches and cutting to pieces two British regiments. However, on the arrival of the siege train from Tournai, the powerful batteries poured such a destructive fire against the defences and the news of the critical state of the fortress caused such alarm at Versailles, that Villars was ordered to relieve the town immediately at all costs.

Though he had hardly recovered from the severe wound he had received at Malplaquet, he had, by dint of the greatest energy, managed to collect an army some 90,000 strong. He had also been joined by the Duke of Berwick, and the two commanders, fully prepared to fight a pitched battle for the relief of Douai, marched from Cambrai *via* Lens towards Vitry with their men, carrying a four days' ration of bread to avoid all difficulties of supply. Leaving some twenty battalions to continue the siege, Marlborough with 80,000 men moved to a strong position on the Scarpe, near Vitry, which he immediately strengthened by the construction of redoubts and fieldworks. He looked forward with the greatest eagerness to a decisive battle, which he hoped would end the war, as it was becoming increasingly evident that the Grand Alliance would not hold together much longer.

He had selected such a strong position, however, that Villars, reconnoitring the lines on the 1st of June, decided that it would be madness to attack, an opinion in which Berwick and Montesquieu thoroughly concurred, so, much to Marlborough's disappointment, the French Army eventually fell back without risking a battle. On their retreat the siege was pressed with renewed vigour, and Villars again made a show of advancing, but Marlborough moved to meet him while Eugene continued the investment, and the French marshal again retreated. A desperate assault on the outworks of the fortress was made by the Prince of Orange, but was beaten off with heavy loss. Two days later, however, a second attempt proved successful, though the assailants suffered heavily from the explosions of several mines.

Seeing that the besiegers were about to make a general assault and that there was no chance of relief, Albergotti surrendered after a gallant defence, which had cost the Allies nearly 8,000 men.

About a fortnight later, Marlborough advanced, intending to lay siege to Arras, but found that Villars had protected the city by an almost impregnable line of entrenchments, mounting 130 guns and garrisoned by nearly 100,000 men. Foiled in his original design, the duke decided to reduce Bethune, which, though exceedingly well fortified and held by a strong garrison under the command of Mons. P. Vauban, a nephew of the great engineer, was known to be badly off for supplies. The Allies suddenly appeared before the town, and Villars advanced, apparently to prevent its investment, but when Marlborough reconnoitred the hostile position, he found his opponent busily engaged in the construction of a fresh series of entrenchments.

The French leader had no intention of risking the only available field army unless an exceptionally favourable opportunity was offered; for by his energy and resource he had already foiled the Allies' attempt to capture Arras, and he was now bent on gaining time, not only for France to reorganise her resources, but for the triumph of Marlborough's political opponents in England, whose success would wreck the Grand Alliance more completely than any reverse in the field. The Allies opened their trenches before Douai towards the end of July, but an attempt to capture the covered way was repulsed and much damage inflicted by a vigorous sortie made by the garrison.

General Schulemberg, however, carried on the siege with the greatest vigour, and, strongly reinforced from the covering army, repulsed two desperate sorties. After a most gallant defence, Vauban was eventually forced to surrender, owing to the want of food and ammunition. The garrison, which had originally numbered close on 9,000 men, had been reduced to under 2,500, of whom more than a third were wounded. Marlborough was so struck with their gallant defence that they were allowed to march out with the honours of war.

Though bitterly chagrined by the loss of his frontier fortress, Louis XIV. hoped much from the turn which events were taking in England, while the duke's hands were tied by the knowledge that the slightest reverse or even a costly victory, such as Malplaquet, would ensure the triumph of his political opponents. Under these circumstances, Marlborough determined to reduce the two small but strongly fortified towns of St. Venant and Aire, situated a few miles apart on the Lys, as their capture would give him complete command of the river, open up direct communication with Lille and render the subsequent reduction of Calais comparatively easy.

Both fortresses, which were strongly held and further protected by inundations, were invested at the beginning of September, but the heavy rains, which commenced much earlier than usual, considerably handicapped the besiegers; and Villars, who had been displaying great activity in harassing his opponent's communications, captured a large convoy containing guns and ammunition, and escorted by 1,600 men, on its way from Ghent to the Allied camp.

In spite of this disaster, however, the Prince of Orange pushed forward the siege of St. Venant with such vigour that the place was forced to surrender by the end of September. The garrison of Aire made a most dogged resistance and the siege was carried on under the most adverse conditions. The continual rain turned the trenches into a quagmire, and the misery endured by the besiegers caused an immense amount of sickness before the fortress capitulated about the middle of November.

After the fall of Aire, the Allies went into winter quarters, after a most arduous and trying campaign, during which, with the exception of the capture of Douai, nothing of importance had been achieved.

Thoroughly appreciating the situation, Villars had conducted a purely defensive campaign with the greatest ability, and in spite of the clamour raised in France by the loss of the fortress, he had been successful in thwarting the Allies' attempt on Arras and had foiled their plans of invasion. While Marlborough's hands had been tied by the political situation in England, the operations conducted by his allies in Piedmont and on the Rhine had been so feeble that Louis had been able to mass practically the whole of his available force in northern France.

The triumph of Harley and Bolingbroke, who, he knew, were determined to humble him at all costs, nearly caused Marlborough to throw up his command; but he was dissuaded from adopting this course by Godolphin, Eugene and the Dutch statesman, Heinsius, who clearly foresaw that the resignation of the great Duke would herald the breaking up of the Grand Alliance.

Though the Tory government loudly professed that he enjoyed their full confidence, Marlborough was aware that he had little power left, and that he would now have to face, in addition to the open obstruction of the States General, the secret opposition of his own government; but he had not as yet realised the lengths to which they were prepared to go in their treacherous negotiations with the French monarch. The death of the emperor and the accession of the Archduke Charles, with the latter's consequent resignation of his claim to the Spanish throne, still further complicated matters and caused the withdrawal of Eugene with the bulk of the Imperial forces.

During the following winter and spring Villars laboured unceasingly at the construction of his famous 'Ne Plus Ultra' lines, which completely covered the French frontier from the Channel to Namur. The work was superintended by the ablest engineers in France, who, with large sums of money and unlimited labour at their disposal, constructed a stupendous line of entrenchments stretching from the coast of Picardy along the River Canche to the southern fork of the Scarpe, following the latter river past Arras to Biache, whence the works ran behind the canal to the Senzet. Inundations between the latter river and the Scheldt prolonged the line to Bouchain, whence it followed the Scheldt to Valenciennes, from which town a line of entrenchments carried the barrier to the Sambre and on to Namur.

Running through a country intersected by rivers and rendered still more difficult by vast stretches of inundation, the formidable line of entrenchments, supported by the great fortresses of Arras, Bouchain, Cambrai and Valenciennes, seemed to render an invasion of France impossible and to justify Villars' boast that he had at last fixed a limit to the Allies' advance.

Even before the commencement of the campaign, Marlborough's difficulties were enhanced by the withdrawal of seven battalions of veteran troops to take part in the preposterous expedition to Newfoundland, which achieved no useful result and ended in a disastrous failure.

The Allied Army assembled round Orchies, some miles south-east of Lille, and at the beginning of May, Marlborough advanced with some 80,000 men towards the hostile lines. Whereupon Villars, moving up from his winter quarters round Cambrai, took post with a slightly superior force behind his formidable entrenchments, with his right resting on Bouchain and his left at Oisy.

Eugene joined the Allies, but was shortly recalled to the Rhine with the bulk of his army; and about the middle of June, Marlborough moved away from the lines, marching westward towards Lens. Much to his disgust, Villars was also forced to send a large detachment to the Rhine, ere he had an opportunity of using his numerical superiority,

THE PASSAGE OF
THE "NE PLUS ULTRA" LINES
AUGUST 1711.

SCALE
MILES

FORTIFIED CITIES ■
REDOUBTS ★
FRENCH LINES ×××
WOODS
INUNDATIONS

so that the relative strength of the opposing armies remained practically unaltered. A complete deadlock ensued, as Marlborough, dreading the triumph of his enemies at home, dared not risk the losses that even a successful assault on the formidable lines would entail, while Louis XIV., relying on the treachery of the British Cabinet, ordered Villars on no account to risk a battle in the open.

The summer was rapidly slipping away, and so far, nothing but a few unimportant skirmishes had taken place, though Marlborough was already preparing for one of his most brilliant *coups*, which was destined to be carried through with complete success without the loss of a single man.

The inundations caused by the damming of the Senzet between Arras and Bouchain were only passable by two causeways, which were blocked by the redoubts at Arleux and Aubigny respectively. Marlborough could have taken the former work whenever he had wished to, but would have been unable to hold it. So, he deliberately set himself to persuade Villars to destroy it and so remove an obstacle from his path. Accordingly, Rantzau, with a strong force, captured the redoubt on the 6th of July, and immediately commenced to strengthen it, while Hompesch, moving up in close support, camped on the glacis outside Douai with a large force. Making a sudden attack on the latter fortress, Villars was repulsed with some apparent difficulty, whereupon Marlborough reinforced Hompesch, left a weak garrison at Arleux and moved westward for a couple of marches, parallel to his opponent's lines. Encouraged by his partial success at Douai, Villars then attacked Arleux in force.

Marlborough despatched his trusty lieutenant, Cadogan, with a force of all arms to its relief; but acting in compliance with his secret instructions, the latter moved so slowly that ere he had covered half the distance, the redoubt had surrendered. Delighted with his success, the French commander promptly razed the work to the ground, while Marlborough, appearing greatly dejected by the disaster, vowed that he would be revenged even if he had to storm his opponent's lines. Villars now detached a force of all arms to raid Brabant, while Marlborough countered the move by sending Albemarle with 10,000 men to Bethune and all his baggage and heavy artillery to Douai. He then set about repairing all the roads leading to the hostile lines west of Arras, apparently making every preparation for a determined assault.

Watching his opponent's movements with delight, Villars concentrated every available man to meet the threatened attack, even withdrawing some of the troops garrisoning the fortresses, while the Allies, lost in amazement, could only imagine that his want of success and the political situation at home had driven Marlborough out of his mind. On the 2nd of August the duke advanced to within a few miles of the hostile lines and set his cavalry to collect fascines, while next evening he ostentatiously sent away his baggage and heavy artillery under a strong escort.

On the morning of the 4th he rode forward to reconnoitre the position, even pointing out to his brigadiers the exact spot at which they were to press home their attacks.

Meanwhile Cadogan had galloped off to Douai; here he found Hompesch's detachment, which, reinforced by drafts from the various garrisons, now amounted to 12,000 men, and warned him to be ready to move at nightfall.

In the Allies' camp the troops passed a miserable afternoon, uncertain as to what the future held in store for them; and though many of the veterans, taught by experience, were convinced that their beloved 'Corporal John' had some daring scheme on foot, the general opinion was that the great Duke had taken leave of his senses and was about to annihilate his army by hurling it against the impregnable entrenchments held by a powerful and determined force commanded by the hard-fighting Villars.

Sending a strong body of cavalry westward late in the afternoon, Marlborough kept the French on the *qui vive*, but it was not until the troops paraded at *'tattoo'* that the order was passed down the ranks to strike tents and prepare to march at once. During the moonlit night the troops, marching in perfect order and in dead silence, moved towards the Scarpe, over which bridges had been constructed and beyond which the field artillery were already assembled. The river was crossed soon after dawn, and shortly afterwards an *aide-de-camp*, bearing a despatch, dashed up to Marlborough, who was riding at the head of the column.

The weary infantry, plodding doggedly along the road, were suddenly electrified by the news passed down the ranks, that Cadogan and Hompesch, crossing at Arleux at 3 a.m. had occupied the enemy's lines without opposition.

A message was passed along 'that the duke desired that the infantry would step out,' and a strong force of cavalry was halted to form a rear-guard while Marlborough with fifty squadrons moved forward at a trot to support Cadogan. In spite of their fatigue, the staunch infantry, pulling themselves together, eagerly trudged forward to complete their great chief's brilliant manoeuvre. Hundreds dropped in the ranks under the weight of their equipment, many even died of exhaustion but the remainder pressed forward without a halt, and after marching nearly forty miles in eighteen hours the whole force arrived at their appointed positions, inside the enemy's lines, between 4 and 5 o'clock on the afternoon of the 5th of August. Marlborough had once again proved that no system of entrenchments can for long check a vigorous commander, who is capable of manoeuvring, while the discipline and magnificent marching powers of his staunch infantry had enabled him to achieve his object without firing a shot.

Villars had received early information of the Allies' march, but absolutely mystified by his opponent's manoeuvres, he could not anticipate his objective; when, however, he learned that they had crossed at Arleux, the defences of which he had himself destroyed, his mortification knew no bounds.

Collecting a large force of cavalry, and ordering the remainder of his army to concentrate at the threatened point at once, the French marshal pushed madly forward with a small escort and only escaped capture by the Allies' outposts by the merest chance. Marlborough now halted for a couple of days to allow the exhausted stragglers to come in, while Villars, drawing up his whole army under the guns of Cambrai, offered battle in the wild hope of retrieving his strategical reverse by a tactical success.

But the duke had already achieved his object, and had no intention of risking a totally unnecessary battle merely to suit his opponent's convenience. Strangely enough, the Dutch deputies, who by their stubborn refusal to sanction an engagement on countless favourable occasions had, time after time, saved the French Army from defeat, now wished Marlborough to fight, although he had already gained his point.

On the 7th of August the Allies, marching almost within the range of the guns of Cambrai, crossed the Scheldt unmolested, and laid siege to Bouchain, while next day sixty squadrons, recrossing the river at Neuville, closed the road from Douai. Throwing some 12,000 men under Albergotti across the Senzet, Villars seized and commenced to fortify a hill, which enabled him to keep open the route between Bouchain and Cambrai. A strong redoubt garrisoned by 600 men was constructed to protect the road, but the Allies managed, though not without the greatest difficulty, to construct a causeway of fascines across the morass almost up to the work.

On the night of the 16th, 600 picked grenadiers advanced silently along the causeway and struggling through the marsh, rushed the redoubt at the point of the bayonet with the loss of only six men. In spite of the extraordinary difficulties caused by the spongy nature of the soil, and of Villars' continual efforts to keep open communication with the town, the siege was pressed forward with such vigour that the governor was forced to capitulate early in September. Marlborough was most anxious to reduce Quesnoi before the end of the campaign as the possession of that fortress would have rendered the whole of his opponent's elaborate system of entrenchments useless; but the British government had already determined on the conclusion of a shameful peace.

The campaign ended with the fall of Bouchain; and the capture of the strongly fortified town, under the eyes of Villars' powerful army, together with the forcing of the formidable 'Ne Plus Ultra' lines without the loss of a man, were destined to be the last but by no means the least glorious of the long series of the great duke's wonderfully successful operations. The preliminaries of peace were signed at the end of September, and the Cabinet, well knowing that Marlborough would never consent to the disadvantageous terms arranged, formulated a baseless charge of mis-appropriation of public money against him; and on its complete breakdown, Harley took the decisive step of removing the great duke from his command at the end of December 1711.

For months he had been subjected to an organised campaign of calumny; his victories were made light of, he was accused of prolonging the war to serve his own ends, of embezzling public money, of deliberately incurring heavy losses so that he might make money by the sale of Commissions, and, finally, even of personal cowardice! At the beginning of the following year the Duke of Ormond, a gallant gentleman but no soldier, was appointed to the vacant command, though he had few qualifications for the post and had taken no part in the war since his, disgraceful failure before Cadiz, nine years previously. The Dutch, however, would have none of him, and Eugene was appointed to succeed his illustrious friend and colleague in the supreme command of the Allied Armies. The siege of Quesnoi was commenced, but Ormond, carrying out his secret instructions, refused to take any part in the operations, and the British contingent was forced to endure the bitter mortification of remaining in their camp while their

Allies captured the town.

Eugene, who was extremely anxious as to the part which England intended to play, next laid siege to the fortress of Landrecies; but Ormond, who had received instructions to 'engage in no battles or sieges,' and was already in active correspondence with Villars, informed the Allied general that he was about to withdraw the British contingent.

On the 16th of July 1712, Ormond's men were most reluctantly forced to take part in the most melancholy event to be found in the proud history of the British Army. The column marched out of the Allied camp in mournful silence, moving with sullen faces and downcast eyes between the ranks of their gallant comrades in arms, in whose company they had achieved such glorious victories and with whom they had shared the hardships and dangers of ten campaigns.

On reaching their camping-ground that evening, Ormond caused the suspension of hostilities to be read out at the head of every regiment, and even the iron bonds of discipline were powerless to suppress a fierce outburst of indignation. The officers, unable to bear the disgrace, withdrew heart-broken to their tents, while the men raved and tore their hair, cursing the general who had shamed them before their allies, and the government which had so callously betrayed them. Numbers of officers resigned their commissions, many of them and thousands of men taking service under Eugene, and almost weeping as they thought of their great leader, the beloved 'Corporal John,' who had led them for ten long years from victory to victory.

The Dutch refused to allow the wretched army to enter the towns, and, to make their miserable position almost unbearable, they were threatened by starvation, as the bread contract had been cancelled by the callous government. Such was the pitiable end to the gallant part which the British contingent had played in the brilliant series of successes gained by the Allied arms since the commencement of the war in 1702.

With a few exceptions, the German, Prussian and Danish auxiliaries in the pay of England refused to obey the disgraceful order of their paymasters and remained with Eugene until the close of the campaign.

But with the withdrawal of the British contingent fortune deserted the Allies. Villars assumed the offensive with the greatest vigour, cutting to pieces a detachment holding the passage over the Scheldt at Denain, raising the siege of Landrecies and rapidly recapturing Douai, Bouchain and Quesnoi. And so, in the end, in spite of the glorious victories of Marlborough and Eugene, the splendid gallantry of the Allied armies and the vast expenditure of blood and treasure, Louis XIV., aided by his treacherous allies, who misgoverned England, was enabled to conclude the war in a species of triumph.

In forming a just estimate of the Duke of Marlborough's achievements as a general, the extraordinary difficulties with which 'he had to contend must be taken into account. The commander-in-chief of the forces of a coalition engaged in a struggle with the armies of a single nation, whose whole policy is directed towards a well-defined object, is always at a serious disadvantage, for not only is he hampered by the divergent views of the allied governments, but he is also forced to smooth the jealousies which naturally arise between the commanders and the troops of various nationalities.

In Marlborough's case the difficulties were enormously increased, for, in addition to commanding the forces of the confederacy in the field, he was also forced to a great extent to undertake the political direction of the Alliance, and only the remarkable tact, charm of manner and great diplomatic ability that he displayed enabled him to carry out the multifarious duties of his dual role with success. The aims of the Allies were more than usually divergent: England was firmly determined to prevent the union of France and Spain, as their combined navies would have dominated the Mediterranean, crippled her trade and threatened her colonial expansion.

Holland was equally determined to obtain the strong fortresses of Flanders, which would give her a formidable barrier against French aggression, while the emperor desired the whole of the Spanish territories for the House of Hapsburg. When the Duke of Savoy joined the Alliance, it was with the sole object of obtaining the major portion of the Spanish provinces in Italy, and consequently he found himself at once at variance with the emperor, while Hanover and Prussia, not immediately menaced by Louis XIV's ambitious projects, had comparatively little interest in the result of the struggle, and Denmark, simply acting as an auxiliary, had none at all.

Nor were the difficulties less with the force under Marlborough's command: the British contingent throughout his campaigns averaged only about 20,000 men, and the remainder was composed of Dutch, Hanoverian, Prussian and Danish troops as well as contingents from the smaller German states.

Surely it is one of his greatest triumphs that he welded this cosmopolitan army into one harmonious force, actuated by an intense spirit of *esprit de corps*, and bound together by their great personal affection for their leader. At the commencement of every campaign, he had to face the same ever-recurring difficulties. The Dutch forces were always unprepared to commence operations, the contingents of the German principalities were always late in arriving at the positions of assembly and were usually much under strength and badly equipped, while the difficulties of supply and transport were almost insurmountable.

Moreover, he was thwarted by the continual obstruction of the pig-headed Dutch field deputies and the insubordination of their generals, while, during his later campaigns, he had to contend with the ever-increasing opposition of his political opponents in England. His grandest schemes were continually wrecked by the timidity and selfishness of his allies, the difficulty in obtaining the requisite number of troops, and England's fatal habit of frittering away in minor expeditions the forces she should have concentrated in the decisive theatre of operations. Had Marlborough been given a free hand and properly supported, he would undoubtedly have brought the war to an early and triumphant conclusion, probably in 1707 or possibly in 1705, before France had had an opportunity of recovering from her disastrous defeat at Blenheim.

Though he kept his army in the field until much later in the year than the majority of his contemporaries, the necessity of suspending operations by putting the troops into winter quarters tended to prolong the war, as it gave France, with her wonderful recuperative power, the chance of reorganising her resources between each campaign. The cramped nature of the theatre of operations in the Low Countries tended to reduce all military operations to the siege and relief of the important fortified cities which commanded the main roads, for except in the driest weather all but the latter became impassable for wheeled traffic. The usual method of conveying heavy guns, stores and ammunition was by the excellent network of waterways and canals which intersected Flanders, hence the supreme importance of the fortress-studded lines of the various rivers.

Compared with the slow, methodical and indecisive operations of William III., which, however, were typical of the period, Marlborough's strategy appears dazzlingly brilliant; and had he not been hampered by the timidity of his allies, his successes would have been even more remarkable than they were. The carefully planned and perfectly carried out flank march by which he transferred his army to the Danube in 1704, deceiving his opponents until it was too late for them to interfere with his movements, was a typical example of his brilliant strategy. He also continually proved his ability by the manner in which, though always slightly numerically inferior to his opponents, he retained the initiative and forced them to conform to his wishes.

Again, the masterly manner in which he forced his opponent's laboriously constructed lines of formidable entrenchments, often defended by a superior force, are by no means the least remarkable of his achievements, though, owing to the mobility of his army and his wonderful ability in manoeuvring in face of the enemy, they were generally carried out with little loss. Altogether, he was far in advance of his time in his method of waging war, and was one of the few commanders of the period who had a true appreciation of the value and limitations of entrenchments in military operations. In fact, the skill, precision and rapidity with which he carried out his manoeuvres stamped him as a commander of the highest class, while as a tactician, no man, not even the great Napoleon, ever exercised a closer control over the course of the battle, or used his reserves with greater effect.

The irresistible cavalry charge which shattered Tallard's centre at Blenheim, the manoeuvres by which he outgeneralled Villeroi and crushed his centre and right at Ramillies, the ability with which he took advantage of his opponent's blunder in making a partial attack at Oudenarde, and the promptitude with which he seized his opportunity and broke through the weakened hostile centre at Malplaquet, were masterpieces of personal control on the field of battle. Some of his opponents, moreover, were leaders of no mean ability, and, had they not been called upon to face Marlborough, Vendôme and Villars would most certainly have caused Europe to ring with their victories. The army under his command, though composed of so many different nationalities, with its ranks filled with a large proportion of vagrants and criminals, was famous for its discipline. Drunkenness and profanity were sternly suppressed, and on the Sabbath, even immediately before battle, Divine Service was always punctiliously celebrated.

In one respect Marlborough was exceedingly fortunate, for in Eugene he found a colleague after his own heart; no petty jealousy ever marred their relations, while their mutual understanding and the harmony with which the two greatest commanders of the time carried out their schemes were little short of marvellous. Marlborough's great military ability was thoroughly appreciated by his contemporaries, and recognised even by his opponents and political adversaries. Voltaire said of him that:

'He had to a degree above all other generals of his time, that calm courage in the midst of tumult, that serenity of soul in danger, which the English call a 'cool head.'

Bolingbroke, his great political opponent, also did him ample justice in his *memoirs*, vol 2:

'By his (William III.'s) death, the Duke of Marlborough was raised to the head of the army and indeed of the confederacy; where he, a new, a private man, a subject, acquired by merit and management a more deciding influence than high birth, confirmed authority and even the crown of Great Britain had given to King William. Not only all the parts of that vast machine, the Grand Alliance, were kept more compact and entire; but a more rapid and vigorous motion was given to the whole; and instead of languishing and disastrous campaigns, we saw every scene of the war full of action. All those wherein he appeared, and in many of those wherein he was not then an actor, but an abettor, however, of their action, were crowned with the most triumphant success.'

I take, with pleasure, this opportunity of doing justice to that great man whose faults I knew, whose virtues I admired, and whose memory, as the greatest general and as the greatest minister that our or perhaps any country has produced, I honour. After the lapse of nearly a century, Napoleon had such a high opinion of his military abilities, that he caused—a history of Marlborough's campaigns to be prepared by his staff in 1808.

In fact, the art of war had altered comparatively little in the space of ninety years intervening between the campaigns of the two great masters of modern war, and the methods of the two great commanders, in numerous cases, show a remarkable similarity.

But when all has been said, Marlborough's reputation as a general may well be allowed to rest on the fact that 'he never fought a battle without winning a victory or besieged a town without taking it.'

Whatever his political or private character may have been—as a commander he was beyond compare, and he deserves to live in the history of his country as England's greatest general, and the man who, by his transcendent ability, made the scarlet coat of the British Army known and respected throughout Europe.

Chronological Summary of the Principal Events of the War of the Spanish Succession 1701—1711

Spain—Northern Italy—The Valley of the Rhine, etc.

1701.

July.—Commencement of hostilities between France and the Empire in Northern Italy.

1702.

January.—Eugene makes an unsuccessful attempt to surprise Cremona (N. Italy).

August.—Failure of the British Expedition under the Duke of Ormond and Admiral Rooke to capture Cadiz (Spain).

September.—The Imperialists capture Landau (Valley of the Rhine).

October—Rooke and Ormond capture the Spanish Treasure fleet at Vigo (Spain).

24th October.—Villars defeats Lewis of Baden at Friedlingen (Valley of the Rhine).

The Netherlands

1701.

February.—Louis XIV. seizes the Barrier Fortresses.

June.—The Earl of Marlborough proceeds to Holland with twelve battalions of British troops.

September.—The Grand Alliance formed between England, the Empire and Holland.

September.—James II. dies and his son is acknowledged as King of England by Louis XIV.

1702.

8th March.—William III. dies and is succeeded by Queen Anne.

18th April—The Dutch and Prussian troops besiege Kaiserworth—surrenders 15th June.

5th May.—England declares war against France.

30th June.—Boufflers makes an unsuccessful attempt to surprise Nimeguen.

2nd July—Marlborough joins the Allied Army near Nimeguen.

26th July—The Allies commence their advance.

2nd August—The Dutch Field Deputies refuse to allow Marlborough to attack.

22nd August.—Marlborough intercepts the French, but the Deputies still refuse to fight.

29th August.—The Allies invest Venlo—surrenders on 24th September.

29th September—Roermond invested—surrenders on 7th October.

29th September—Stevenswaert and Maeseyck captured.

12th October—Boufflers marches to relieve Liege, but is forestalled by the Allies and forced to retreat; the Dutch still refuse to fight.

14th October.—The siege of the citadel of Liege commenced—stormed on 23rd October.

November.—The Allies go into winter quarters,

The Subsidiary Theatre of Operations
Spain—Northern Italy—The Valley of the Rhine, etc.

1703.

February.—Villars crosses the Rhine and captures Kehl (Valley of the Rhine).

15th April—Villars advances through the Black Forest (Valley of the Rhine).

16th May.—Portugal joins the Grand Alliance.

16th May.—Villars joins the Elector of Bavaria (Valley of the Danube).

7th September.—Tallard captures New Breisach (Valley of the Rhine).

20th September.—Villars defeats the Imperialists at Hochstädt (Valley of the Danube).

5th October—The Duke of Savoy joins the Grand Alliance (N. Italy).

5th October—The French besiege Landau—surrenders on the 21st October (Valley of the Rhine).

15th November.—Tallard defeats the Imperialists at Spiers (Valley of the Rhine).

1704.
May.—Tallard advances into the Black Forest to hand over re-inforcements and supplies to the Elector of Bavaria (Valley of the Danube).

THE MAIN THEATRE OF OPERATIONS
The Netherlands
(The main theatre of operations transferred to the Valley of the Danube, June—September.)

1703.
17th March.—The Earl of Marlborough returns to Holland.

3rd May—The Allies besiege Bonn—surrenders on 15th May.

June.—Marlborough manoeuvres to keep Villeroi occupied near Namur.

June.—The Allies make an unsuccessful attempt to capture Antwerp.

30th June—Boufflers defeats Opdam's detachment at Eckeren.

23rd July—Marlborough advances against the French entrenched lines on the Scheldt, but the Dutch refuse to permit him to attack.

August.—Marlborough returns to the Valley of the Meuse.

August.—The Allies capture Huy.

27th September—Limburg surrenders.

October.—The Allies go into winter quarters.

1704.
April—Marlborough returns to Holland.

lst-8th May.—The Allies assemble on the Meuse.

19th May.—The march to the Danube commences.

23rd May.—Marlborough arrives at Bonn.

29th May.—Marlborough reaches the Main with the Allied cavalry.

31st May.—Marlborough crosses the Main.

3rd June—Marlborough crosses the Neckar at Ladenburg.

10th June.—Marlborough reaches Mondelsheim and meets Eugene.

13th June.—Lewis of Baden arrives in the Allied camp.

14th June—Eugene returns to the Rhine; Marlborough marches towards Ulm.

20th June——Marlborough effects the passage of the defile of Geislingen.

THE SUBSIDIARY THEATRE OF OPERATIONS
Spain—Northern Italy—The Valley of the Rhine, etc.

1704—continued

July.—Tallard leaves the Valley of the Rhine and marches through the Black Forest to join the Elector (Valley of the Danube).

July.—Eugene follows Tallard, moving parallel to, but north of, the French line of march.

July—Tallard unsuccessfully besieges Villingen (Valley of the Danube).

4th August.—Gibraltar captured by a British expedition under Admiral Rooke and the Prince of Hesse-Darmstadt (Spain).

No events of any importance occurred in the subsidiary theatres of operations.

THE MAIN THEATRE OF OPERATIONS
The Netherlands
(The main theatre of operations transferred to the Valley of the Danube, June—September.)

1704—continued

22nd June—Junction with the Imperial Army, north of Ulm.

23rd June—The Allies halt at Gingen, to await the arrival of General Churchill with the artillery and infantry.

1st July—The Allies advance towards Donauworth.

2nd July—Capture of the Franco-Bavarian position on the Schellenberg.

4th July—The Elector of Bavaria abandons his entrenched camp at Dillingen and retires under the guns of Augsburg.

July—The Allies capture Rain and Marlborough issues an ultimatum to the Elector of Bavaria, giving him the choice of abandoning the French alliance or submitting his country to a 'Military Execution.'

11th July—The Allies commence to ravage Bavaria.

23rd July—Tallard joins the Elector near Augsburg.

6th August.—Marlborough falls back towards Neuburg on the Danube.

9th August—Eugene arrives near Hochstädt (on the Danube); Lewis of Baden marches to besiege Ingolstadt.

9th August.—The Elector, crossing the Danube at Dillingen, moves against Eugene.

10th August—Marlborough makes a forced march to join Eugene.

11th August—The Allies concentrate near Donauworth.

13th August—The Battle of Blenheim.

19th August.—The Allies occupy Augsburg and capture Ulm.

August.—They commence their march back to the Rhine.

16th September—Landau besieged by Lewis of Baden— surrenders on 23rd November.

28th October.—The Allies capture Treves and besiege Trarbach, which surrenders on the 23rd November.

November.—The Allies go into winter quarters.

THE SUBSIDIARY THEATRE OF OPERATIONS
Spain—Northern Italy—The Valley of the Rhine, etc.

1705.
January—The Spanish Army besieges Gibraltar (Spain).

27th January—Combined naval and military assault on the fortress fails (Spain).

April—The siege abandoned (Spain). 4th August—Vendôme defeats Eugene at Cassano (N. Italy).

23rd August—An Anglo-Dutch Expedition under the Earl of Peterborough lands near Barcelona (Spain).

14th September—Fort Montjuich, commanding the city, captured (Spain).

9th October.—Barcelona surrenders (Spain).

December.—A Spanish force besieges San Mateo (Spain).

1706.

January.—Peterborough relieves San Mateo and captures Nules (Spain).

4th February.—Peterborough relieves Valencia (Spain).

27th June.—Galway, with an Anglo-Portuguese force, occupies Madrid (Spain).

April—The French besiege Barcelona without success (Spain).

7th September.—Eugene defeats the French and relieves Turin (N. Italy).

28th September.—Galway evacuates Madrid (Spain).

THE MAIN THEATRE OF OPERATIONS
The Netherlands

1705.

May.—Villeroi assumes the offensive in the Netherlands.

24th May.—The French capture Huy.

26th May.—Marlborough joins the Allied Army near Treves.

17th June—Owing to the non-arrival of the German contingents, Marlborough is forced to abandon his projected invasion of France.

2nd July—He joins Overkirk near Maestricht.

11th July—The Allies recapture Huy.

17th June—Marlborough outmanoeuvres Villeroi and forces the French Lines at Tirlemont.

29th July.—He forces the crossing of the Dyle, but the Dutch refuse to follow up his success.

16th August—The Allies march towards Genappe.

19th August.—The Dutch refuse to allow an attack on the French position.

September.—Indecisive manoeuvres, the French avoid a general action and the Dutch refuse to attack.

October—The Allies go into winter quarters.

1706.

May.—Marlborough joins the army near Liege.

19th May.—Villeroi advances towards Namur.

23rd May.—The Battle of Ramillies.

24th May.—The Allies occupy Louvain.

26th-31st May.—Brussels, Oudenarde, Mechlin, Ghent and Bruges surrender.

6th June—Antwerp surrenders.

17th June.—Overkirk besieges Ostend—surrenders on 5th July.

22nd August.—Menin surrenders.

5th September.—Dendermonde surrenders.

4th October.—Ath surrenders.

October—The Allies go into winter quarters.

THE SUBSIDIARY THEATRE OF OPERATIONS
Spain—Northern Italy—The Valley of the Rhine, etc.

1707.

25th April.—Berwick defeats the Allies at Almanza (Spain).

22nd May.—Villars captures the entrenched camp at Stolhofen (Valley of the Rhine).

27th July—Eugene invades France and besieges Toulon (S. France).

21st August.—Eugene abandons the siege and retires into Piedmont (S. France).

1708.

April.—Failure of the French attempt to invade Scotland.

29th September.—Stanhope captures Minorca (Mediterranean).

May/October Futile operations by small detachment of the Allies on the Rhine.

THE MAIN THEATRE OF OPERATIONS
The Netherlands

1707.

May-June.—Marlborough and Vendôme manoeuvre in Brabant.

4th June—The Dutch refuse to attack the French position near

Waterloo.

July.—Marlborough goes to Dresden to arrange the dispute between the Emperor and Charles XII. of Sweden.

August—Marlborough pursues Vendôme and drives him under the guns of Mons but without succeeding in bringing him to action.

September.—The Allies go into winter quarters after a futile campaign.

1708.
April.—Marlborough returns to Holland.

23rd May.—Vendôme threatens Antwerp, but is forestalled by the Allies.

25th May.—He then moves towards Louvain, but is again forestalled.

5th July.—Ghent and Bruges surrender to the French.

9th July—Vendôme invests Oudenarde and Marlborough marches to relieve it.

11th July—The Battle of Oudenarde.

14th July—Count Lottum seizes the French entrenchments at Ypres.

12th August—Large convoy of guns, etc., arrives at the Allied camp at Helchin.

13th August—Eugene commences the siege of Lille.

31st August—Vendôme and Berwick concentrate near Lessines and march to Tournai.

3rd September.—They advance to raise the siege of Lille; Marlborough takes up a strong position to cover it and the French eventually retreat.

6th September.—First assault on Lille, part of the covered way captured.

20th September.—Second assault, some outworks captured.

The Subsidiary Theatre of Operations
Spain—Northern Italy—The Valley of the Rhine, etc.

1708—continued
November.—The French besiege Alicante (Spain).

1709.

18th April—Alicante relieved by Byng and Stanhope and the garrison transferred to Port Mahon (Spain).

7th May.—A small Anglo-Portuguese force is defeated by the Spaniards at the Caya (Spain).

No events of any importance occurred in the subsidiary theatres of operations.

THE MAIN THEATRE OF OPERATIONS
The Netherlands

1708—continued

28th September—Webb defeats de la Motte's attempt to capture a convoy at Wynendael.

3rd October—Third assault, the Allies strengthen their position.

21st October—The city surrenders, Bouffiers retires into the citadel.

24th November—The Elector of Bavaria endeavours to surprise Brussels.

27th November.—Marlborough forces the Lines of the Scheldt and relieves Brussels.

9th December.—The citadel of Lille surrenders.

18th December.—Bruges surrenders.

1709.

1st January.—Ghent surrenders.

January.—The Allies go into winter quarters.

28th May.—An Ultimatum presented to Louis XIV.

12th June—Louis XIV. refuses the terms offered by the Allies.

23rd June—Marlborough commences his advance.

28th June.—The Allies invest Tournai, the citadel surrenders on the 3rd September.

6th September.—Hesse-Cassel crosses the Haine at Obourg.

7th September—Marlborough and Villars march towards Mons.

9th September—The Dutch refuse to attack the French position at Malplaquet.

11th September—The Battle of Malplaquet.

15th September—The Allies besiege Mons—surrenders on the 9th October.

October.—The Dutch refuse to besiege Quesnoi.

October.—The Allies go into winter quarters.

The Subsidiary Theatre of Operations
Spain—Northern Italy—The Valley of the Rhine, etc.

1710.
July.—Failure of the British Expedition to Cette (S. France).

27th July—Stanhope defeats the French at Almanara (Spain).

20th August.—Stanhope and Staremberg defeat the French outside Saragossa.

November.—The Allies enter Madrid; but evacuate it about a month later (Spain).

9th December—Vendôme defeats Stanhope at Brihuega (Spain).

10th December.—Indecisive action between Vendôme and Staremberg at Villa-Viciosa (Spain).

1711.
January.—Marshall Noailles captures Gerona (Spain).

April—The Emperor Joseph (of Austria) dies.

The Main Theatre of Operations
The Netherlands

1710.
March-April—Abortive Peace Congress at Gertruydenberg.

22nd April—The Allies force the Lines of la Bassée on the Scarpe.

24th April—Douai besieged—surrenders on the 26th of June.

28th August——Bethune surrenders.

28th September.—St. Venant surrenders.

9th November.—Aire surrenders.

November.——The Allies go into winter quarters.

1711
1st May.—The Allies advance towards the 'Ne Plus Ultra' Lines.

13th June——Eugene is recalled to the Rhine; Marlborough marches towards Lens.

6th July—The Allies capture the redoubt at Arleux.

9th July —Villars attacks Hompesch at Douai.

22nd July—The French recapture the redoubt at Arleux and destroy it.

28th July—Marlborough feints at the French lines near Arras.

4th-5th August—The Allies force the '*Ne Plus Ultra*' Lines at Arleux.

7th August—They cross the Scheldt near Cambrai.

8th August—Bouchain invested—surrenders on 12th September.

14th-16th August—The redoubts erected by Villars are captured.

27th September.—Secret negotiations between Louis and the British Government.

September.—The Allies go into winter quarters.

November.—Marlborough returns to England and is charged with misappropriating public money.

31st December. The Duke of Marlborough is dismissed from the command of the army.

The Battle of Blenheim

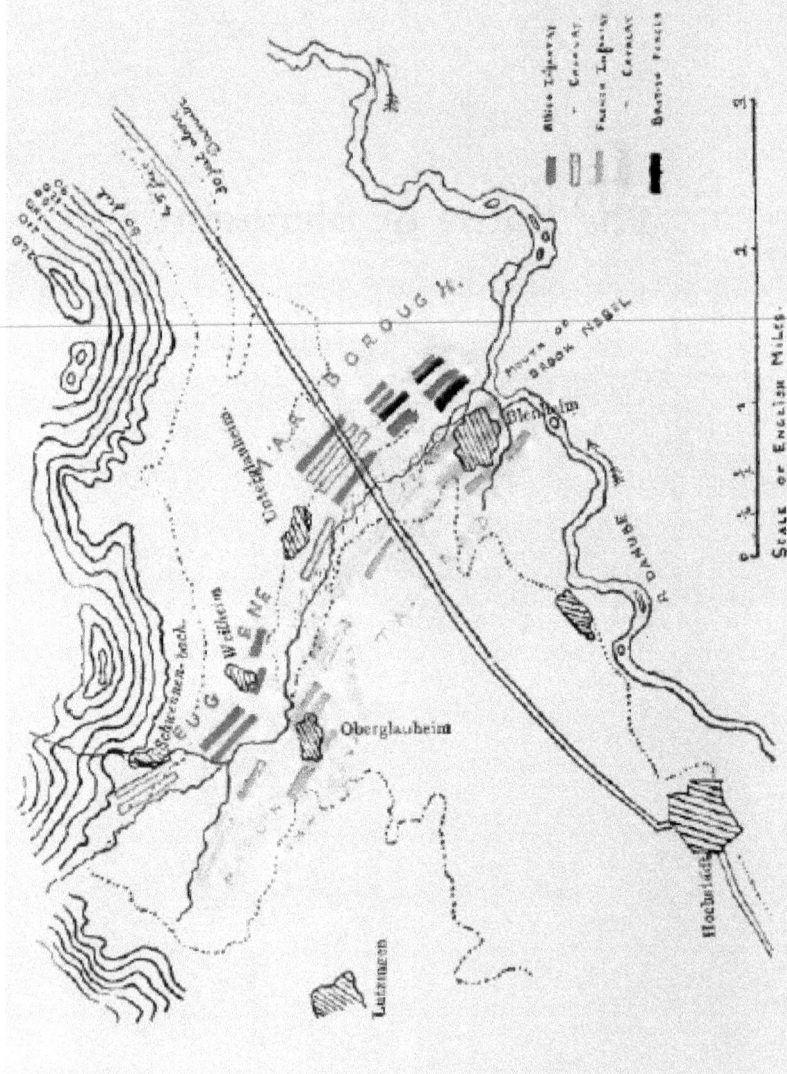

Contents

PART 1

The Political Objective

The proper understanding of a battle and of its historical significance is only possible in connection with the campaign of which it forms a part; and the campaign can only be understood when we know the political object which it was designed to serve.

A battle is no more than an incident in a campaign. However decisive in its immediate result upon the field, its value to the general conducting it depends on its effect upon the whole of his operations, that is, upon the campaign in which he is engaged.

A campaign, again, is but the armed effort of one society to impose its will in some particular upon another society. Every such effort must have a definite political object. If this object is served the campaign is successful. If it is not served the campaign, is a failure. Many a campaign which began or even concluded with a decisive action in favour of one of the two belligerents has failed because, in the result, the political object which the victory was attempting was not reached. Conversely, many a campaign, the individual actions of which were tactical defeats, terminated in favour of the defeated party, upon whom the armed effort was not sufficient to impose the will of his adversary, or to compel him to that political object which the adversary was seeking. In other words, military success can be measured only in terms of civil policy.

It is therefore essential, before approaching the study of any action, even of one so decisive and momentous as the Battle of Blenheim, to start with a general view of the political situation which brought about hostilities, and of the political object of those hostilities; only then, after grasping the measure in which the decisive action in question affected the whole campaign, can we judge how the campaign, in its turn, compassed the political end for which it was designed.

The war whose general name is that of the Spanish Succession was undertaken by certain combined powers against Louis XIV. of France (and such allies as that monarch could secure upon his side) in order to prevent the succession of his grandson to the crown of Spain.

With the various national objects which Holland, England, the Empire and certain of the German princes, as also Savoy and Portugal, may have had in view when they joined issue with the French monarch, military history is not concerned. It is enough to know that their objects, though combining them against a common foe, were not identical, and the degrees of interest with which they regarded the compulsion of Louis XIV. to forego the placing of his grandson upon the Spanish throne were very different. It is this which will largely explain the various conduct of the allies during the progress of the struggle; but all together sought the humiliation of Louis, and joined on the common ground of the Spanish Succession.

The particular object, then, of the campaign of Blenheim (and of those campaigns which immediately preceded and succeeded it) was the prevention of the unison of the crowns of France and Spain in the hands of two branches of the same family. Tested by this particular issue alone, the campaign of Blenheim, and the whole series of campaigns to which it belongs, failed. Louis XIV. maintained his grandson upon the throne of Spain; and the issue of the long war could not impose upon him the immediate political object of the allies.

But there was a much larger and more general object engaged, which was no less than the defence of Austria—more properly the Empire—and of certain minor States, against what had grown to be the overwhelming power of the French monarchy.

From this standpoint the whole period of Louis XIV.'s reign—all the last generation of the seventeenth century and the first decade and more of the eighteenth—may be regarded as a struggle between the soldiers of Louis XIV. (and their allies) upon the one hand, and Austria, with certain minor powers concerned in the defence of their independence or integrity, upon the other.

In this struggle Great Britain was neutral or benevolent in its sympathies in so far as those sympathies were Stuart; but all that part of English public life called Whig, all the group of English aristocrats who desired the abasement of the Crown, perhaps the mass of the nation also, was opposed, both in its interests and in its opinions, to the supremacy of Louis XIV. upon the Continent.

William of Orange, who had been called to the English throne by the Revolution of 1688, was the most determined opponent Louis had in Europe. Apart from him, the general interests of the London merchants, and the commercial interests of the nation as a whole, were in antagonism to the claims of the Bourbon monarchy. We therefore find the forces of Great Britain, in men, ships, guns, and money, arrayed against Louis throughout the end of his reign, and especially during this last great war.

Now, from this general standpoint—by far the most important—the war of the Spanish Succession is but part of the general struggle against Louis XIV.; and in that general struggle the campaign of 1704, and the battle of Blenheim which was its climax, are at once of the highest historical importance, and a singular example of military success.

For if the general political object be considered, which was the stemming of the French tide of victory and the checking of the Bourbon power, rather than the particular matter of the succession of the Spanish throne, then it was undoubtedly the campaign of 1704 which turned the tide; and Blenheim must always be remembered in history as the great defeat from which dates the retreat of the military power of the French in that epoch, and the gradual beating back of Louis XIV.'s forces to those frontiers which may be regarded as the natural boundaries of France.

Not all the French conquests were lost, nor by any means was the whole great effort of the reign destroyed. But the peril which the military aptitude of the French under so great a man as Louis XIV. presented to the minor States of Europe and to the Austrian empire was definitely checked when the campaign of Blenheim was brought to its successful conclusion. That battle was the first of the great defeats which exhausted the resources of Louis, put him, for the first time in his long reign, upon a close defensive, and restored the European balance which his years of unquestioned international power had disturbed.

Blenheim, then, may justly rank among the decisive actions of European history.

In connection with the campaign of which it formed a part, it gave to that campaign all its meaning and all its complete success.

In connection with the general struggle against Louis, that campaign formed the turning point between the flow and the ebb in the stream of military power which Louis XIV. commanded and had set in motion.

From the day of Blenheim, August 13th, 1704, onwards, the whole

French effort was for seven years a desperate losing game, which, if its end was saved from disaster by the high statesmanship of the king and the devotion of his people, was none the less the ruin of that ambitious policy which had coincided with the great days of Versailles.

The war was conducted, as I have said, by various allies. Its success depended, therefore, upon various commanders regarded as coequal, acting as colleagues rather than as principals and subordinates. But the story of the great march to the Danube and its harvest at Blenheim, which we are about to review, sufficiently proves that the deciding genius in the whole affair was that of John Churchill, Duke of Marlborough. The plan was indeed Eugene's; and in the battle itself he shared the glory with his English friend and colleague.

Again, the British troops present were few indeed compared with the total of the allied forces. At Blenheim, in particular, they amounted to less than a third of the numbers present. The excellence of their material, however, their magnificent work at the Schellenberg and on Blenheim field itself, coupled with the fact that the general to whom the final success is chiefly due was the great military genius of this country, warrants the historian in classing this battle among British actions, and in treating its story as a national affair.

I will approach the story of the campaign and of the battle by a conspectus of the field of war in which Marlborough was so unexpectedly to show the military genius which remains his single title to respect and his chief claim to renown.

PART 2

The Early War

In order to grasp the strategic problem presented to Marlborough and the allies in the spring of 1704, it is first necessary to understand the diplomatic position at the outbreak of the war, and the military disposition of the two years 1702 and 1703, and thus the general position of the armies which preceded Marlborough's march to the Danube.

Louis XIV. recognised his grandson as king of Spain late in 1700 The coalition immediately formed against him was at first imperfect. Savoy, with its command of the passes over the Alps into Austrian territory, was in Louis' favour. England, whose support of his enemies was (for reasons to be described) a capital factor in the issue, had not yet joined those enemies. But, from several causes, among the chief of which was Louis' recognition of the Pretender as king of England after James the II.'s death, the opinion of the English aristocracy, and perhaps of the English people, was fixed, and in the last months of 1701 the weight of England was thrown into the balance against France.

Why have I called this—the decision of the English Parliament—a capital factor in the issue of the war?

Excepting for a moment the military genius of Marlborough— whose great capacity had not yet been tested in so large a field—two prime characters gave to Great Britain a deciding voice in what was to follow. The first of these was her wealth, the second that aristocratic constitution of her polity which was now definitely established, and which, for nearly a century and a half, was to make her strength unique in its quality among all the elements of European competition.

As to the first of these—the *Wealth* of England—it is a matter of such importance to the comprehension of all the eighteenth century and most of the nineteenth that it should merit a far longer analysis and affirmation than can be devoted to it in these few lines. It must be enough for our purpose to say that Great Britain, from about 1680 onwards, was not only wealthier (in proportion to her population) than the powers with whom she had to deal as enemies or allies, but was also proceeding to increase that wealth at a rate far exceeding that of her rivals. Again, what was perhaps, for the purposes of war, the chief point of all, England held that wealth in a mobile, fluid form, which could at once be translated into munitions, the wages of mercenaries, or the hire of transports, within the shortest time, and at almost any point in Western and Northern Europe.

Essentially commercial, already possessed of a solid line of enterprises beyond the seas, having defeated and passed the Dutch in the race for mercantile supremacy, England could afford or withhold at her choice the most valuable and rapid form of support—money.

How true this was, even those in Europe who had not appreciated the changed conditions of Great Britain immediately perceived when the determination of Parliament, at the end of 1701, to support the alliance against Louis XIV., took the form of voting 40,000 men, all of whom would be immediately supplied and paid with English money.

True, of the 40,000 not half were British; but (save for the excellent quality of the British troops), the point was more or less indifferent. The important thing was that England was able to provide and to maintain this immense accretion to the coalition against France, and to use it where she would. We shall see later how this power turned the fate of the war.

If I have insisted so strongly upon the financial factor, it is both because that factor is mis-appreciated in most purely military histories, and also because, in the changed circumstances of our own time, it is not easy for the reader to take for granted, as did his ancestors, the overwhelming superiority which England once enjoyed in mobilised wealth, usable after this kind. It can best be compared to the similar superiority enjoyed in the Middle Ages by the Republic of Venice, to whose fortunes, both good and ill, the story of modern England affords so strange a parallel.

The second factor I have mentioned—the aristocratic constitution of the country—though almost equally important, is somewhat more elusive, and might be more properly challenged by a critic.

England had not, in the first years of the eighteenth century, reached that calm and undisturbed solidity which is the mark of an aristocratic State at its zenith.

Faction was bitter, the opposition between the old loyalty to the Crown and the new national regime was so determined as to make civil war possible at any moment. This condition of affairs was to last for a generation, and it was not until the middle of the eighteenth century was passed that it disappeared.

Nevertheless, compared with the Continental States, Great Britain already presented by 1701 that elasticity in substance and tenacity in policy which accompany aristocratic institutions. Corruption might be rife, but it was already growing difficult to purchase the services of a member of the governing class against the national interests. That knowledge of public affairs, diffused throughout a small and closely combined social class, which is the mark of an aristocracy, was already apparent. The power of choosing, from a narrow and well-known field, the best talents for any particular office (which is another mark of aristocracy), was already a power apparent in the government of this country. The solidarity which, in the face of a common enemy, an aristocracy always displays, the long-livedness, as of a corporate body, which an aristocracy enjoys, and which permits it to follow with such strict continuity whatever line of foreign policy it has undertaken, was clearly defining itself at the moment of which I write.

In a word, the new settlement of English life upon the basis of class government, the exclusion of the mass of the people from public affairs, the decay (if you will) of a lively public opinion, the presence of that hopeless disinherited class which now forms the majority of our industrial population; the organisation of the universities, of justice, of the legislature, of the executive, as parts of one social class; the close grasp which that class now had upon the land and capital of the whole country, which it could utilise immediately for interior development or for a war—all this marked the youth and vigour of an oligarchic England, which was for so long to be at once invulnerable and impregnable.

At what expense in morals, and therefore in ultimate strength and happiness, such experiments are played, is no matter for discussion in a military history. We must be content to remark what vigour her new constitution gave to the efforts of England in the field, while yet that constitution was young.

England, then, having thrown this great weight into the scale of the Empire, and against France, the campaign of 1702 was entered upon with the chances in favour of the former, and with the latter in an anxiety very different from the pride which Louis XIV. had taken for granted in the early part of his reign.

If the reader will consider the map of Western Europe, the effect of England's joining the allies will be apparent.

The frontier between the Spanish Netherlands and Holland—that is, between modern Belgium and Holland—was the frontier between the forces of Louis XIV. and those of opponents upon the north. Thus, Antwerp and Ostend were in the hands of the Bourbon, for the Spanish Netherlands had passed into the hands of the French king's grandson, and the French and Spanish forces were combined. Further east, towards the Upper Rhine, a French force lay in the district of Cleves, and all the fortresses on the Meuse, running in a line south of that post, with the exception of Maestricht, were in French hands.

French armies held or threatened the Middle Rhine. Upon the Upper Rhine and upon the Danube an element of the highest moment in favour of France had appeared when the Elector of Bavaria had declared for Louis XIV., and against Austria.

Had not England intervened with the great weight of gold and that considerable contingent of men (in all, eighteen of the new forty thousand), France would have easily held her northern position upon the frontier of Holland and the Lower Rhine, while the Elector of Bavaria, joining forces with the French Army upon the Upper Rhine, would have marched upon Vienna.

The emperor was harried by the rising of the Hungarians behind him; and as the principal forces of the French king would not have been detained in the north, the whole weight of France, combined with her new ally the Elector of Bavaria, would have been thrown upon the Upper Danube.

As it was, this plan was, in its inception at least, partially successful, but only in its inception, and only partially.

For, with the summer of 1702, Marlborough, though hampered by the fears of the Dutch with whom he had to act in concert, cleared the French out of Cleves, caused them to retire southward in the face of the great accession of strength which he brought with the new troops in English pay and the English contingents. Following the French retirement, he swept the whole valley of the Meuse, and took its fastnesses from Liege downwards, all along the course of the stream. (It was this success which to Marlborough's existing earldom added the high dignity of Duke, by letters patent of December 16, 1702.)

By the end of the year this northern front of the French armies was imperilled, and Marlborough and his allies in that part hoped to undertake with the next season the reduction of the Spanish Netherlands.

It must be remembered, in connection with this plan, that France has always been nervous with regard to her north-eastern frontier; that the loss of this frontier leaves a way open to Paris: an advance from Belgium was to the French monarchy what an advance along the Danube was to Austria—the prime peril of all. As yet, France was nowhere near grave peril in this quarter, but pressure there marred her general plans upon the Danube.

Nevertheless, the march upon Vienna by the Upper Danube had been prepared with some success. While part of the northern frontier was thus being pressed and part menaced, while the Meuse was being cleared of French garrisons, and the French fortresses on it taken by Marlborough and his allies, the Elector of Bavaria had seized Ulm. The French upon the Upper Rhine, under Villars, defeated the Prince of Baden at Friedlingen, and established a road through the New Forest by which Louis XIV.'s forces, combined with those of the Elector of Bavaria, could advance eastward upon the emperor's capital. It was designed that in the next year, 1703, the troops of Savoy, in alliance with those of France, should march from North Italy through the passes of the Alps and the Tyrol upon Vienna, while at the same time the Franco-Bavarian forces should march down the Danube towards the same objective.

When the campaign of 1703 opened, however, two unexpected events determined what was to follow.

The first was the failure of Marlborough in the north to take Antwerp, and in general his inability to press France further at that point; the second, the defection of Savoy from the French alliance.

As to the first—Marlborough's failure against Antwerp. The Spanish Netherlands were now solidly held; the forces of the allies were indeed increasing perpetually in this neighbourhood, but it appeared as though the attempt to reduce Brabant, Hainault, and Flanders, which are here the bulwark of France, would be tedious, and perhaps barren. A sort of "consolation" advance was indeed made upon the Rhine, and Bonn was captured; but no more was done in this quarter.

As to the second point, the solid occupation of the Upper Danube by the Franco-Bavarians was indeed fully accomplished. The imperial forces were defeated upon the bank of that river at Hochstadt, but the advance upon Vienna failed, for the second half of the plan, the march from Northern Italy upon Austria, through the Tyrol, had come

The General Situation in 1703.

to nothing, through the defection of Savoy. The turning of the scale against Louis by the action of England was beginning to have its effect; Portugal had already joined the coalition, and now Savoy had refused to continue her help of the Bourbons.

The year 1704 opened, therefore, with this double situation: to the south Austria had been saved for the moment, but was open to immediate attack in the campaign to come; meanwhile, the French had proved so solidly seated in the Spanish Netherlands (or Belgium) that repeated attacks on them in this quarter would in all probability prove barren.

It was under these circumstances that Eugene of Savoy came to the great decision which marked the year of Blenheim. He determined that it was best—if he could persuade his colleagues—to carry the war into that territory which was particularly menaced. He conceived the plan of marching a great force from the Netherlands right down to the field of the Upper Danube.

There could be checked the proposed march upon the heart of the coalition, which was Vienna. There, if fortune served the allies, they would by victory make all further chance of marching a Franco-Bavarian force down the Danube impossible; meanwhile, and at any rate, the new step would alarm all French effort towards the Upper Rhine, weaken the French organisation upon its northern frontier, and so permit of a return of the allies to an attack there at a later time.

Eugene of Savoy was a member of the cadet branch of that royal house. His grandfather, the younger son of Charles Emmanuel, had founded the family called Savoy Carignan. His father had been married to one of Mazarin's nieces. Eugene was her fifth son, and at this moment not quite forty years of age.

His character, motives, and genius must be clearly seized if we are to appreciate the campaign and the Battle of Blenheim.

It was the Italian blood which formed that character most, but he was thoroughly French by birth and training. Born in Paris, and desiring a career in the French Army, it was a slight offered to his mother by the French king that gave his whole life a personal hatred of Louis XIV. for its motive. From boyhood till his death, between sixty and seventy, this great captain directed his energies uniquely against the fortunes of the French king. When, later in life, there was an attempt to acquire his talents for the French service, he replied that he hoped to re-enter France, but only as an invader. It has been complained that he lacked precision in detail, and that as an organiser he was somewhat at fault; but he had no equal for rapidity of vision, and for seizing the essential point in a strategic problem. From that day in his twentieth year when he had assisted at Sobiesky's destruction of the Turks before Vienna, through his own great victory which crushed that same enemy somewhat later at Zenta, in all his career this quality of immediate perception had been supremely apparent.

He was at this moment—the end of the campaign of 1703—the head of the imperial council of war; and he it was who first grasped the strategic necessity which 1703 had created. The determination to carry the defence of the empire into the valley of the Upper Danube was wholly his own. He wrote to Marlborough suggesting a withdrawal of forces as considerable as possible from the northern field to the southern.

By a happy accident, the judgment of the Englishman exactly coincided with his own, and indeed there was so precise a sympathy between these two very different men that when they met in the course of the ensuing campaign there sprang up between them not only a lasting friendship, but a mutual comprehension which made the combination of their talents invincible during those half dozen years of the war which all but destroyed the French power.

Such was the origin of Marlborough's advance southward from the Netherlands in the early summer of 1704, an advance famous in history under the title of "*the march to the Danube.*"

PART 3

The March to the Danube

The position of the enemy at the moment when Marlborough's march to the Danube from the Netherlands was conceived may be observed in the sketch map later on.

Under Villeroy, who must be regarded as the chief of the French commanders of the moment, lay the principal army of Louis XIV., with the duty of defending the northern front and of watching the Lower Rhine.

It was this main force which was expected to have to meet the attack of Marlborough and the Dutch in the same field of operations as had seen the troops in English pay at work during the two preceding years. But Villeroy was, of course, free to detach troops southwards somewhat towards the Middle Rhine, or the valley of the Moselle, if, as later seemed likely, an attack should be made in that direction.

On the Upper Rhine, and in Alsace generally, lay Tallard with his corps. This marshal had captured certain crossing-places over the Rhine, but had all his munitions and the mass of his strength permanently on the left bank.

Finally, Marcin, with his French contingent, and Max-Emanuel, the Elector of Bavaria, with the Bavarian Army, held the whole of the Upper Danube, from Ulm right down to and past the Austrian frontier.

Over against these forces of the French and their Bavarian allies we must set, first, the Dutch forces in the north, including the garrisons of the towns on the Meuse which Marlborough had conquered and occupied; and, in the same field, the forces in the pay of England (including the English contingents). These amounted in early 1704 to 50,000 men, which Marlborough was to command.

Next, upon the Middle Rhine, and watching Tallard in Alsace, was Prince Eugene, who had been summoned from Hungary by the Imperial government to defend this bulwark of Germany, but his army was small compared to the forces in the north.

Finally, the Margrave of Baden, Louis, with another separate army, was free to act at will in Upper Germany, to occupy posts in the Black Forest, or to retire eastward into the heart of Germany or towards the Danube as circumstances might dictate. This force was also small. It was supplemented by local militia raised to defend particular passes in the Black Forest, and these, again, were supported by the armed peasantry.

It is essential to a comprehension of the whole scheme to understand that *before* the march to the Danube the whole weight of the alliance against the French lay in the north, upon the frontier of Holland, the valley of the Meuse, and the Lower Rhine. The successes of Bavaria in the previous year had given the Bavarian army, with its French contingent, a firm grip upon the Upper Danube, and the possibility of marching upon Vienna itself when the campaign of 1704 should open.

The great march upon the Danube which Eugene had conceived, and which Marlborough was to execute so triumphantly, was a plan to withdraw the weight of the allied forces suddenly from the north to the south; to transfer the main weapon acting against France from the Netherlands to Bavaria itself; to do this so rapidly and with so little leakage of information to the enemy as would prevent his heading off the advance by a parallel and faster movement upon his part, or his strengthening his forces upon the Danube before Marlborough's should reach that river.

Such was the scheme of the march to the Danube which we are now about to follow; but before undertaking a description of the great and successful enterprise, the reader must permit me a word of distinction between a strategic move and that tactical accident which we call a battle. In the absence of such a distinction, the campaign of Blenheim and the battle which gives it its name would be wholly misread.

A great battle, especially if it be of a decisive character, not only changes history, but has a dramatic quality about it which fixes the attention of mankind.

The general reader, therefore, tends to regard the general movements of a campaign as mere preliminaries to, or explanations of, the decisive action which may conclude it.

This is particularly the case with the readers attached to the victorious side.

The French layman, in the days before universal service in France, wrote and read his history of 1805 as though the march of the Grand Army were deliberately intended to conclude with Austerlitz. The English reader and writer still tends to read and write of Marlborough's march to the Danube as though it were aimed at the field of Blenheim.

This error or illusion is part of that general deception so common to historical study which has been well called "*reading history backwards.*" We know the event; to the actors in it the future was veiled. Our knowledge of what is to come colours and distorts our judgment of the motive and design of a general.

The march to the Danube was, like all strategic movements, a general plan animated by a general objective. It was not a particular thrust at a particular point, destined to achieve a highly particular result at that point.

Armies are moved with the object of imposing political changes upon an opponent. If that opponent accepts these changes, not necessarily after a pitched battle, but in any other fashion, the strategical object of the march is achieved.

Though the march conclude in a defeat, it may be strategically sound; though it conclude in a victory, it may be strategically unsound. Napoleon's march into Russia in 1812 was strategically sound. Had Russia risked a great battle and lost it, the historical illusion of which I speak would treat the campaign as a designed preface to the battle. Had Russia risked such a battle and been successful, the historical illusion of which I speak would call the strategy of the advance faulty.

As we know, the advance failed partly through the weather, partly through the spirit of the Russian people, not through a general action. But in conception and in execution the strategy of Napoleon in that disastrous year was just as excellent as though the great march had terminated not in disaster but in success.

Similarly, the reputation justly earned by Marlborough when he brought his troops from the Rhine to the Danube must be kept distinct from his tactical successes in the field at the conclusion of the effort. He was to run a grave risk at Donauwörth, he was to blunder badly in attacking the village of Blenheim, he was to be in grave peril even in the last phase of the battle, when Eugene just saved the centre with his cavalry.

Had chance, which is the major element in equal combats, foiled him at Donauwörth or broken his attempt at Blenheim, the march to the Danube would still remain a great thing in history. Had Tallard refused battle on that day, as he certainly should have done, the march to the Danube would still deserve its great place in the military records of Europe.

When we have seized the fact that Marlborough's great march was but a general strategic movement of which the action at Blenheim was the happy but accidental close, we must next remark that the advance to the Danube was the more meritorious, and gives the higher lustre to Marlborough's fame as a general, from the fact that it was an attempt involving a great military hazard, and that yet that attempt had to be made in the face of political difficulties of peculiar severity.

In other words, Marlborough was handicapped in a fashion which lends his success a character peculiar to itself, and worthy of an especial place in history.

This handicap may be stated by a consideration of three points which cover its whole character.

The first of these points concerns the physical conditions of the move; the other two are peculiar to the political differences of the allies.

It was in the nature of the move that a high hazard was involved in it. The general had calculated, as a general always must, the psychology of his opponent. If he were wrong in his calculation, the advance on the Danube could but lead to disaster. It was for him to judge whether the French were so nervous about the centre of their position upon the Rhine as to make them cling to it to the last moment, and tend to believe that it was either along the Moselle or (when he had left that behind) in Alsace that he intended to attack. In other words, it was for him to make the French a little too late in changing their dispositions, a little too late in discovering what his real plan was, and therefore a little too late in massing larger reinforcements upon the Upper Danube, where he designed to be before them.

Marlborough guessed his opponent's psychology rightly; the French marshals hesitated just too long, their necessity of communicating with Louis at Versailles further delayed them, and the great hazard which he risked was therefore risked with judgment. But a hazard it remained until almost the last days of its fruition. The march must be rapid; it involved a thousand details, each requiring his supervision and his exact calculation, his knowledge of what could be expected of his troops, and his survey of daily supply.

There was another element of hazard.

Arrived at his destination upon the plains of the Danube, Marlborough would be very far from any good base of supply.

The country lying in the triangle between the Upper Danube and the Middle Rhine, especially that part of it which is within striking distance of the Danube, is mountainous and ill provided with those large towns, that mobilizable wealth, and those stores of vehicles, munitions, food, and remounts which are the indispensable sustenance of an army.

The industry of modern Germany has largely transformed this area, but even today it is one in which good depots would be rare to find. Two hundred years ago, (at time of writing), the tangle of hills was far more deserted and far worse provided.

By the time Marlborough should have effected his junction with his ally in the upper valley of the Danube only two bases of supply would be within any useful distance of the new and distant place to which he was transferring his great force.

The most important of these, his chief base, and his only principal store of munitions and every other requisite, was Nuremberg; and that town was a good week from the plains upon the bank of the Danube where he proposed to act. As an advanced base nearer to the river, he could only count upon the lesser town of Nördlingen.

Therefore, even if he should successfully reach the field of action which he proposed, cross the hills between the two river basins without loss or delay, and be ready to act as he hoped upon the banks of the Danube before the end of June, his stay could not be indefinitely prolonged there, and his every movement would be undertaken under the anxiety which must ever haunt a commander dependent on an insufficient or too distant base of supply. This anxiety, be it noted, would rapidly increase with every march he might have to take southward of the Danube, and with every day's advance into Bavaria itself, if, as he hoped, the possibility of such an advance should crown his efforts.

We have seen that the great hazard which Marlborough risked made it necessary, as he advanced southward up the Rhine during the first half of his march, to keep Villeroy and Tallard doubtful as to whether his objective was the Moselle or, later, Alsace; and while they were still in suspense, abruptly to leave the valley of the Rhine and make for the crossing of the hills towards the Danube. So long as the French marshals remained uncertain of his intentions, they would not dare to detach any very large body of troops from the Rhine valley to the Elector's aid: under the conditions of the time, the clever handling of movement and information might create a gap of a week at least between his first divergence from the Rhine and his enemy's full appreciation that he was heading for the south-east.

He so concealed his information and so ordered his baffling movements as to achieve that end.

So much for the general hazard which would have applied to any commander undertaking such an advance.

But, as I have said, there were two other points peculiar to Marlborough's political position.

The first was, that he was not wholly free to act, as, for instance, Caesar in Gaul was free, or Napoleon after 1799. He must perpetually arrange matters, in the first stages with the Dutch commissioner, later with the imperial general, Prince Louis of Baden, who was his equal in command. He must persuade and even trick certain of his allies in all the first steps of the great business; he must accommodate himself to others throughout the whole of it.

Secondly, the direction in which he took himself separated him from the possibility of rapidly communicating his designs, his necessities, his chances, or his perils to what may be called his moral base. This moral base, the seat both of his own Government and of the Dutch (his principal concern), lay, of course, near the North Sea, and under the immediate supervision of England and the Hague. This is a point which the modern reader may be inclined to ridicule until he remembers under what conditions the shortest message, let alone detailed plans and the execution of considerable orders, could alone be performed two hundred years ago. By a few bad roads, across a veritable dissected map of little independent or *quasi*-independent polities, each with its own frontier and prejudices and independent government, the messenger (often a single messenger) must pass through a space of time equivalent to the passage of a continent today, and through risks and difficulties such as would today be wholly eliminated by the telegraph. The messenger was further encumbered by every sort of change from town to town, in local opinion, and the opportunities for aid.

More than this, in marching to the Danube, Marlborough was putting between himself and that upon which he morally, and most of all upon which he physically, relied, a barrier of difficult mountain land.

Having mentioned this barrier, it is the place for me to describe the physical conditions of that piece of strategy, and I will beg the reader to pay particular attention to the accompanying map, and to read what follows closely in connection with it.

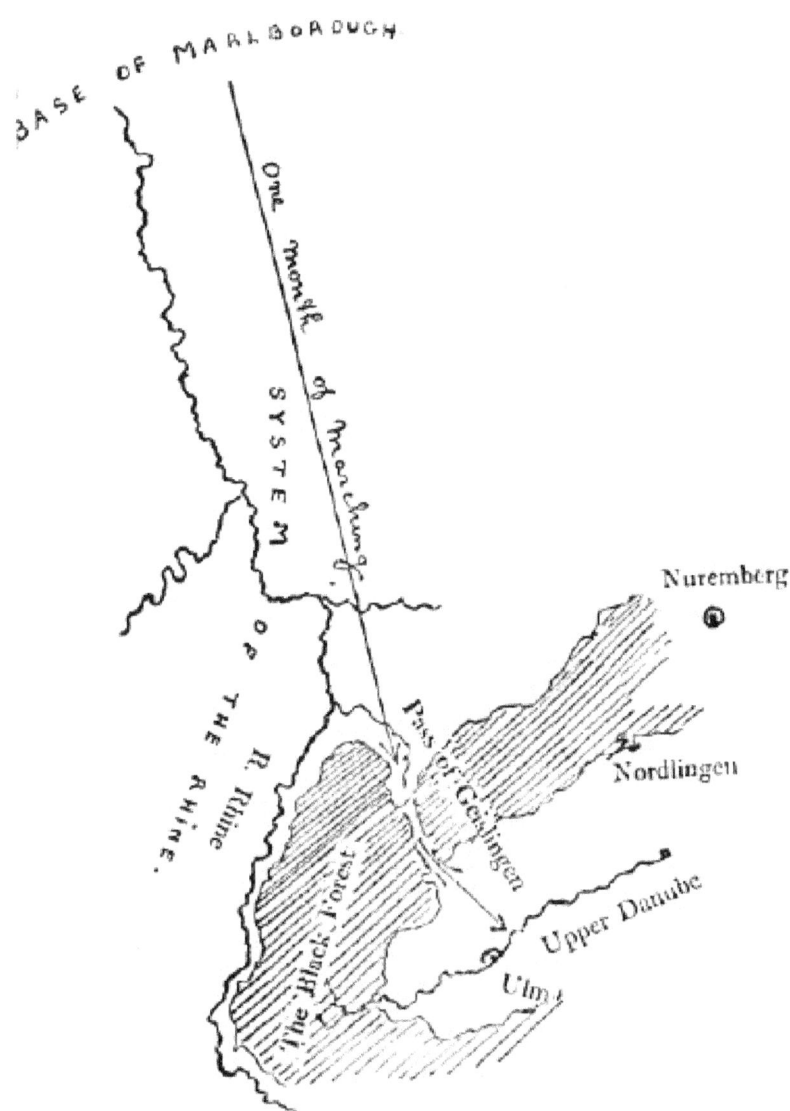

BASE OF MARLBOROUGH

One month of marching

SYSTEM

OF THE RHINE.

R. Rhine

Nuremberg

Pass of Geislingen

The Black Forest

Nordlingen

Upper Danube

Ulm

Map showing the peril of Marlborough's march to the Danube, beyond
the hills which separate the Rhine from the Danube.

In all war, strategy considers routes, and routes are determined by obstacles.

Had the world one flat and uniform surface, the main problems of strategy would not exist.

The surface of the world is diversified by certain features—rivers, chains of hills, deserts, marshes, seas, etc.—the passage across which presents difficulties peculiar to an army, and it is essential to the reading of military history to appreciate these difficulties; for the degrees of impediment which natural features present to thousands upon the march are utterly different from those which they present to individuals or to civilian parties in time of peace.

Since it is to difficulties of this latter sort that we are most accustomed by our experience, the student of a campaign will often ask himself (if he is new to his subject) why such and such an apparently insignificant stream or narrow river, such and such a range of hills over which he has walked on some holiday without the least embarrassment, have been treated by the great captains as obstacles of the first moment.

The reason that obstacles of any sort present the difficulty they do to an army, and present it in the high degree which military history discovers, is twofold.

First, an army consists in a great body of human beings, artificially gathered together under conditions which do not permit of men supplying their own wants by agriculture or other forms of labour. They are gathered together for the principal purpose of fighting. They must be fed; they must be provided with ammunition, usually with shelter and with firing, and if possible, with remounts for their cavalry; reinforcements for every branch of their service must be able to reach them along known and friendly (or well-defended) roads, called their lines of communication. These must proceed from some base, that is from some secure place in which stores of men and material can be accumulated.

Next, it is important to notice that variations in speed between two opposed forces will nearly always put the slow at a disadvantage in the face of the more prompt. For just as in boxing the quicker man can stop one blow and get another in where the slower man would fail, or just as in football the faster runner can head off the man with the ball, so in war superior mobility is a fixed factor of advantage—but a factor far more serious than it is in any game. The force which moves most quickly can "walk round" its opponent, can choose its field for action, can strike in flank, can escape, can effect a junction where the slower force would fail.

It is these two causes, then—the artificial character of an army, with its vast numbers collected in one place and dependent for existence upon the labour of others and the supreme importance of rapidity—which between them render obstacles that seem indifferent to a civilian in time of peace so formidable to a general upon the march.

The heavy train, the artillery, the provisioning of the force, can in general only proceed upon good ways or by navigable rivers. At any rate, if the army departs from these, a rival army in possession of such means of progress will have the supreme advantage of mobility.

Again, upon the flat an army may proceed by many parallel roads, and thus in a number of comparatively short columns, marching upon one front towards a common rendezvous. But in hilly country it will be confined to certain defiles, sometimes very few, often reduced to *one* practicable pass. There is no possibility of an advance by many routes in short columns, each in touch with its neighbours; the whole advance resolves itself into one interminable file.

Now, in proportion to the length of a column, the units of which must each march one directly behind the other, do the mechanical difficulties of conducting such a column increase Every accident or shock in the long line is aggravated in proportion to the length of the line. Finally, a force thus drawn out on the march in one exiguous and lengthy trail is in the worst possible disposition for meeting an attack delivered upon it from either side.

All this, which is true of the actual march of the army, is equally true of its power to maintain its supply over a line of hills (to take that example of an obstacle); and therefore, a line of hills, especially if these hills be confused and steep, and especially if they be provided with but bad roads across them, will dangerously isolate an army whose general base lies upon the further side of them.

What the reader has just read explains the peculiar character which the valley of the Upper Danube has always had in the history of Western European war.

The Rhine and its tributaries form one great system of communications, diversified, indeed, by many local accidents of hill and marsh and forest, with which, for the purposes of this study, we need not concern ourselves.

In a lesser degree, the upper valley of the Danube and its tributaries, though these are largely in the nature of mountain torrents, forms another system of communications, nourishing considerable towns, drawing upon which communications, and relying upon which towns as centres of supply, an army may manoeuvre.

But between the system of the Rhine and that of the Danube there runs a long sweep of very broken country, the Black Forest merging into the Swabian Jura, which in a military sense cuts off the one basin from the other.

At the opening of the eighteenth century, when that great stretch of hills had but a score of roads, none of them well kept up, when no town of any importance could be found in their valleys, and when no communication, even of a verbal message, could proceed faster than a mounted man, this sweep of hills was a very formidable obstacle indeed.

It was these hills, when Marlborough determined to strike across them, and to engage himself in the valley of the Upper Danube, which formed the chief physical factor of his hazard; for, once engaged in them, still more when he had crossed them, his appeals for aid, his reception of advice, perhaps eventually a reinforcement of men or supplies, must depend upon the Rhine valley.

True he had, the one within a week of the Danube, the other within two days of it, the couple of depots mentioned above, the principal one at Nuremberg, the advanced one at Nördlingen. Nevertheless, so long as he was upon the further or eastern side of the hills, his position would remain one of great risk, unless, indeed, or until, he had had the good fortune to destroy the forces of the enemy.

All this being before the reader, the progress of the great march may now be briefly described.

In the winter between 1703 and 1704 domestic irritation and home intrigues, with which we are not here concerned, almost persuaded Marlborough to give up his great role upon the Continent of Europe.

Luckily for the alliance against Louis and for the history of British arms, he returned upon this determination or phantasy, and with the very beginning of the year began his plans for the coming campaign.

He crossed first to Holland in the middle of January 1704, persuaded the Dutch Government to grant a subsidy to the German troops in the South, pretended (since he knew how nervous the Dutch would be if they heard of the plan for withdrawing a great army from their frontiers to the Danube) that he intended operating upon the Moselle, returned to England, saw with the utmost activity to the raising of recruits and to the domestic organisation of the expedition, and reached Holland again to undertake the most famous action of his life in the latter part of April.

It was upon the 5th of May that he left the Hague. He was at Maestricht till the 14th, superintending every detail and ordering the construction of bridges over the Meuse by which the advance was to begin. Upon the 16th he left by the southward road for Bedburg, and immediately his army broke winter quarters for the great march.

It was upon the 18th oi May that the British regiments marched out of Ruremonde by the bridges constructed over the Meuse, aiming for the rendezvous at Bedburg.

The very beginning of the march was disturbed by the fears of the Dutch and of others, though Marlborough had carefully kept secret the design of marching to the Danube, and though all imagined that the valley of the Moselle was his objective.

Marlborough quieted these fears, and was in a better position to insist from the fact that he claimed control over the very large force which was directly in the pay of England.

He struck for the Rhine, up the valley of which he would receive further contingents, supplied by the minor members of the Grand Alliance, as he marched.

By the 23rd he was at Bonn with the cavalry, his brother Churchill following with the infantry. Thence the heavy baggage and the artillery proceeded by water up the river to Coblentz, and when Coblentz was reached (upon the 25th of May) it was apparent that the Moselle at least was not his objective, for on the next day, the 26th, he crossed both that river and the Rhine with his army, and continued his march up the right bank of the Rhine.

But this did not mean that he might not still intend to carry the war into Alsace. He was at Cassel, opposite Mayence, three days after leaving Coblentz; four days later the head of the column had reached the Neckar at Ladenberg, where bridges had already been built by Marlborough's orders, and upon the 3rd of June the troops crossed over to the further bank.

Here was the decisive junction where Marlborough must show his hand: the first few miles of his progress south-eastward across the bend of the Neckar would make it clear that his object was not Alsace, but the Danube.

He had announced to the Dutch and all Europe an attack upon the valley of the Moselle; that this was a ruse all could see when he passed Coblentz without turning up the valley of that river. The whole week following, and until he reached the Neckar, it might still be imagined that he meditated an attack upon Alsace, for he was still following the course of the Rhine. Once he diverged from the valley of this river and struck across the bend of the Neckar to the south and east, the alternative he had chosen of making the Upper Danube the seat of war was apparent.

It is therefore at this point in his advance that we must consider the art by which he had put the enemy in suspense, and confused their judgment of his design.

The first point in the problem for a modern reader to appreciate is the average rate at which news would travel at that time and in that place. A very important dispatch could cover a hundred miles and more in the day with special organisation for its delivery, and with the certitude that it had gone from one particular place to another particular place. But general daily information as to the movements of a moving enemy could not be so organised.

We must take it that the French commanders upon the left bank of the Rhine at Landau, or upon the Meuse (where Villeroy was when Marlborough began his march), would require full forty-eight hours to be informed of the objective of each new move.

For instance, on the 25th of May Marlborough's forces were approaching Coblentz. To find out what they were going to do next, the French would have to know whether they were beginning to turn up the valley of the Moselle, which begins at Coblentz, or to cross that river and be going on further south. A messenger might have been certain that the latter was their intention by midday of the 26th, but Tallard, right away on the Upper Rhine, would hardly have known this before the morning of the 29th, and by the morning of the 29th Marlborough was already opposite Mayence.

It is this gap of from one to three days in the passage of information which is so difficult for a modern man to seize, and which yet made possible all Marlborough's manoeuvres to confuse the French.

Villeroy was bound to watch until, at least, the 29th of May for the chance of a campaign upon the Moselle.

Meanwhile, Tallard was not only far off in the valley of the Upper Rhine, but occupied in a remarkable operation which, had he not subsequently suffered defeat at Blenheim, would have left him a high reputation as a general.

This operation was the reinforcement of the army under the Elector of Bavaria and Marcin by a dash right through the enemy's country in the Black Forest.

Early in May the Elector of Bavaria had urgently demanded reinforcements of the French king.

The mountains between the Bavarian army and the French were held by the enemy, but the Elector hurried westward along the Danube, while Tallard, with exact synchrony and despatch, hurried eastward; each held out a hand to the other, as it were, for a rapid touch; the business of Tallard was to hand over the new troops and provisions at one exact moment, the business of the Elector was to catch the junction exactly. If it succeeded it was to be followed by a sharp retreat of either party, the one back upon the Danube eastward for his life, the other back westward upon the Rhine.

Tallard had crossed the Rhine on the 13th of May with a huge convoy of provisionment and over 7000 newly recruited troops. Within a week the thing was done. He had handed over in the nick of time the whole mass of men and things to the Elector. (As the French dispatch goes, 7,500 men, every horse, and all the waggons, save 120, which had got into difficulties on the way; Fortescue's note suggesting that 1,500 men only reached the Franco-Bavarians is based on Quincy.) He had done this in the midst of the Black Forest and in the heart of the enemy's country, and he immediately began his retirement upon the Rhine. Tallard was thus particularly delayed in receiving daily information of Marlborough's march.

On the 29th of May Tallard, retiring from the dash to help Bavaria, was still at Altenheim, on the German bank of the Rhine. It was only on that day that he learnt from Villeroy that Marlborough had no idea of marching up the Moselle, but had gone on up the Rhine towards Mayence. Marlborough had crossed the Moselle and the Rhine on the 26th, but it took Tallard three days to know it. Tallard, knowing this, would not know whether Marlborough might not still be thinking of attacking Alsace: to make that alternative loom large in the mind of the French commanders, Marlborough had had bridges prepared in front of his advance at Philipsburg—though he had, of course, no intention at all of going as far up as Philipsburg.

It was on June 3rd, as we have seen, that the foremost of Marlborough's forces were nearing the banks of the Neckar, and upon the 4th that anyone observing his troops would have clearly seen for the first time that they were striking for the Danube. But it was twenty-four hours before Tallard, who had by this time come down the Rhine as far as Lauterberg to defend a possible attack upon Alsace, knew certainly that the Danube, and not the Rhine, would be the field of war.

All this time it was guessed at Versailles, and thought possible by the French generals at the front, that the Danube was Marlborough's aim. But a guess was not good enough to risk Alsace upon.

By the time it was certain Marlborough was marching for the Danube—June 4th and 5th—Tallard's force was much further from the Elector of Bavaria than was Marlborough's, as a glance at the map will show. There was no chance then for heading Marlborough off, and the chief object of the English commander's strategy was accomplished. He had kept the enemy in doubt as to his intentions up to the moment when his forces were safe from interference, and he could strike for the Danube quite unmolested.

★★★★★★★★★★

It is, of course, an error to say, as is too often done in our school histories and the official accounts of our universities, that the French commanders had no idea of a march upon the Danube. A child could have seen that the march upon the Danube was one of the possible plans open to Marlborough, and Villeroy expressly mentions the alternative in his letter of the 30th of May. The whole point of Marlborough's manoeuvres was to leave the enemy in doubt until the very last moment as to which of the three, the Danube, the Moselle, or Alsace, he would strike at; and to be well away upon the road to the former before the French had discovered his final decision.

★★★★★★★★★★

Villeroy at once came south in person, and joined Tallard at Oberweidenthal. The two commanders met upon the 7th of June to confer upon the next move, but at this point appeared that capital element of delay which hampered the French forces throughout the campaign, namely, the necessity of consulting with the King at Versailles. The next day, the 8th, Tallard and Villeroy, who had gone back to their respective commands after their conference, sent separate reports to Versailles. It was not until the 12th that Louis answered, leaving the initiative with his generals at the front, but advising a strong offensive upon the Rhine in order to immobilise there a great portion of the enemy's forces.

The advice was not unwise. It did, as a fact, immobilise Eugene for the moment, and kept him upon the Rhine for some weeks, but, as we shall see later, that General was able to escape when the worst pressure was put upon him, to cross the Black Forest with excellent secrecy and speed, and to effect his junction with Marlborough in time for the battle of Blenheim.

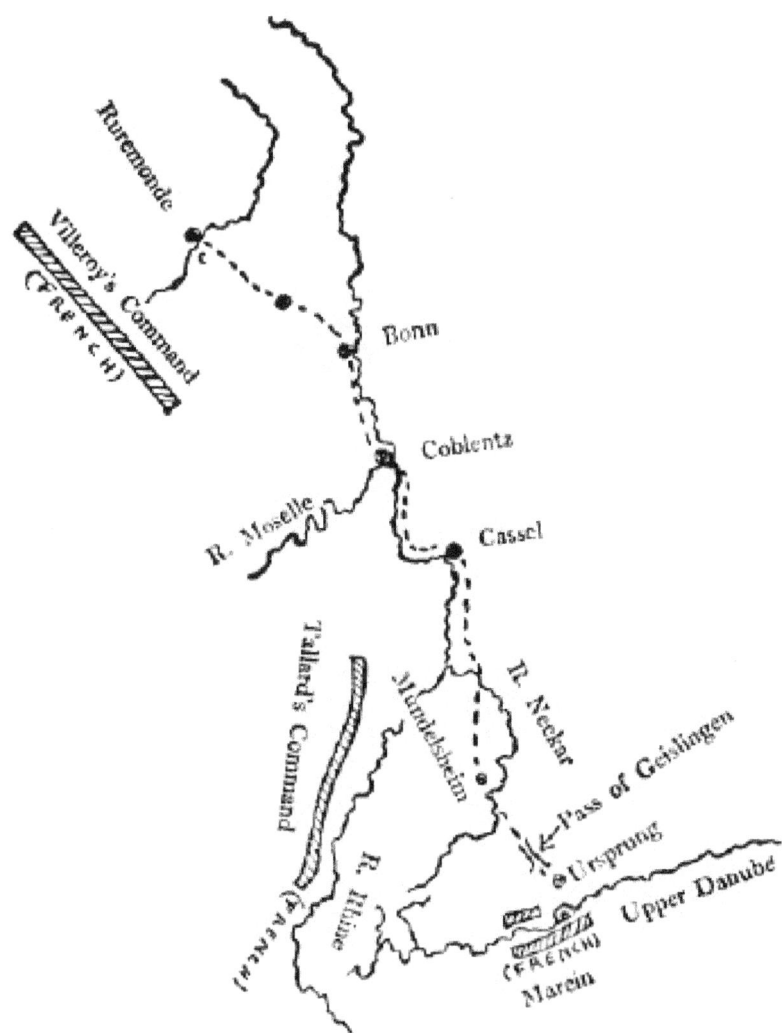

Map illustrating Marlborough's march to the Danube.

But, meanwhile, Baden had chased the Elector of Bavaria out of the Black Forest and down on to the Upper Danube. Marlborough might, at any moment, join hands with Baden. The Elector sent urgent requests for yet more reinforcements from the French, and Tallard, in a letter to Versailles of the 16th of June, advised the capture and possession of such points in the Black Forest as would give him free access across the mountains, the proper provisioning of his line of supply when he should cross them, and the accomplishment of full preparations for joining the Elector of Bavaria in a campaign upon the Upper Danube.

Let the day when the French court received this letter be noted, for the coincidence is curious. At the very moment when Tallard's letter reached Versailles, the 22nd of June, Marlborough was effecting his junction with Baden outside the gates of Ulm at Ursprung. The decision of Louis XIV., that Tallard should advance beyond the hills in force to the aid of the Elector, exactly coincides with the appearance of the English General upon the Danube, and it was on the 23rd of June, the morrow, that the King wrote to Villeroy the decisive letter recommending Tallard to cross over from Alsace towards Bavaria with forty battalions and fifty squadrons, say 25,000 men.

But this advance of Tallard's across the Black Forest and his final junction with the Elector and Marcin before the battle of Blenheim did not take place until after Marlborough had joined Baden and the march to the Danube was accomplished. It must therefore be dealt with in the next division, which is its proper place. For the moment we must return to Marlborough's advance upon the Danube, which we left at the point where he crossed the Neckar upon the 3rd and 4th of June. He had, as we have just seen, and by methods which we have reviewed, completely succeeded in saving the rest of his advance from interference.

Safe from pursuit, and with no further need for concealing his plan, Marlborough lingered in the neighbourhood of the Neckar, partly to effect a full concentration of his forces, partly to rest his cavalry. It was a week before he found himself at Mundelsheim, between Heilbron and Stuttgart, and at the foot of the range which still divided him from the basin of the Danube. Here Eugene, the author of the whole business, met Marlborough; between them the two men drew up the plans which were to lead to so momentous a result, and knitted in that same interview a friendship based upon the mutual recognition of genius, which was to determine seven years of war.

Upon the 13th of June these great captains met and conferred also with the Margrave, Louis of Baden, who commanded all the troops in the hills, and who was to be the third party to their plan. He was a man, cautious, but able, easily ruffled in his dignity, often foolishly jealous of another's power. He insisted that Marlborough and he should take command upon alternate days—he would not serve as second—and in all that followed, the personal relations between himself and Marlborough grew less and less cordial up to the eve of the great battle. His prudence and arrangement, however, his exact synchrony of movement and good hold over his troops, made Marlborough's decisions fruitful.

Upon the 14th of June the passage of Marlborough's column over the hills between the Rhine and the Danube began. Baden went back to the command of his army, which already lay in the plain of the Upper Danube, and awaited the arrival of Marlborough's command, and the junction of it with his own force before Ulm.

A heavy rain, drenched and bad roads, marked Marlborough's crossing of the range. It was not until the 20th that the cavalry reached the foot of the final ascent, but in two days the whole body had passed over. It was thus upon the 22nd of June that the junction between Marlborough and Baden was effected. From that day on their combined forces were prepared to operate as one army upon the plain of the Upper Danube. They stood joined at the gates of Ulm, and in their united force far superior to the Franco-Bavarians, who had but just escaped Baden's army, and who lay in the neighbourhood watching this fatal junction of their rivals.

I say, "who had but just escaped Baden's army," for it was part of the general plan (and a part most ably executed) that not only should the seat of war be brought into the valley of the Upper Danube by Marlborough's march to join Baden, but, as a preparation for this, that the army of the Elector, with his French allies under Marcin, should be driven eastward out of the mountains and cut off from the main French forces upon the Rhine.

This chasing of the Franco-Bavarians down on to the Danube and out of the Black Forest was begun just after the spirited piece of generalship by which Tallard had, as we have seen, reinforced the Elector of Bavaria in the middle of May. That rapid and brilliant piece of work had been effected only just in time. Hardly was it accomplished when Baden's force in the mountains marched, as part of Marlborough's general plan, against the Elector, with the object of forcing him back into the Danube valley at full speed.

It was on the 18th of May that the British regiments were crossing the Meuse, and the advance upon the Danube had begun.

It was on the 18th of May that Louis of Baden appeared at the head of his army in the Black Forest and initiated that separation of the Bavarian forces from the French which was a necessary part of the general plan we have spoken of. It was but a few hours since Tallard had stretched out his hand and passed the recruits and the provisions over to the Franco-Bavarian forces.

The Elector of Bavaria had with him certain French regiments, and Marshal Marcin was under his commands, while Marlborough's plan was still quite unknown. Therefore, no large French force could apparently be spared from the valley of the Rhine to help the Elector in that of the Danube; the Duke of Baden could have things his own way against the lesser force opposed to him.

On the 19th he was advancing on Ober and Neder Ersasch. The Duke of Bavaria had evacuated these villages upon the 20th, and on the same night the Duke of Baden reached Meidlingen. Pursuer and pursued were marching almost parallel, separated only by the little river of Villingen. Now and then they came so close that Baden's artillery could drop a shot into the hurrying ranks of the Elector.

On the 21st Baden was at Geisingen, threatening Tuttlingen. On the 23rd he had reached Stockach, and was pressing so hard that his van had actually come in contact with the rear of the Bavarians, a situation reminiscent of the Esla Bridge in Moore's retreat on Coruña.

The valley of the Danube opened out before the two opponents. The Elector found it possible to maintain his exhausted but rapid retreat, and, ten days later, he had escaped. For by the 3rd of June the Franco-Bavarian forces lay at Elchingen, the Duke of Baden was no nearer than Echingen, (Hechingen?) and the former was saved after a fortnight of very anxious going; but though saved, they were now completely cut off for the moment from French reinforcement. Marlborough was approaching the hills; he would cross them in a few days. He would join Baden's army; and the moment Marlborough should have joined Baden, the Elector would be in peril of overwhelming adversaries.

We have seen how the plan matured. Three weeks after the Bavarian army's escape from the Black Forest, upon the 22nd of June, Marlborough's force had crossed the range and made one with Baden's before Ulm.

PART 4

The Seven Weeks—The Three Phases

From the day when the duke had appeared upon the southern side of the mountains, and was debouching into the plains of the Danube, to the day when he broke the French line at Blenheim, is just over seven weeks; to be accurate, it is seven weeks and three days. It was on the last Sunday but one of the month of June that he passed the mountains; it was upon the second Wednesday of August that he won his great victory.

These seven weeks divide themselves into three clear phases.

The first is the march of Marlborough and Baden upon Donau-wörth and the capture of that city, which was the gate of Bavaria.

The second is the consequent invasion and ravaging of Bavaria, the weakening of the Elector, and his proposal to capitulate; the consequent precipitate advance of Tallard to the aid of the Elector, and the corresponding secret march of Eugene to help Marlborough.

The third occupies the last few days only: it is concerned with the manoeuvres immediately preceding the battle, and especially with the junction of Marlborough and Eugene, which made the victory possible.

THE FIRST PHASE
From the junction of Marlborough and Baden
to the fall of Donauwörth

When the Duke of Marlborough had joined hands with the forces of Baden upon the 22nd of June 1704 his general plan was clear: the last of his infantry, under his brother Churchill, would at once effect their junction with the rest at Ursprung, and he and Baden had but to go forward.

His great march had been completely successful. He had eluded and confused his enemy. He was safe on the Danube watershed, and within a march of the river itself. The only enemies before him on this side of the hills were greatly inferior in number to his own and his ally's. His determination to carry the war into Bavaria could at once be carried into effect.

With this junction the first chapter in that large piece of strategy which may be called "the campaign of Blenheim" comes to an end.

Between the successful termination of his first effort, which was accomplished when he joined forces with Baden upon the Danube side of the watershed in the village of Ursprung, and the great battle by which Marlborough is chiefly remembered, there elapsed, I say, seven summer weeks. These seven weeks are divided into the three parts just distinguished.

In order to understand the strategy of each part of those seven weeks, we must first clearly grasp the field.

The accompanying map shows the elements of the situation.

East of the Black Forest lay open that upper valley of the Danube and its tributaries which was so difficult of access from the valley of the Rhine. In the hills to the north of the Danube, and one day's march from the town of Ulm, were now concentrated the forces of Marlborough and the Duke of Baden. They were advancing, ninety-six battalions strong, with two hundred and two squadrons and forty-eight guns: in all, say, somewhat less than 70,000 men.

At Ulm lay Marcin, and in touch with him, forming part of the same army, the Elector of Bavaria was camped somewhat further down the river, near Lauingen.

The combined forces of Marcin and the Elector of Bavaria numbered, all told, some 45,000 men, and their inferiority to the hostile armies, which had just effected their junction north of Ulm at Ursprung, was the determining factor in what immediately followed.

Marcin crossed the Danube to avoid so formidable a menace, and took up his next station behind the river at Leipheim, watching to see what Marlborough and the Duke of Baden would do. The Elector of Bavaria, in command of the bridge at Lauingen, stood fast, ready to retire behind the stream. The necessity of such a retreat was spared him. The object of his enemies was soon apparent by the direction their advance assumed.

For the immediate object of Marlborough and Baden was not an attack upon the inferior forces of the Elector and Marcin, but for reasons that will presently be seen, the capture of Donauwörth, and

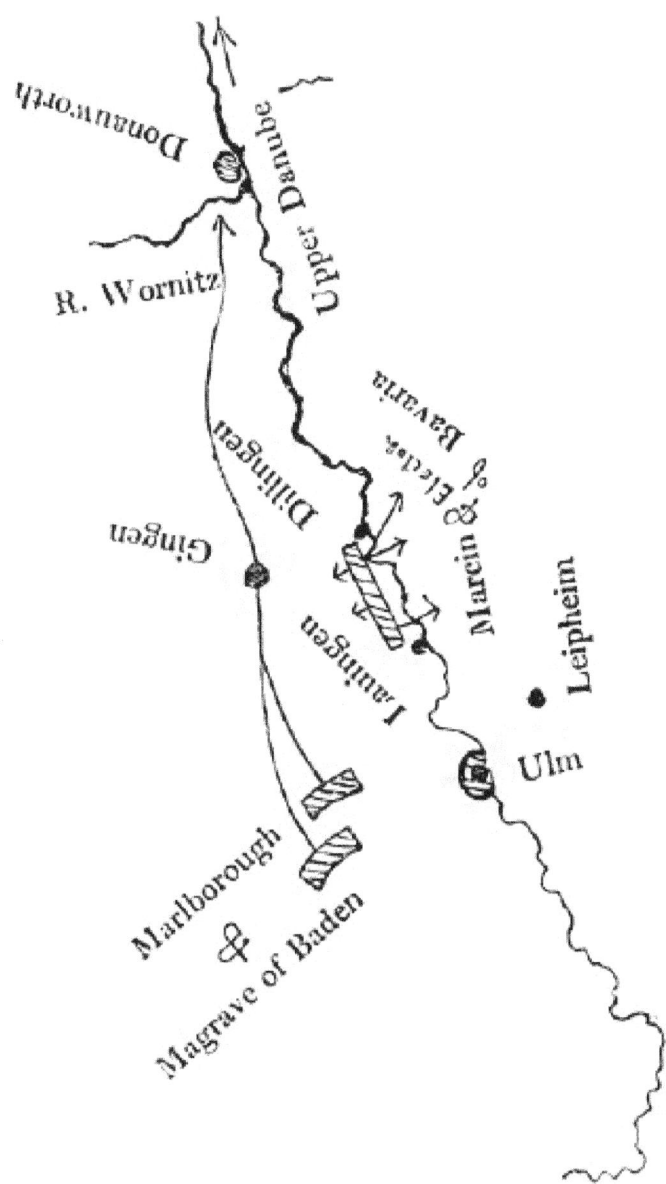

Map illustrating the march of Marlborough and Baden across Marcin's front from the neighbourhood of Ulm to Donauwörth.

their direct march upon Donauwörth took them well north of the Danube. On the 26th, therefore, Marcin thought it prudent to recross the Danube. He and the Elector joined forces on the north side of the Danube, and lay from Lauingen to Dillingen, commanding two bridges behind them for the crossing of the stream, and fairly entrenched upon their front. Meanwhile their enemies, the allies, passed north of them at Gingen. This situation endured for three days.

★★★★★★★★★★

It is worthy of remark that the opportunity for victory which the weak forces under Marcin and the Elector of Bavaria offered at this moment to the superior forces of the allies would have led to an immediate attack of the last upon the first when, two generations later, war had developed into something more sudden and less formal, through the efforts of the Revolution.

Marlborough and the Duke of Baden, with their superior forces, would have attacked Marcin and the Elector had they been their own grandsons. Napoleon, finding himself in such a situation as Marlborough's a hundred years later, would certainly have fallen on the insufficient forces to his south, for it was known that reinforcements were coming over the Black Forest to save the Franco-Bavarian forces. To break up those forces before reinforcement should come was something which a sudden change of plan could have effected, but not even the genius of Marlborough was prepared, in his generation, for a movement necessitating so great a disturbance of calculations previously made. Donauwörth was his objective, and upon Donauwörth he marched, leaving intact this inferior hostile force which watched his advance from the south.

★★★★★★★★★★

When it was apparent that the allied forces of the English general and the Duke of Baden intended to make themselves masters of Donauwörth (and the Elector of Bavaria could have no doubt of their intentions after the 29th of July, when their march eastward from Gingen was resumed), a Franco-Bavarian force was at once detached by him to defend that town, and it is necessary henceforward to understand why Donauwörth was of such importance to Marlborough's plan.

It was his intention to enter Bavaria so as to put a pressure upon the Elector, whose immediate and personal interests were bound up with the villages and towns of his possessions. The Elector could not afford to neglect the misfortunes of its civilian inhabitants, even for the ends of his own general strategy; still less could he sacrifice those subjects of his for the strategic advantage of the King of France and his marshal.

This Marlborough knew. To enter Bavaria, to occupy its towns (only one of which, Ingolstadt, was tolerably fortified), and if possible, to take its capital, Munich, had been from its inception the whole business and strategic motive of his march to the Danube.

But if Marlborough desired to enter Bavaria, Donauwörth was the key to Bavaria from the side upon which he was approaching.

This word "key" is so often used in military history, without any explanation of it which may render it significant to the reader, that I will pause a moment to show *why* Donauwörth might properly be called in metaphor the "key" of Bavaria to one advancing from the north and west.

Bavaria could only be reached by a general coming as Marlborough came, on condition of his possessing and holding some crossing-place over the Danube, for Marlborough's supplies lay north of that river (principally at Nördlingen), and the passing of the enormous supply of an army over one narrow point, such as is a bridge over such an obstacle as a broad river, demands full security.

It will further be seen from the map that yet another obstacle, defending Southern Bavaria and its capital towards the west, as the Danube does towards the north, is the river Lech; a passage over this was therefore also of high importance to the Duke of Marlborough and his allies. Now, a man holding Donauwörth can cross both rivers at the same time unmolested, for they meet in its neighbourhood.

Further, Donauwörth was a town amply provisioned, full of warehouse room, and in general affording a good advanced base of supply for any army marching across the Danube. It afforded an opportunity for concentration of supplies, it contained waggons and horses and food. Supplies, it must be remembered, were the great difficulty of each of the two opposed forces, in this moving of great numbers of men east of the Black Forest, in a comparatively poor country, largely heath and forest, and ill populated.

No serious permanent defences, such as could delay the capture of the town, surrounded Donauwörth; but up above it lies a hill, called from its shape "the Schellenberg" or "Bell Hill." This hill is not isolated, but joins on the higher ground to its north by a sort of flat isthmus, which is level with the summit or nearly so. (As a fact, the advance along this "isthmus" on to the Schellenberg is slightly downhill, and against artillery of modern range and power the Schellenberg could

Rhain

To Munich

R. Lech

Bridge

Upper Danube

THE GREAT ROAD

The Schellenberg

Donauwörth

TO BASE

BRIDGE

R. Wornitz

Frontier of Bavaria.

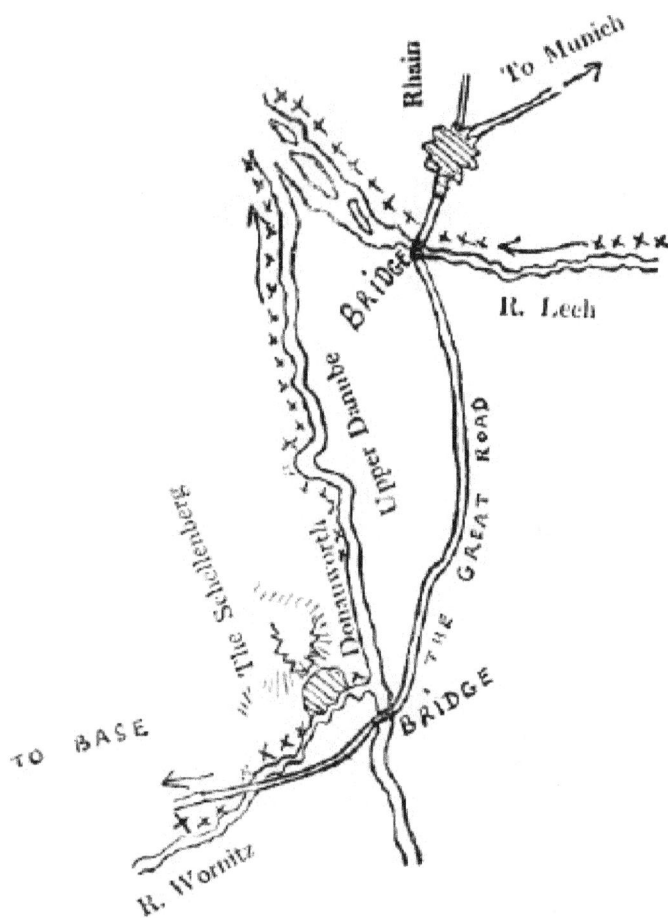

Map showing how Donauwörth is the key of Bavaria from the North-West.

not be held.)

The force which, on perceiving the Duke of Marlborough's intention of capturing Donauwörth, the Elector of Bavaria very rapidly detached to defend that town, was under the command of Count d'Arco; it consisted of two regiments of cavalry and about 10,000 infantry (of whom a quarter were French). D'Arco had orders to entrench the hill above the town as rapidly as might be and to defend it from attack; for whoever held the Schellenberg was master of Donauwörth below. But the Elector could only spare eight guns for this purpose from his inferior forces.

Upon the 2nd of July, in the early morning, Marlborough, by one of those rapid movements which were a prime element in his continuous success, marched before dawn with something between seven and eight thousand infantry carefully chosen for the task and thirty-five squadrons of horse for the attack on the Schellenberg. It was Marlborough's alternate day of command.

With all his despatch, he could not arrive on the height of the hill nor attack its imperfect but rapidly completing works until the late afternoon. It is characteristic of his generalship that he risked an assault with this advance body of his without waiting for the main part of the army under the Duke of Baden to come up. With sixteen battalions only, of whom a third were British, he attempted to carry works behind which a force equal to his own in strength was posted. The risk was high, for he could hardly hope to carry the works with such a force, and all depended upon the main body coming up in time. There was but an hour or two of daylight left.

The check which Marlborough necessarily received in such an attempt incidentally gave proof of the excellent material of his troops. More than a third of these fell in the first furious and undecided hour. They failed to carry the works. They had already once begun to break and once again rallied, but had suffered no final dissolution under the ordeal—though it was both the first to which the men were subjected during this campaign, and probably also the most severe of any they were to endure.

Whether they, or indeed any other troops, could long have survived such conditions as an attempt to storm works against equal numbers is not open to proof; for, while the issue was still doubtful (but the advantage naturally with the force behind the trenches), the mass of the army under the Duke of Baden came up in good time upon the right (that is, from the side of the town), poured almost unopposed over the deserted earthworks of that side, and, five to one, overwhelmed the 12,000 Franco-Bavarians upon the hill.

After one of those short stubborn and futile attempts at resistance which such situations discover in all wars, the inevitable dissolution of d' Arco's command came before the darkness. It was utterly routed; and we may justly presume that not 4,000—more probably but 3,000—rejoined the Army of Marcin and of the Elector of Bavaria.

The loss of the Schellenberg had cost Marlborough's enemies, whose forces were already gravely inferior to his own, eight guns and close upon one-fifth of their effective numbers. The Franco-Bavarians hurried south to entrench themselves under Augsburg, while Donauwörth, and with it the passage of the two great rivers and the entry into Bavaria, lay in the possession of Marlborough and his ally.

The balance of military and historical opinion will decide that Marlborough played for too high stakes in beginning the assault so late in the evening and with so small a force. But he was playing for speed, and he won the hazard.

It was a further reward of his daring that he could point after this first engagement to the fine quality of his British contingent. (Of seventeen officers of the Guards, twelve were hit; of the total British force at least a third fell; more than a third of these, again, were killed.)

It was upon the evening of July the 2nd, then, that this capital position was stormed. It was upon the 5th that Marcin and the Elector lay hopeless and immobile before Augsburg, while their enemies entered a now defenceless Bavaria by its north-western gate. And this complete achievement of Marlborough's plan was but the end of the first phase in the campaign upon the Danube.

Meanwhile, a large French reinforcement under Tallard was already far up on its way from the Rhine, across the Black Forest, to join Marcin and the Elector of Bavaria and set back the tide of war, and, when it should have effected its junction with those who awaited it at Augsburg, to oppose to Marlborough and the Duke of Baden a total force greater than their own.

The French marshal, Tallard, was in command of the army thus rapidly approaching in relief of the Franco-Bavarians. His arrival, if he came without loss, disease, or mishap, promised a complete superiority over the English and their allies, unless, indeed, by some accident or stroke of genius, reinforcement should reach *them* also before the day of the battle.

This reinforcement, in the event, Marlborough did receive. He owed it, as we shall see, to the high talents of Prince Eugene; and it is upon the successful march of this general, his junction with Marlborough, and the consequent success of Blenheim, that the rest of the campaign turns.

We turn next, then, to follow the second phase of the seven weeks, which consists in Tallard's advance to join the Elector, and in Eugene's rapid parallel march, which brought him, just in time, to Marlborough's aid.

THE SECOND PHASE
The Advance of Tallard

To follow the second phase of the seven weeks, that is, the phase subsequent to the capture of the Schellenberg and the retirement of Marcin and the Elector of Bavaria on to Augsburg, it is necessary to hark back a little, and to trace from its origin that advance of Tallard's reinforcements which was to find on the field of Blenheim so disastrous a termination.

We shall see that in this second phase Tallard did indeed manage to effect his junction with the Elector and Marcin with singular despatch; that this junction compelled Marlborough and Baden to cease the ravaging of Bavaria upon which they had been engaged, and to join in closely watching the movement of the Franco-Bavarian forces, lest their own retreat or their line of supplies should be cut off by that now large army.

The Schellenberg was stormed, as we have seen, on the 2nd of July.

Tallard, as we have also seen, had orders from Versailles, when Marlborough's plan of reaching the Danube was clear, to put himself in motion for an advance to the Elector's aid.

He moved at first with firmness and deliberation, determined to secure every post of his advance throughout the difficult hills, and thoroughly to provision his route. He crossed the Rhine upon July 1st, and during the very hours that, far to the east, the disaster of Donauwörth was in progress, he was assembling his forces upon the right bank of the river before beginning to secure his passage through the Black Forest. Upon the 4th he began his march over the hills.

A week later he was in the heart of the broken country at Hornberg, and on the 16th of July he had contained the garrison of Villingen, the principal stronghold which barred his route to the Danube, and which, did he leave it untaken, would jeopardise his provision and supply, the health and even the maintenance of his horses and men by the mountain road.

Upon the 18th he opened fire upon the town; but on the very day that the siege thus began he received from Marcin the whole story of the disaster of the Schellenberg, which had taken place a fortnight before, and a most urgent request for immediate reinforcement.

Tallard's deliberation, his attempt to secure the enemy's one stronghold upon the line of his passage across the hills, and amply to provision his advance, were fully justified. He knew nothing of the fall of Donauworth. He believed himself to have full time for a properly organised march to join the Elector of Bavaria, and that meant the capture of Villingen. And the siege of that fortress had the further advantage that it compelled Eugene and his army to remain near the Rhine. Only at this late day, the 18th of July, did Tallard learn that the forces of Marlborough and of Baden had captured the crossing of the Danube and the Lech, and were pouring into Bavaria.

He should have known it earlier, but the despatch which bore him the information had miscarried.

Already, upon the 9th, Marcin had written from Augsburg a pressing letter to Tallard, bidding him neglect everything save an immediate march, and, ill provisioned as he was, and insecure as he would leave his communications, to hasten to the aid of the Elector. Marlborough and Baden (he wrote) had crossed the Danube and the Lech on the 5th and 6th of July. They were before Rhain; and when Rhain fell (as fall it must), all Bavaria would be at their mercy.

This letter Tallard never received.

Marcin was right. Rhain could not possibly hold out: none of the Bavarian strongholds except Ingolstadt were tolerably fortified. Rhain was destined to fall, and with its fall all Bavaria would be the prey of the allied generals.

The Elector, watching all this from just beyond the Lech, was in despair. He proposed to sue for terms unless immediate news of help from the French upon the Rhine should reach him. And if the Elector sued for terms and retired from the contest, France would be left alone to bear the whole weight of the European alliance: its forces would at once be released to act upon the Rhine, in Flanders, or wherever else they would.

When, upon the 14th, Marcin wrote that second letter to Tallard, telling him to neglect everything, to march forward at all costs, and to hasten to Bavaria's relief—the letter which Tallard did receive, and which came to him on the 18th of July, just as he was beginning the siege of Villingen—Rhain still held out; but, even as Tallard read the letter, Rhain had fallen, and the terrible business of the harrying of Bavaria had begun. For Baden and Marlborough proceeded to ravage the country, a cruel piece of work, which Marlborough believed necessary, because it was his supreme intention to bring such pressure to bear upon the Elector as might dissuade him from taking further part in the war.

The villages began to burn (one hundred and twenty were destroyed), the crops to be razed. The country was laid waste to the very walls of Munich, and that capital itself would have fallen had the Englishman and his imperial ally possessed a sufficient train to besiege it.

Tallard was still hesitating to abandon the siege of Villingen when, upon the 21st of July, came yet a *third* message from Marcin, which there was no denying. Tallard learnt from it of the fall of Rhain, of the ravaging of Bavaria, of the march of Marlborough and Baden upon Munich, of the crucial danger in which France lay of seeing the Elector of Bavaria abandon her cause.

Wholly insufficient as the provisioning of the route was, Marcin assured Tallard it was just enough to feed his men and horses during the dash eastwards; and, with all the regret and foreboding necessarily attached to leaving in his rear an unconquered fortress and marching in haste upon an insufficiently provided route, Tallard, on the next day, the 22nd, raised the siege of Villingen and risked his way across the mountains down to the valley of the Danube.

The move was undoubtedly necessary if the Bavarian alliance was to be saved, but it had to be accomplished in fatal haste.

Sickness broke out among Tallard's horses; his squadrons were reduced in a fashion that largely determined the ultimate issue at Blenheim.

His troops, ill fed and exhausted, marched upon wretched rations of bread and biscuit alone, and with that knowledge of insecurity behind them which the private soldier, though he can know so little of the general plan of any campaign, instinctively feels when he is taking part in an advance of doubtful omen.

A week later, upon the 29th of July, the army was in sight of Ulm. It found there but six thousand sacks of flour. It knew that it would find no sufficient provisionment in Augsburg at the end of its advance, yet advance it must unless the forces of Bavaria were to be lost to the cause of Louis XIV.

Five days later the junction was effected, and upon Monday the

4th of August the united armies of Tallard and the Elector of Bavaria faced, in the neighbourhood of Augsburg, the opposing armies of Marlborough and Baden upon the further side of the Lech.

In spite of the deplorable sickness and loss among his horse, the absence of remounts, the exhaustion of his men, the poor provisioning, and the insecurity of the line of supply behind him, Tallard could now present forces somewhat superior (counted by battalions and nominal squadrons)—far superior in artillery—to the forces of the allies.

Had this reluctant and tardy advance of Tallard's on the one hand, the ravaging of Bavaria by Baden and Marlborough on the other, between them constituted the whole of the second phase in the preliminaries of Blenheim, the result of the campaign might have been very different, in spite of the impoverished condition of the Franco-Bavarian Army.

But a third element, of the utmost importance, must be added: the rapid, the secret, and the successful march of Eugene during these same days across the northern part of these same hills which the French had just traversed by their southern passes, and the debouching of that formidable captain with his admirably disciplined force, especially strong in cavalry, upon the upper valley of the Danube to reinforce Marlborough and to decide the war.

So long as Tallard proceeded, with soldierly method, to the proper affirmation of his line of advance and to the reduction of Villingen, Eugene had been pinned to the neighbourhood of the Rhine.

Would Eugene, when the siege of Villingen was raised, and when Tallard had been persuaded to that precipitous eastern move, go back to hold the line of the Rhine against the French forces there situated, or would he decide for the risk of detaching a large command, perhaps of leading it himself, and of joining Marlborough? That was the doubtful factor in Tallard's plans.

As in the case of Marlborough's own march to the Danube, either alternative was possible. The safer course for Eugene, and that one therefore which seemed in the eyes of his enemies the more probable, was for him to remain on the Rhine. But it was conceivable that he would run the risk of leading a force to the Danube; and did he so decide, the whole business of the French remaining on the Rhine was to discover his intention, the whole business of Eugene to hide it.

As in the case of Marlborough's march to the Danube, Eugene was led by a just instinct to gamble on the chance of the French Army in Alsace not noting his move, and of the few troops he left opposite them upon the Rhine sufficing to screen his movements and to give the effect of much larger numbers. In other words, though his task in the coalition was to watch the central Rhine, he decided to take the risk of seeing the Rhine forced, and to march in aid of the English general whom he had himself summoned to Bavaria, with whose genius his own had such sympathy, and at whose side he was to accomplish the marvels of the next seven years.

Like Marlborough, he was successful in concealing his determination, but, with a smaller force than Marlborough's had been, he was able to be more successful still.

Villeroy, who commanded the French upon the Middle Rhine, was informed by numerous deserters and spies that Eugene, after the fall of Villingen, was at Radstadt, and intended detaching but two or three battalions at most from his lines upon the right bank of the Rhine, and these not, of course, for work upon the Danube, but only to cover Wurtemburg by garrisoning Rottweil.

This information, coming though it did from many sources, was calculatedly false, and Eugene's movements, after the siege of Villingen had been raised, were arranged with a masterly penetration of his enemy's mind. A leisurely two days after the siege of Villingen was raised he entered that fortress, ordered the breaches to be repaired, and, in his every order and disposition, appeared determined to remain within the neighbourhood of the Upper Rhine. Nearly a week later he was careful to show himself at Rottweil, hardly a day's march away, apparently doing no more than cover Wurtemburg against a possible French attack from beyond the Rhine; and, so far as such leisure and immobility could testify to his intentions, he proclaimed his determination to remain in that neighbourhood, and in no way to preoccupy himself with what might be going on in the valley of the Upper Danube.

With due deliberation, he left eight battalions in Rottweil to garrison that place, posted seventeen upon his lines upon the Rhine, and himself openly proceeded—and that at no great speed—to march for the valley of the Neckar with 15,000 men.... Those 15,000 had been picked from his army with a particular care; nearly one-third were cavalry in the highest training, and the command, which seemed but one of three detachments all destined to operate upon the Rhine, was in fact a body specially chosen for a very different task. Eugene continued to proceed in this open fashion and slow as far as Tubingen....

It was many days since Tallard had begun his advance; many days since Villeroy, on the Rhine, had been watching the movements of

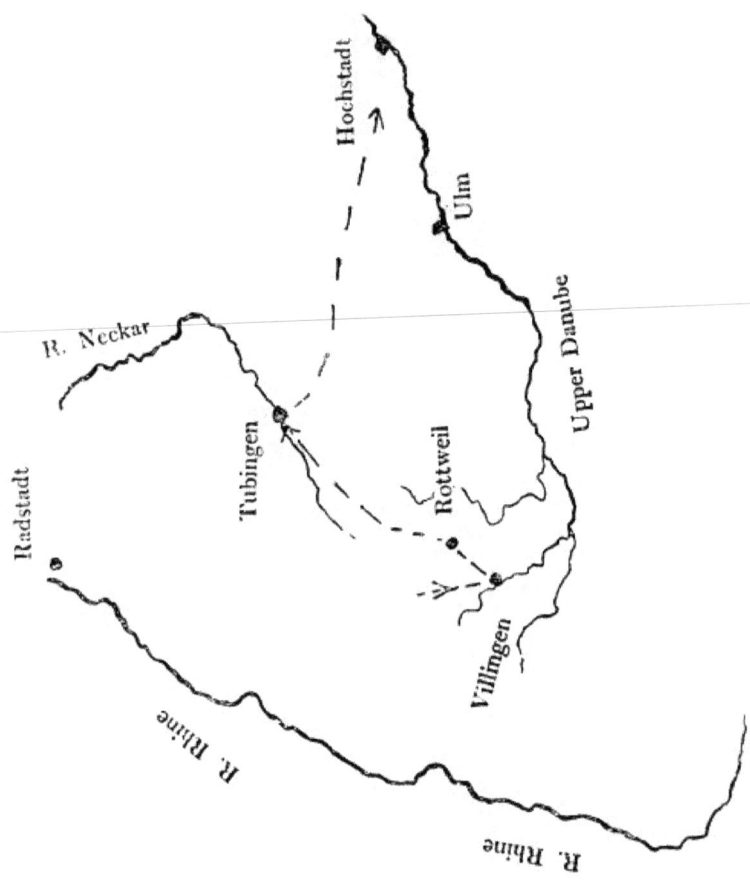

Map showing Eugene's march on the Danube from the Black Forest.

Radstadt

R. Neckar

Tubingen

Rottweil

Villingen

R. Rhine

R. Rhine

Upper Danube

Ulm

Hochstadt

Eugene; and during all these days that great general had done no more than assure his original positions with ample leisure, and to begin, with what was apparently a gross lack of concealment, a return by the Neckar round the north of the Black Forest to the Rhine valley.

Suddenly, from the moment of his reaching Tubingen, all this slow and patient work ceases. Eugene and his 15,000 abruptly disappear.

In place of the open march which all might follow, friend and foe alike, there is a void; in place of clear and reiterated information upon his unhurried movements, there is nothing but a fog, contradictory rumours, fantastic and ill-credited.

Never was a design better kept or concealed to a moment so near its accomplishment. When that design was accomplished, it was to determine, as we shall see in what follows, the whole issue of the campaign of Blenheim.

THE THIRD PHASE

The Appearance of Eugene

The third phase in the operations which led up to the battle of Blenheim is one of no more than nine days.

It stands distinct from all that went before, and must be regarded in history as a sort of little definite and enclosed preface to the great action. The distinctive character of this, the third phase, resides in the completion of the Franco-Bavarian force, its manoeuvring in the presence of the enemy, and its finding itself unexpectedly confronted with the reinforcements of Eugene.

To seize the character of this third phase, the sketch map over the page must be referred to.

It is the 5th of August. Tallard has fully effected his junction with Marcin and the Elector of Bavaria, and the united Franco-Bavarian force lies in and to the east of Ausgburg. On the opposite bank of the river Lech this force is watched by the Army of Marlborough and Baden, which has been ravaging Bavaria. But Marlborough and Baden, though they have an advanced depot at Donauwörth, have their forward munitions and supplies far up northwards. Nördlingen is their advanced base, two days' marching beyond the Danube. A week away to the north Nuremberg contains their only large and perma-nent collection of stores. Marlborough and Baden are in perpetual difficulty for food, for ammunition, and for forage—especially for am-munition.

Since the whole object of Marlborough in marching to the Upper

191

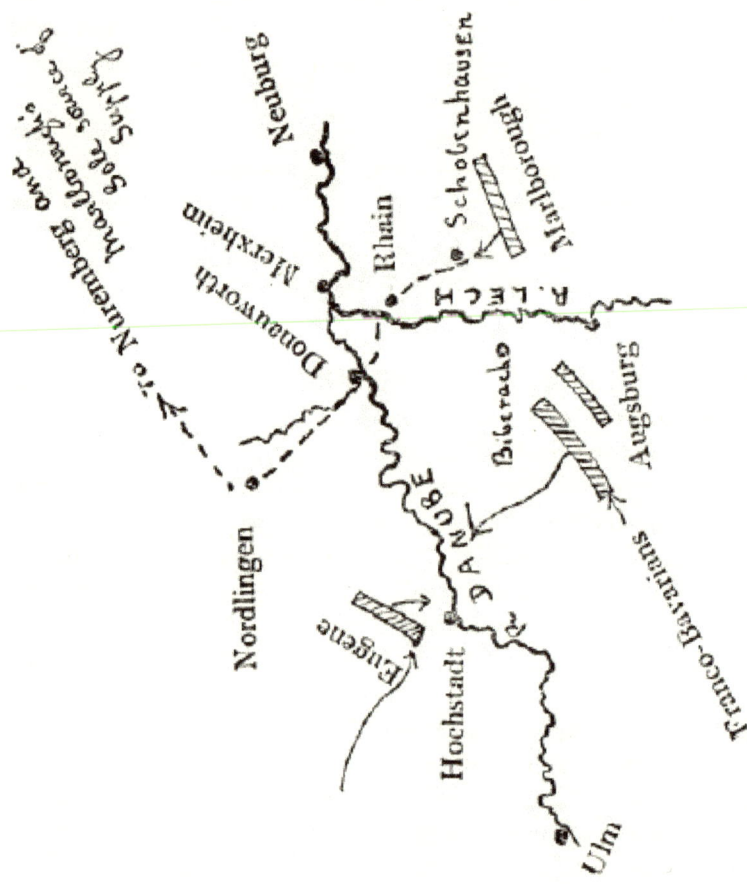

Map showing the situation when Eugene suddenly appeared at Hochstadt, August 5-7, 1704.

Danube was to embarrass in this new seat of war the alliance of the French and Bavarian forces, it is, conversely, the business of the French commander to get him out of the valley of the Upper Danube and restore the liberty of action of the French monarch and of his ally the Elector of Bavaria.

The surest way of getting Marlborough out of the Upper Danube is to threaten his line of supply. He will then be compelled to fall back northward upon his base. Further (though Tallard did not know it at the moment), there is present the very real difficulty of friction between the two commanders of the army opposing him. Marlborough and Baden are not getting on well together. If it were possible for Marlborough to persuade Baden to go off on some little expedition of his own, withdrawing but a few soldiers, Marlborough would be well content, and Marlborough is by far the more formidable of the two men. But though the opportunity for such a riddance of divided command is open, for Prince Louis of Baden is anxious to besiege Ingolstadt, Marlborough dares not weaken the combined forces, even by a few battalions, now that Tallard has effected his junction with the Elector and with Marcin, and that a formidable force is opposed to him.

These elements in the situation, once clearly seized, the sequel follows from them logically enough.

The above describes the situation on the 5th of August.

On the 6th, Wednesday, the united Franco-Bavarian force began its march northward towards the Danube, a march parallel with Marlborough's line of supply, and threatening that line all the way, ready to cut it when once the northern bank of the Danube was reached. Marlborough was compelled, in view of that march, to go back northward, step for step with his opponents. The artery that fed him was in danger, and everything else must be neglected.

In the evening of that Wednesday, August the 6th, Tallard and the Elector were at Biberach, Marlborough and Baden at Schobenhausen, which, as the map shows, lies also a day's march to the north from the last position these troops had held, and was on the way to the crossing of the Danube at Neuburg, as the Franco-Bavarians were on the way to the crossing of the same great river at Dillingen.

On the 7th there was no movement, but on the 8th, the Friday, as the Franco-Bavarian host approached the crossing of the Danube at Dillingen, their leader (if Tallard may be regarded as their leader—he was nominally under the orders of the Elector, but he was the marshal of Louis XIV.) heard suddenly that Eugene *had appeared at Hochstadt with thirty-nine squadrons and twenty battalions.*

The trick was done. The rapid and secret march of Eugene had been accomplished with complete success, and his force was within speaking distance of Marlborough's.

When the news came to the French camp, it was even there evident what a sudden transformation had come over the campaign; but to one who could see, as the historian sees, the moral condition of both forces, the event is more significant still.

A great commander, whose name was henceforth to be linked most closely with that of Marlborough's himself, was present upon the Upper Danube. He brought with him troops not only equivalent in number to a third of his colleague's existing forces, but trained under his high leadership, disciplined in his excellent school, and containing, what will prove essential to the fortunes of the coming battle, a very large proportion of cavalry. Further, the appearance of Eugene at this critical moment permitted Marlborough to rid himself of Louis of Baden, to despatch him to the siege of Ingolstadt in the heart of Bavaria, at once to be free of the clog which the slow decision and slow movements of that general burdened him with, to threaten the heart of the enemy's country by that general's departure on such a mission, and to unite himself and his forces with a man whose methods were after his own heart.

It is true that a minor problem lay before Eugene and Marlborough which must be solved before the great value of the junction they were about to effect could be taken advantage of. Their forces were still separated by the Danube: Marlborough lay a day's march to the south of it, and were he to cross the Danube at Neuburg he would be two days' march from Eugene. But each army was free to march towards the other, and all that their commanders had to decide was upon which side of the river the junction should be effected. Were the junction effected to the south—that is, were Eugene to cross the Danube and join Marlborough in Bavaria—Tallard, crossing the Danube at Dillingen, could strike at the great northern line of communications which conditioned all these movements. It was, therefore, the obvious move for Eugene and Marlborough to join upon the *northern* bank of the Danube, and to move upon and defend that all-important line of communications, point for point, as Tallard might threaten it.

It was on the 8th, the Friday, as I have said, that Eugene's presence was known both to Tallard and to Marlborough, for Eugene had ridden forward and met his colleague.

Upon the 9th, the Saturday, the French marched towards the bridge of Dillingen. Eugene, who was already on the way back to his army, returned to inform Marlborough of this, then rode westward again to his forces, and, while the French made their arrangements for crossing the river on the morrow, he busied himself in conducting his 15,000 eastward down the north bank of the Danube. Three thousand of Marlborough's cavalry went forward to meet him, and to begin that junction between the two forces which was to determine the day at Blenheim.

The next day, Sunday the 10th, the Franco-Bavarian army passed the river and lay in the position with which their forces had in the past been so familiar, the position from Lauingen to Dillingen which Marcin and the Elector had held when, six weeks before, Marlborough and Baden had passed across the Franco-Bavarian front to the north in their march upon Donau worth and the Schellenberg.

On the same Sunday, the 10th, Marlborough had brought up his main force to Rhain, within an hour of the Danube, and Eugene was drawing up his force at a safe distance from the French position north of the village of Münster, and behind the brook of Kessel, where that watercourse joins the Danube.

But, though junction with Marlborough was virtually effected, it must be effected actually before Eugene could think himself safe from that Franco-Bavarian force a day's march behind him, which was three times his own and more. His urgent messages to Marlborough led that commander to march up his men through the night. Before the dawn of August, the 11th broke, Churchill, with twenty battalions, had crossed at Merxheim, and the whole army, marching in two columns, was upon the move—the right-hand column following Churchill to the bridge of Merxheim, the left-hand column crossing the Lech by the bridge of Rhain, to pass the Danube at Donauwörth.

In the afternoon of that Monday the whole of Marlborough's command was passing the Wornitz, and long after sunset, following upon a march which had kept the major part of the great host afoot for more than twenty hours, Eugene and Marlborough were together at the head of 52,000 men, established in unison, and defending, with now no possibility of its interruption, the line of communications from the north.

Every historian of this great business has justly remarked the organisation and the patient genius of the man who made such a concentration possible under such conditions and in such a time, without appreciable loss, at hurried notice, and with a complete success.

It is a permanent example and masterpiece in that inglorious part of war, the function of transport and of marching orders, upon which strategy depends as surely as an army depends on food.

Fully accompanied by his artillery, Marlborough's force could not have accomplished the marvel that it did; yet even this arm was brought up, in the rear of the army, by the morning of Tuesday the 12th, and from that moment, given a sufficient repose, the whole great weapon under the two captains could act as one.

On that same morning, Tuesday the 12th, the Franco-Bavarian army under Tallard and the Elector were choosing out with some deliberation a camp so situated as to block any movement of their enemy up the valley of the Danube. The situation of the camp was designed to make this advance up the Danube so clearly impossible that nothing would be left but what the strategy of the last few days had imposed upon Marlborough, namely, a retreat upon his base northward, away from the Danube, towards Nördlingen. It was not imagined that the two commanders of the imperial forces would attack this Franco-Bavarian position, and so risk a general action; for by a retreat upon Nördlingen their continued existence as an army was assured, while an indecisive result would do them far more harm than it would do their opponents. Did Marlborough and Eugene force an action, it is doubtful whether Tallard had considered the alternative of refusing it.

At any rate, on this Tuesday, the 12th of August, Tallard and the Elector had no intention but to take up a position and camp which would make a retreat up the Danube impossible to Marlborough and Eugene; and certainly, neither imagined that any attempt to force the camp would be made, since an alternative of retreat and complete safety was offered the enemy towards Nördlingen.

While the French *fourriers* were ordering the lines of the encampment—the tents stretching, the streets staking out—the English duke and Eugene overlooked the business from the church tower of Tapfheim and saw what Tallard designed. Between the main of their own forces and the camp which the Franco-Bavarians were pitching was a distance of about five miles. The location of each body was therefore perfectly well known to the other, and rarely have two great hosts lain in mutual presence for full twenty-four hours in so much doubt of an issue, in such exact opposition, and each with so complete an apprehension of his opponent's power.

At this point—let us say noon of Tuesday, August 12th—it is essential for us to dwell upon the character of such battles as that upon which Marlborough was already determined; for by the time, he had seen the French disposition of their camp, the duke had determined upon forcing an action.

It is the characteristic of great captains that they live by and appreciate the heavy risk of war.

When they suffer defeat, history—which soldiers and those who love soldiers so rarely write—contemns the hardiness of their dispositions. When victory, that capricious gift, is granted them, history is but too prone to fall into an opposite error, and to see in their hardihood all of the calculating genius and none of the determined gambler.

Justice would rather demand that the great captain should be judged by the light in the eyes of his men, by the endurance under him of immense fatigues, by the exact accomplishment of one hundred separate things a day, each clearly designed and remembered, by his grasp of great sweeps of landscape, by his digestion of maps and horizons, and finally and particularly by this—that the great captain, whether he loses or he wins, *risks* well: he smells the adventure of war, and is the opposite of those who, whether in their fortunes or their bodies, chiefly seek security.

Judged by all these tests, John Churchill, Duke of Marlborough, was a supreme commander; and it is not the least part in our recognition of this, that the first and chief of the great actions upon which his fame reposes was an action essentially and typically hazardous, and one the disastrous loss of which was as probable as, or more probable than, the successful issue which it obtained.

He could not know the special factor of weakness in his opponent's cavalry; he was to misjudge the first element in the position when he broke his best infantry in the futile attack upon the village. But he was to benefit by those small, hidden, momentary things which determine great battles, and which make of soldiers, as of men who follow the sea, determined despisers of success, and as determined worshippers of the merit which may or may not attain it.

To have led his army as he had led it for now three months, to have designed the general plan that he had designed, and to have accomplished it; to have effected the splendid concentration but a few hours since upon the Kessel—these formed a work sufficient to deserve the reward of victory, Marlborough had the fortune not only to deserve, but to achieve.

The night of that Tuesday fell with no alarm upon the one side or upon the other. In the camp of Marlborough and of Eugene was the knowledge that the twin commanders had determined upon an action; in that of Tallard and the Elector the belief that it was more probable their opponents would follow the general rules of war, and fall back to recruit their supplies by the one route that was widely open to them.

Midnight passed. It was already the morning of Wednesday the 13th before the one had moved, or the other had guessed the nature of his enemy's plan.

It was moonless and pitch-dark, save for the dense white mist which, in the marshy lands of that river valley, accompanies the turn of the August night. This mist had risen and covered the plain. The little villages were asleep after their disturbance by the advent of so many armed men. The cockcrows of midnight were now well past when there was stir in Marlborough's camp, and from this moment, somewhere about two of the morning of Wednesday, August the 13th, the action of Blenheim begins.

PART 5

The Action

The field of Blenheim has changed in its physical aspect less than any other of the great battlefields of Europe during the two hundred years and more that have passed since Marlborough's victory.

He who visits today this quiet Bavarian cornland, with its pious and happy peasantry, its modest wealth, and its contempt for haste and greed, sees, if he come in the same late summer of the year, just what the mounted parties saw who rode out upon that Wednesday before the eight columns of Marlborough and Eugene under the early morning.

Thus, approaching the field of Blenheim from the east, the view consists in a low and strangely regular line of closely-wooded hills to the right and northwards; southwards, and to the left, a mass of under-growth, the low trees of the marshes, occasional gaps of rank herbage which make bright green patches interspersing the woodland, mark the wide and marshy course of the Danube, with its belt of alluvial soil and swamp on either side.

Between this stretch of damp river-ground to the south and the regular low wooded hills to the north lies a plain just lifted above the level of the river by such few feet as are sufficient to drain it and no more. Crossing this plain transversely, on their way to the Danube, ooze and trickle rather than run certain insignificant streams; each rises in the wooded hills to the north, falls southward, and in the length of a very few miles reaches the main river. These streams are found, as one goes up the great valley, at every mile or so. With one, the Nebel, we shall be particularly concerned, for during the action at Blenheim it formed the only slight obstacle separating the two armies. This plain, which in August is all stubble, is some three miles across, such a space separates the hills from the river, and that distance, or a trifle more, is the full length of the little muddy brooks which thus occasionally intersect it.

To the eye which takes in that landscape at a first glance, bare of crops and under a late summer sun, the plain seems quite even and undisturbed by any hollows or rolls of land. It is, in fact, like most such apparently simple terrains, slightly diversified: its diversity is enough to affect in some degree the disposition of soldiers, to afford in certain places occasional cover, and to permit of opportunities for defence.

But these variations from the flat are exceedingly slight. The hollow which the Nebel has made, for instance, is not noticed on foot or even in mechanical traction as one follows the main road which runs the whole length of the plain, though if one goes across country on foot, one notices the slight bank of a few feet separating the cultivated land from a narrow belt of rough grass, which is boggy in wet weather, and which, in varying breadth, accompanies the course of the stream.

The plain also, as might be expected, rises slightly from its low shelf just above the Danube swamps and meadows, to the base of the hills. Its ascent in its whole three miles of breadth is but sixty feet.

Over this level sweep of tilled land rise at intervals the spires of rare villages, round which scattered houses and gardens of the Bavarian sort—broad-eaved, flat-roofed, gay with flowers—are gathered. But for these few human groups there is no break in the general aspect of the quite open fields.

As might be expected, an interrupted chain of such villages marks the line of the great river from Donauwörth to Ulm, each standing just on the bank and edge of what for long was the flood-ground of the Danube, and is still in part unreclaimed marsh and water meadow. Each is distant a mile or two from its next fellow. Thus, nearest Donauwörth we have Münster, upon which the left of the allied army reposed when it lay in camp before the battle. Next in order come Tapfheim and Schwenningen, through which that army marched to the field. Further up-stream another group stretches beyond the Nebel, the hamlet of Sonderheim, the little town of Hochstadt, the village of Steinheim, etc.; and, in the middle of this line, at the point where the Nebel falls into the old bed of the Danube, is built that large village of *Blindheim*, which, under its English form of Blenheim, has given the action the name it bears in this country.

I say "the old bed of the Danube," for one feature, and one alone, in that countryside has changed in the two hundred years, though the change is not one which the eye can note as it surveys the plain, nor one which greatly affects the story of the action. This change is due to the straightening of the bed of the great river.

At the time when Blenheim was fought, the Danube wound in great loops, with numerous islands and backwaters complicating its course, and swung back and forth among the level swamps of its valley. It runs to-day in an artificial channel, which takes the average, as it were, of these variations, drains the flood-ground, and leaves the old bed in the form of stagnant, abandoned lengths of water or reeds, in which the traveller can trace the former vagaries of the river. Thus Blindheim, which stood just above the broad and hurrying water at the summit of one such loop, is now 800 yards away from the artificial trench which modern engineering has dug for the river. But the new channel has no effect upon the landscape to the eye. The floor on which the Danube runs is still a mass of undergrowth and weeds and grass, which marks off the cultivated land on the south, as it has been limited since men first ploughed.

I have said that the little slow and muddy streamlet called the Nebel must particularly meet with our attention, because it formed at the beginning of the action of Blenheim a central line dividing the two hosts, and round its course may be grouped the features of the terrain upon which the battle was contested.

Blindheim, or, as we always call it, Blenheim, lay, as we have seen, just above the bank of the Danube at the mouth of this stream. Following up the water (which is so insignificant that in most places a man can cross it unaided in summer), at the distance of about one mile, is the village of Unterglauheim, lying above the *left* bank, as Blenheim does above the right. Further on, another three-quarters of a mile up the *right* bank, is the village of Oberglauheim; and where the water dribbles in various small streams from the hills, and at their base, where the various tiny rivulets join to form the Nebel, at the edge of the woods, is Schwennenbach.

The tiny hamlet of Weilheim may be regarded as an appendix of this last or of Oberglauheim indifferently. It lies opposite the latter village, but on the further side of the stream, and about half a mile away.

Right behind Oberglauheim, at the base of the hills to the westward, and well away from the Nebel, is the larger village of Lutzingen.

These names, and that of the Nebel, are sufficient for us to retain as we follow the course of the battle, remembering as we do so that one good road, the road by which the allies marched in the morning to the field from Münster, and the road by which the Franco-Bavarian forces retreated after the defeat—the main road from Donauwörth to Ulm—traversed, and still traverses, the terrain in its whole length. (The railway from Ulm to Donauwörth follows the line of this road exactly, and is almost the only modern feature upon the field.)

It was at two in the morning of Wednesday the 13th of August that the allies broke camp and began their march westward towards the field of Blenheim.

That they intended to reach that field was not at first apparent. They might equally well have designed a retirement upon Nördlingen, and it was this that the commanders of the Franco-Bavarian army believed them to intend. The dense mist which covered the marshes of the river and the plain above clung to the soil long after sunrise. It was not until seven o'clock that the advancing columns of the enemy were observed from the French camp, distant about a mile away, and beginning to deploy in order to set themselves in line of battle. But though they were then first seen, their arrival had been appreciated two hours before, (Mr Fortescue writes as though this were not the case. He has overlooked Tallard's letter to the minister of war of the 4th of September), and the French line was already drawn up opposite them on the further bank of the Nebel as they deployed. (A small body was left at Unterglauheim, but withdrawn as the allies advanced; and outposts lay, of course, upon the line of Marlborough's advance, and fell back before it.)

The French order of battle is no longer to be found in the archives, though we can reconstruct it fairly enough, and in parts quite accurately, from the separate accounts of the action given by Tallard, by Marcin himself, by Eugene, and from English sources. The line of battle of the allies we possess in detail; and the reader can approach with a fair accuracy the dispositions of the two armies at the moment when the action began, though it must be understood that the full deployment of Marlborough and Eugene was not accomplished until after midday on account of the difficulty the latter commander found in posting his extreme right at the foot of the hills and in the woods of Schwennenbach; while it must be further noted that the first shots of the battle sounded long before its main action began, that is, long before noon—for the French guns upon the front of their line opened at long range as early as nine o'clock, and continued a lively cannonade until, at half-past twelve, Eugene being at last ready, the first serious blows were delivered by the infantry.

All this we shall see in what followed. Meanwhile we must take a view of the two armies as they stood ranged for battle before linesman or cavalryman had moved.

The map on following page indicates in general terms the situation of the opposing forces.

The French stood upon the defensive upon the western bank of the Nebel. Their camp lay behind their line of battle, a stretch of tents nearly two miles long.

It is particularly to be noted that though, for the purpose of fighting this battle, they formed but one army, the two separate commands, that of the Elector (with Marcin) and that of Tallard, were separately treated and separately organised. The point is of importance if we are to understand the causes of their defeat, for it made reinforcement difficult, and put two loosely joined wings where a strong centre should have stood.

Tallard's command, thirty-six battalions and (nominally) forty-four squadrons, extended from Blindheim to the neighbourhood of Oberglauheim. Its real strength may be taken at about 10,000 to 18,000 infantry, and at the most 5,200 cavalry; but of these last a great number could not be used as mounted men.

The village of Oberglauheim itself, and all that stretched to the left of it up the Nebel as far as the base of the hills, was occupied by the army of Marcin and the Elector of Bavaria. This force was forty-two battalions and eighty-three squadrons strong. The cavalry in this second army, the left of the whole force, had been less severely tried by disease, rapid marching, and ill provisionment than that of Tallard. We may reckon it, therefore, at its full or nearly its full strength, and say that Marcin and the Elector commanded over 20,000 men and close upon 10,000 horse.

In a word, the total of the Franco-Bavarian forces, though we have no documents by which to estimate their exact numbers, may be regarded, from the indications we have of the losses of the cavalry, etc., as certainly more than fifty and certainly less than fifty-three thousand men, infantry and cavalry combined. To these we must add ninety guns, disposed along the whole front after the fashion of the time, and these under the general and separate command of Frézelière.

★★★★★★★★★★

Mr Fortescue gives the total force of cavalry under Marcin and the Elector at one hundred and eight squadrons and the infantry at forty-six battalions. The French official record gives forty-two battalions (not forty-six) and eighty-three squadrons in the place of one hundred and eight. Mr Fortescue gives no authority for his larger num-

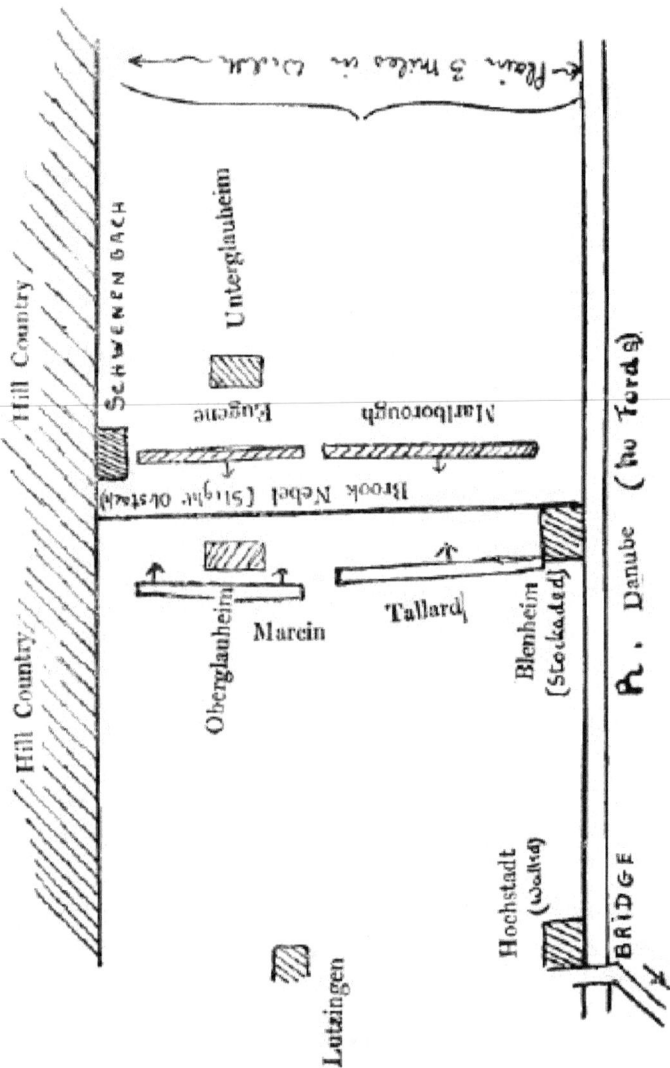

The Elements of the Action of Blenheim.

bers; and, on the general principle that, in a contested action, each force knows best about its own organisation, I have followed these official records of the French as the most trustworthy.

★★★★★★★★★★

This disposition of the guns in a chain along the whole front of the line the reader is begged especially to note.

The particular dispositions of the Franco-Bavarian forces must now be seized, and to appreciate these let us first consider the importance of the village of Blenheim.

Blenheim, a large scattered village, with the characteristic Bavarian gardens round each house, lay so close to the course of the Danube as it then ran that there was no possibility of an enemy's force passing between it and the river. It formed a position easy to be defended, lying as it did on a slight crest above the brook Nebel, where that brook joined the main river.

Blenheim, therefore, if it were soundly held, blocked any attempt to turn the French line upon that side; but if it were carried by the enemy, that enemy would then be able to enfilade the whole French line, to take it in flank and to roll it up.

Tallard, therefore, with perfect judgment, posted in the village a very strong force of his infantry. This force consisted at first of nine battalions, shortly after, by reinforcement, of sixteen battalions of foot, and further of four regiments of dragoons *dismounted*.

★★★★★★★★★★

It is essential to note this point. Mr Fortescue talks of the dragoons "trotting" to "seal up the space between the village and the Danube." If they trotted it was as men trot in their boots, for they were on foot. The incident sufficiently proves the ravages which disease accompanying an insufficiently provided march had worked in Tallard's cavalry.

★★★★★★★★★★

Not content with throwing into Blenheim between 8000 and 10,000 men, Tallard placed behind the village and in its neighbourhood a further reserve of at least eleven battalions. Of his thirty-six battalions, therefore, only nine remained to support his cavalry over the whole of the open field between Blenheim and Oberglauheim, a distance of no less than 3500 yards. Consequently, this great gap had to be held in the main by his insufficient and depleted cavalry. Eight squadrons of these (of the red-coated sort called the *Gendarmerie*) formed the first section of this line, stretching from Blenheim to the neighbourhood of the main road and a little beyond it. Further along, towards Oberglauheim, another ten squadrons of cavalry were lined up to fill the rest of the gap. In a second line were ten more squadrons of cavalry under Silly; and the nine battalions of infantry remaining, when those in and near Blenheim had been subtracted, lay also in the second line, in support of the cavalry of the first line.

Such was Tallard's disposition, of which it was complained both at the time and afterwards that in putting nearly the whole of his infantry upon his right in the village of Blenheim and behind it he far too greatly weakened the great open gap between Blenheim and Oberglauheim. His chief misfortune was not, however, lack of judgment in this, but the character of the man who commanded the troops in Blenheim. This general officer, whose name was Clérambault, was of the sort to be relied upon when orders are strict and plain in their accomplishment: useless in an emergency; but it is only an emergency that proves the uselessness of this kind of man. The army of the Elector and Marcin, which continued the line, similarly disposed their considerable force of cavalry in front, along the banks of the stream; their infantry lay, in the main, in support of this line of horse and behind it; they had also filled Oberglauheim with a mass of infantry; but the disposition of this left half of the French line is of less interest to the general reader, for it held its own, and contributed to the defeat only in this, that it did not at the critical moment send reinforcements to Tallard upon the right.

In general, then, we must see the long French line set out in two main bodies. That on the right, under Tallard, had far the greater part of its infantry within or in support of Blenheim, while the cavalry, for the most part, stretched out over the open centre of the field, with Silly's ten squadrons and what was left of the infantry in reserve.

★★★★★★★★★★

Nearly all the English authorities and many of the French authorities speak of the whole twenty-seven battalions out of Tallard's thirty-six as being in Blenheim from the beginning of the action, and Mr Fortescue adds the picturesque, but erroneous, touch that "Marlborough" (before the action) "had probably counted every one of the twenty-seven battalions into it" (Blenheim).

This error is due to the fact that at the close of the battle there actually were twenty-seven battalions within the village, but they were not there at the beginning of the action; and Marlborough cannot, therefore, have "counted" them going in. The numbers, as I have said, were first nine battalions, with four regiments of dismounted dragoons; then, a little later, another seven, making sixteen; then, *much later,* and

206

when the French were hard pressed, yet another *eleven*, lying as a reserve *behind* Blenheim, were called into the village by the incompetence of Clérambault who commanded in Blenheim. He should have sent them to help the centre—as will be seen in the sequel.

★★★★★★★★★★

That on the left, under Marcin and the Elector, had its far more numerous cavalry similarly disposed upon its front along the brook, most of its infantry behind, and a great number of these holding the village of Oberglauheim, with cavalry in front of them also. Along the whole line the ninety guns were disposed in a chain, as I have described.

Such being the disposition of the French troops, let us now turn to that of the Imperialists and their English and other allies under Eugene and Marlborough. These appeared within a mile of the French position by seven in the morning, and all that part of their left which lay between the river and the highroad was drawn up within long range of the French artillery somewhat before nine o'clock. But, as a glance at the map will show, their right had to march much further in order to come into line along the course of the Nebel, the course of which leans away from the line of Marlborough's advance. The difficulty of swampy land under the hills and of woods made the final disposition of the extreme left particularly tardy and tedious, nor was it fully drawn up until just after midday. During all the interval of three hours a brisk cannonade at long range had been proceeding from the guns in front of the French line—and, as nearly always the case with artillery before the modern quick-firer, was doing less damage than the gunners imagined.

When the allied line was finally formed its disposition was as follows:—

On the extreme left six columns of infantry, half of which consisted of British regiments. (1st battalion Royal Scots; 1st battalion First Guards; 8th, 20th, 16th, 24th, and 10th Foot; 3rd battalion 23rd Royal Welsh, 21st Royal Scots Fusiliers.)

These stood immediately opposite the village of Blenheim, and were designed for that attack upon it, which Marlborough, in his first intention, desired to make the decisive feature of the action.

Next, towards the main road, came four lines, two of infantry before and behind, and in the midst two parallel lines of cavalry, the foremost of which was British, and in which could be distinguished the mounting and horsemanship of the Scots Greys. (From one to

207

three squadrons each of the 1st, 3rd, 5th, 6th, 17th Dragoon Guards, 5th Royal Irish Dragoons, and a squadron of the Scots Greys.)

Next again, to the north, and astraddle of the great road, lay the main force; this it will be remarked was drawn up precisely in front of that part in the long French line which was the weakest, and which indeed consisted of little more than the ten squadrons of horse which filled the gap between the *Gendarmerie* and Oberglauheim. This main force was also drawn up in four great lines; the first of infantry, the two next of cavalry, the rear of infantry: it contained no British troops, and, with the others already mentioned, formed Marlborough's command. All the rest, along the north and the east, along the left bank of the Nebel, from Willheim up into the woods, and the gorge at the source of the brook, was Eugene's command—not a third of the whole.

As to the total strength of the allied forces which we must attempt to estimate as we estimated that of the Franco-Bavarians, we know it accurately enough—it was some 52,000 men. The opposing hosts were therefore little different in numbers. But it is of great importance to note the disproportion of cavalry. In that of the Imperialists under Marlborough and Eugene, not only was the cavalry better mounted and free from the fatigue and disease that had ravaged Tallard's horses, but it was nearly double in number that of its opponents. On the other hand, the artillery of the allies was far inferior. Only sixty-six guns at the most were opposed to the French ninety. (This is the number given by Eugene. Fortescue and most English authorities give fifty-two.)

Blenheim, in the issue, turned out to be a cavalry battle—a battle won by cavalry, and its effect clinched by cavalry. The poor role played by the guns and the inability of the French to make use of their numerical superiority in this arm was a characteristic of the time, which had not yet learnt to use the cannon as a mobile weapon.

A general action is best understood if the reader is first told the main event, and later observes how the details of its progress fit in with that chief character of it.

The main event of the battle of Blenheim was simply this:—

Marlborough first thought to carry Blenheim: he failed. Having failed before the village of Blenheim, he determined to break through Tallard's left, which formed the centre of the French line, and was successful in doing so. By thus breaking through the centre of the French line, he isolated all Tallard's army upon the right, except such small portion of it as broke and fled from the field. The remainder crowded into the village of Blenheim, was contained, surrounded, and compelled to surrender.

The undefeated left half of the French line was therefore compelled to retire, and did so through Lutzingen upon the Danube, crossing which river in hurried retreat, it fell back upon Ulm. In one conspectus, the position at the beginning of the action was this:—

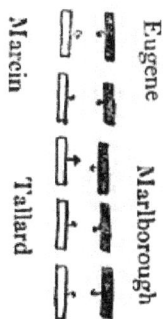

Marcin   Eugene

Tallard   Marlborough

and at the end of it this:—

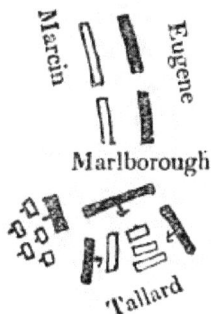

Marcin   Eugene

Marlborough

Tallard

Now let us follow the details of the fight which brought about such a result.

First, at half-past twelve when all was ready, came Marlborough's attack upon Blenheim.

We have seen some pages back how well advised was Tallard to treat Blenheim as the key of his position, and how thoroughly that large village, once properly furnished with troops and fortified with palisades, would guarantee his right. On that very account, Marlborough was determined to storm it; for if it fell, there would instantly follow upon its fall a complete victory. The whole French line would be turned.

It may be argued that Marlborough here attempted the impossible, but it must be remembered, in the first place, that he was by temperament a man of the offensive and of great risks. His first outstanding action, that of the Schellenberg, proved this, and proved it in his favour. Five years later, in one of his last actions, that of Malplaquet, this characteristic of his was to appear in his disfavour. At any rate, risk was in the temperament of the man, and it is a temperament which in warfare accounts for the greatest things.

First and last, some 10,000 men were employed against the one point of Blenheim; and the assault upon the village, though a failure, forms one of the noblest chapters in the history of British arms.

It was one o'clock of the afternoon when the serious part of the action opened by the two first lines of Marlborough's extreme left advancing under Lord Cutts to pass the Nebel, to cross the pasture beyond, and to force the palisades of the village. The movement across the stream was undertaken under a fire of grape from four guns posted upon a slight rise outside the village.

Cutts' body crossed the brook in face of this opposition, re-formed under the bank beyond, left their Hessian contingent in shelter there as a reserve, while the British, who were the remainder of the body, advanced against the palisades.

The distance is one of about 150 yards. The Guards and the four regiments with them, (the 10th, 21st, 23rd, and 24th), came up through the long grass of the aftermath, Row at their head. Two thirds of that short distance was passed in silence. The guns upon the slope beyond could not fire at a mark so close to their own troops behind the palisades. The English had orders not to waste a shot until they had carried the line of those palisades with the bayonet. The French behind the palisades reserved their fire.

It was one of those moments which the eighteenth century, with its amazingly disciplined professional armies, alone can furnish in all the history of war, an episode of which the Guards at Fontenoy were, a generation later, to afford the supreme example, and one depending on that perfection of restraint for which the English service was deservedly renowned. When a distance but a yard or two longer than a cricket pitch separated the advancing English from the palisades, the French volley crashed out. One man in three of the advancing line fell agonised or dead.

The British regiments, still obedient to Row's instructions, reserved their fire until their leader touched the woodwork with his sword. Then they volleyed, and having fired, wrestled with the palisades as though to drag them down by sheer force. Perhaps some few parties here and there pressed in through a gap, but as the English soldiers struggled thus, gripped and checked by the obstacle, the French fire poured in again was deadly; the British assault was broken, and fled in disorder over the little field to the watercourse. As it fled, the Gendarmerie charged it in flank, captured the colours of the 21st, were repelled again by the Hessians in reserve (who recaptured the flag), and the first fierce moment of the battle was over.

One-third of Cutts' command had been concerned in this first failure against Blenheim village. Two-thirds remained to turn that failure into a success. But before this second two-thirds was launched, there took place an episode in the battle, not conspicuously noted at the time, and given a minor importance in all accounts save Tallard's own. It was significant in the extreme.

As Cutts' broken first line was passing out of range and was effecting its retirement after the first disorder, and after the Hessians had repelled the first and partial cavalry charge of the French, the *Gendarmerie*, eight squadrons strong, prepared to charge again as a whole. They came upon the English before these had regained safety. Cutts naturally begged for cavalry to meet this cavalry danger, and Lumley sent five British squadrons to cross the stream and check the French charge. The English horse came to the further bank after some little difficulty with the mud of the sluggish stream, which difficulty has been exaggerated, and in no way affected the significance of what followed.

★★★★★★★★★★

For some reason or other, the exaggeration of this feature—the marshiness of the banks of the Nebel—mars many an English account of the action. The Nebel, of course, was something of an obstacle, slight as it was, and in places the meadows on its bank widen out and are soft even in the dry weather which had as a whole distinguished the three weeks before Blenheim. But the crossing of that obstacle by the cavalry was nothing in the story of the battle. It was what the cavalry did *after they crossed* that counted.

★★★★★★★★★★

For what followed was the singular sight of eight French squadrons charging down a slope against only five, those five cramped in the hollow near a stream bed, and yet succeeding in receiving the shock of the charge of numbers so greatly superior, and, so far from yielding, breaking the offensive of their opponents into a confusion.

I repeat, it was but an episode, one that took place early in the day, and apparently of no weight. But, in a general historical view of the battle, it is of the first importance, for it showed what different stuff the opposed cavalries were made of, and that the Allied Army, which was already numerically the superior in cavalry—nearly double its opponents—had also better mounts, better riders, and a better discipline in that arm. A universal observer, seeing this one early detail in the battle of Blenheim, might have prophesied that the action would be a cavalry action as a whole, and that the cavalry of Marlborough would decide it.

I left Cutts prepared to launch the remaining two-thirds of his force at Blenheim village, in the hope of accomplishing what the first third had failed to do.

The whole combined body which the French had estimated at 10,000 men, and which seems to have been at least of some 8000, surged up in the second attempt against the palisades of the village. Part of that line and many of the outer gardens were carried, but the attack could not be driven home. It was, perhaps, at this moment that Tallard sent in those extra men which raised the French battalions in Blenheim from nine to sixteen, and gave the defenders, behind their walls, a force equal to the attackers. At any rate, the main attack was thrust back as the first had been, and the great corps of men, huddled, confused, rallied here and there as best they could be, broke from before the village.

The loss was terrible, and Marlborough having failed, not only failed, but saw that he had failed. It was his salvation. His subordinates would have returned to the fruitless attack with troops already shaken and dreading the ground. Marlborough ordered a false attack to be kept up from the further bank, upon the village, and, with that elasticity of command which is the prime factor of tactical success, and which commonly distinguishes youth rather than middle age in a general, turned all his efforts upon the centre. (Marlborough was at this moment fifty-four years and two months old.)

Here the main road crosses the Nebel by a stone bridge. Four other bridges had been thrown across at other points between this stone bridge and Unterglauheim. By these the infantry were crossing, which infantry, it will be remembered, stood as to their first line in front of the cavalry in the main central body. This almost undisputed passage of the Nebel would not have been possible had not the distance between

Blenheim and Oberglauheim been what it was. The gap was great, the French line defending it too thin, and the possibility of a cross fire defending the centre was eliminated by the width of that centre.

Even as it was, the passage of the Nebel led to one very difficult moment which might by accident or genius have turned the whole action in favour of the French; and in connection with this episode it must be remembered that the French commanders asserted that the passage of the Nebel was no success on the part of their enemy, but was deliberately permitted to that enemy in order that he might be overwhelmed upon the opposing slope, with the marshy stream behind him, when the time for a counter-attack should come.

The moment came when the greater part of Marlborough's cavalry had crossed, but before they had fully formed upon the further bank. While they were still in the disorder of forming, the French cavalry upon their left—that is, between the main road and Blenheim—charged down the slight slope, and something like a dismemberment of the whole of Marlborough's mounted line began. It was checked for a moment by the fire of the British infantry, during which check Marlborough brought over certain Danish and Hanoverian squadrons which had remained upon the further bank. But the French charged again, and though infantry of Marlborough's which was pouring over the stream up beyond the stone bridge came up in time to prevent a complete breakdown, the moment was critical in the extreme. All Marlborough's centre was pressed and shaken; a further spurt against it and it would break.

It was such a moment as commanders of rapid decision and quick eye have always seized; and if it be asked how Tallard should have seized it, the answer is that there were French guns to mass, there was French infantry in Blenheim unused, and more in reserve behind Blenheim wholly useless. There were the ten squadrons of Tallard's second line of cavalry under Silly, a couple of hundred yards away, to be summoned in a few moments.

Rapid decision and keen sight of this sort would have done the business; but Tallard was slow of perception; an excellent strategist, but short-sighted and a great gentleman; one, moreover, who had advanced by favour rather than by intrigue. He lost the moment.

Marlborough's cavalry managed to form, struggling beyond the brook, and the last final phase of the action was at hand—for Marlborough's cavalry would reiterate that general lesson which the whole battle teaches, to wit, that the horse of the allies was not only far stronger numerically, but far better trained than the French cavalry before them, and, with equal chances, must destroy it. Tallard, by missing his moment, had permitted those equal chances to be restored. Even so, yet one other last accident favoured the French. The hour was about five, or rather later in the mid-afternoon.

In order to be able to form his cavalry beyond the Nebel, Marlborough wanted to have a clear right flank, and with that object he had launched from 6,000 to 7,000 Hanoverians against Oberglauheim. The excellent infantry of Blainville, less in numbers, emerged from the village, threw the Hanoverians into gross disorder, and captured their commander. At this point there was beginning to be a rout. This new French success, properly followed up, would again have had a chance to break the allied centre at its weakest point, just at the link where Marlborough joined on to Eugene.

Marcin, inferior as was his command, gripped the opportunity, sent cavalry at once to Oberglauheim, and that cavalry charged. But here the greatness of Marlborough as a personal commander suddenly appeared. He seized the whole character of the moment in a way that Tallard on his first chance had wholly failed to do. He put himself in person at the head of the Danish brigade that lay in reserve, brought it across the rivulet, and came just in time to take the charge of the French cavalry. Even as that charge was preparing, Marlborough sent to Eugene for cavalry at the gallop. He (Marlborough) must hold fast with his Danes against the French horse—five minutes, ten, fifteen at the most—till help should come from the right.

Here, again, another factor in the success of the day appeared—that Eugene and Marlborough understood each other.

Eugene had just suffered a sharp check upon the extreme right; he was re-forming for a new attack when he got Marlborough's message. Without the loss of a moment in weighing his own immediate necessities, he sent Fugger thundering off, and Fugger, with the imperial cuirassiers, came galloping full speed upon Marlborough's right flank just as the French charge was at its hardest pressure upon the Danish line. He took that French charge in flank, broke its impetus, permitted the Danish infantry to hold their own, and so compelled the French horse to fall back; within a quarter of an hour from its inception the peril of a breach in Marlborough and Eugene's centre was thus dissolved.

Here, then, is yet another incident in the battle, which shows not only on which side rapidity of perception lay, but also on which side lay sympathy between commanders, and, most important of all, the discipline and material eminence of the dominating arm.

It was now nearly six o'clock, and the August sun was red and low in the face of the English General. The French line still stood intact before him.

Marlborough's first great effort against Blenheim had disastrously failed all during the earlier afternoon; he had but just escaped a terrible danger, and had but barely been saved, by Eugene's promptitude in reinforcement, from seeing his line cut in two. Nevertheless, he was the master of the little daylight that remained. His cavalry, and indeed nearly all his troops, were now formed beyond the Nebel; he had the mass of his forces now all gathered opposite the weakest part of the French line. It was his business to pierce that line and to conquer.

As he advanced upon it, the French infantry, then stationed over the long evening shadows of the slope, though there deplorably few in numbers, met his advance by so accurate a fire that his own line for a moment yielded. Even then the day might have been retrieved if the French cavalry under Tallard's command had been capable of a charge. To charge—if we may trust the commander's record—they received a clear order. As a point of fact, charge they did not. A failure to comprehend, a tardy delivery of the dispatch, fatigue, or error was to blame—we have no grounds on which to base a decision. There was a discharge of musketry from the saddle, an abortive attempt to go forward, which in a few minutes was no more an attempt but a complete failure, and in a few more minutes not a failure but a rout. The words of Tallard himself, who saw that almost incredible thing, and who writes as an eye-witness, are sufficiently poignant. They are these:—

"I saw one instant in which the battle was won if the cavalry had not turned and abandoned the Line."

What happened was that the incipient, doubtful, and confused French charge had broken before a vigorous and united countercharge of Marlborough's cavalry: the French horse backed, turned, bunched, fell into a panic; and when the mass of their cavalry had fled in that panic, the French centre, that is, the thin line of infantry still standing there, were ridden through and destroyed.

They lay in heaps of dead or wounded, cut down with the sword, for the most part unbroken in formation, their feet eastward whence the charge had come, and their faces to the sky. Over and beyond those corpses rode the full weight of Marlborough's cavalry, right through Tallard's left, which was the centre of the French line, while

215

Tallard vainly called for troops to come out of Blenheim and check the fury, and as vainly sent for reinforcements to come from Marcin on the left, which should try and dam the flood that was now pouring through the bulwark of his ranks. On the left, Marcin heard too late. As to the messenger to Blenheim on the right he was taken prisoner; Tallard himself, hastening to that village, was taken prisoner in turn.

What followed, at once something inevitable and picturesque, must not be too extended in description for the purpose of a purely military recital. The centre being pierced, while the left under Marcin and the Elector still held its own against Eugene, the right, that is, the huddled battalions—now twenty-seven—within Blenheim village, and the four mounted regiments of dragoons therein, were the necessary victims of the victory. The piercing of the centre had cut them off from all aid. They were surrounded and summoned to surrender.

Clérambault: their commander, had already drowned himself in despair, or had been drowned in a deplorable attempt at flight—at any rate, was dead.

Blausac, an honest man, the second in command, refused to surrender. British cavalry rode round to prevent all egress from the village upon its western side. Churchill brought up the mass of Marlborough's infantry. Upon the side towards the Danube the churchyard was stormed and held. Still Blausac would not ask for terms.

It looked for a moment, under the setting sun of that fatal day, as though the 11,000 thus isolated within the streets of Blenheim would be massacred for mere glory, for Blausac was still obstinate. A subordinate officer, who saw that all was lost, harangued the troops into surrender, and the last business of the great battle was over.

As darkness gathered, the undefeated left under Marcin and the Elector—the half now alone surviving out of the whole host, the other half or limb being quite destroyed or surrendered—retreated with such few prisoners and such few colours as they had taken. They retreated hastily with all their train and their artillery, abandoning their camp, of course, and all through the night poured towards the Danube and built their bridges across the stream.

Darkness checked the pursuit. Some few remnants of Tallard's escaped to join the retreat. The rest were prisoners or dead.

Of the fifty odd thousand men and ninety guns that had marshalled twelve hours before along the bank of the Nebel, 12,000 men had fallen, 11,000 had surrendered, and one-third of the pieces were in the hands of the enemy.

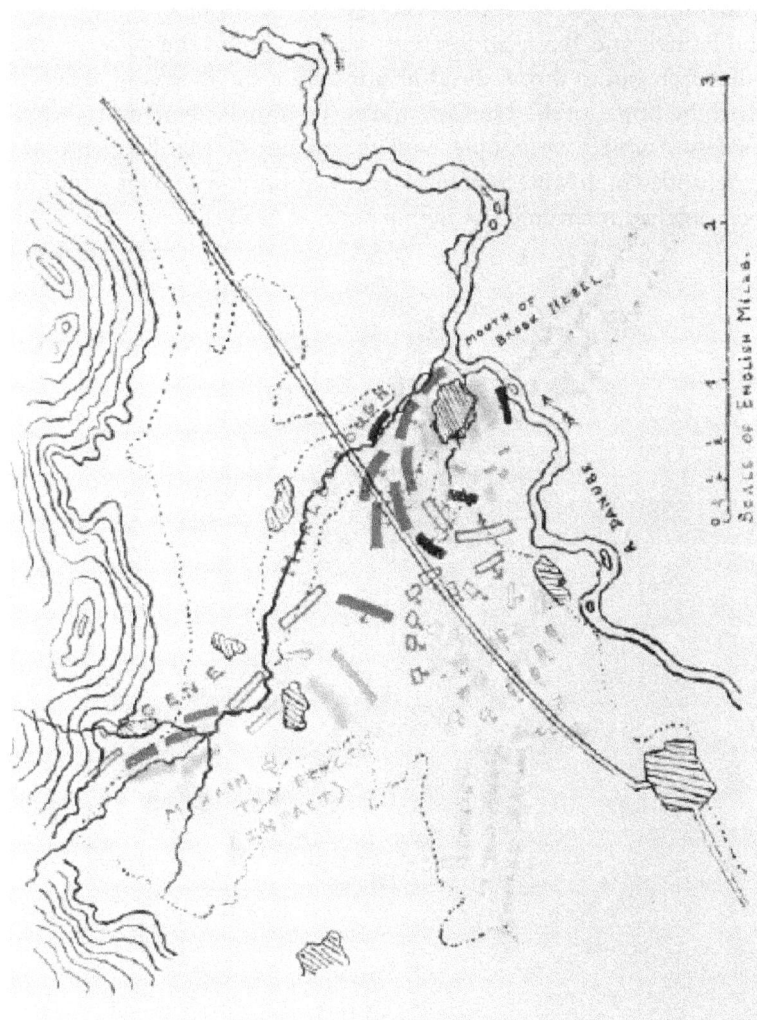

THE BATTLE OF BLENHEIM

SCALE OF ENGLISH MILES.

The political consequences of this great day were more considerable by far than was even its character of a military success. It was the first great defeat which marked the turn of the tide against Louis XIV. It was the first great victory which stamped upon the conscience of Europe the genius of Marlborough. It wholly destroyed all those plans, of which the last two years had been full, for an advance upon Vienna by the French and Bavarian forces. It utterly cleared the valley of the Danube; it began to throw the Bourbons upon the defensive at last. It crushed the hopes of the Hungarian insurrection. It opened that series of successes which we couple with the names of Marlborough and Eugene, and which were not to be checked until, five years later, the French defence recovered its stubbornness at Malplaquet.